Volume 1 of the Empire Blueprint Series: Case Studies for
Business Success

70 Case Studies in Vision, Strategy, and Personal Branding

ALSO BY AUTHORSDOOR GROUP

Volume 1 of the Empire Blueprint Series: Case Studies for
Business Success

70 Case Studies in Vision, Strategy, and Personal Branding

The Foundations of Success

L. A. MOESZINGER

AuthorsDoor Group
an imprint of The Ridge Publishing Group

Library of Congress Control Number: 2024922965

70 Case Studies in Vision, Strategy, and Personal Branding: The Foundations of Success / by L. A. Moeszinger

ISBN 978-1-956905-39-7 (e-book)
ISBN 978-1-956905-38-0 (softcover)

1. Business & Economics / Entrepreneurship. 2. Business & Economics / Small Business. 3. Business & Economics / Management. 4. Self-Help / Motivational & Inspiration. 5. Business & Economics / Leadership. I. Title. II. Series

Printed in the United States of America

Dedicated to the dreamers, strategists, and personal brand builders who dare to envision the future, chart bold paths, and leave their unique mark on the world.

AuthorsDoor Group
Coeur d'Alene, Idaho

INTRODUCTION TO THE
AUTHORSDOOR LEADERSHIP PROGRAM

The AuthorsDoor Leadership Program, separate from the Builders Empire Series, is a new initiative designed to empower authors and publishers with the skills to effectively sell books. It features three tailored series: (1) AuthorsDoor Series: *Publisher & Her World*, (2) AuthorsDoor Advanced Series: *Publisher & Her World*, and (3) AuthorsDoor Masterclass Series: *Publisher & Her World*; each series is meticulously structured to guide participants from foundational concepts to advanced strategies in selling books, book by book, in a chronological format. The courses, offered for free on our YouTube channels—Publisher & Her World at Ridge Publishing Group, AuthorsDoor Group: Publisher & Her World, and Authors Red Door #Shorts—complement the books and workbooks, each providing unique and valuable teachings.

Explore additional resources to enhance your journey:

- Follow our blog at AuthorsRedDoor.com.
- Subscribe to our Newsletters at AuthorsDoor.com.
- Join our AuthorsDoor Strategy Forum Facebook Group.
- Connect with our Facebook Page at AuthorsDoor Group.
- Become a fan on our social media channels @AuthorsDoor1.

For feedback or questions, contact us at info@authorsdoor.com. We are here to support your journey from writing to successfully selling your books.

Warm regards,

L. A. Moeszinger #PubHerWorld

Contents

Introduction

70 Case Studies in Vision, Strategy, and Personal Branding

In today's fast-paced business world, the ability to craft a compelling vision, execute effective strategies, and develop a standout personal brand can set organizations and individuals on a path to success. This first volume of the Empire Blueprint Series dives deep into these essential areas, presenting 70 case studies that provide practical insights and real-world examples from diverse industries.

The volume is structured to guide readers through the foundational elements of business success. It begins with crafting an inspiring vision—the north star that aligns goals and inspires action. From there, readers will explore planning for success, implementing business structures, and executing strategies, providing a roadmap for sustainable growth.

A significant portion of this volume focuses on personal branding, time management, and storytelling in marketing, showing how leaders and professionals can position themselves effectively in competitive markets. In the age of digital marketing, building an audience online and mastering social media platforms are indispensable skills, and this volume offers case studies that reveal how others have succeeded in these areas. Email marketing, website strategy, and business expansion through innovation round out the collection, equipping readers with the knowledge they need to adapt, grow, and thrive.

Each case study not only highlights best practices but also explores the challenges and solutions faced along the way, offering lessons that readers can apply directly to their own endeavors. Whether you are an entrepreneur, a student, or a professional seeking actionable insights, this volume provides a wealth of inspiration and guidance to help you shape your vision, strategize effectively, and build a brand that resonates.

Audience Guidance

This volume, "70 Case Studies in Vision, Strategy, and Personal Branding," has been designed to provide real-world insights and practical tools for a variety of readers—whether you are an entrepreneur, student, or seasoned professional. Each audience will find value in different ways, with flexible learning paths and actionable takeaways that can be applied across industries.

Entrepreneurs

For those launching or scaling businesses, this volume offers concrete examples of how other entrepreneurs have navigated challenges, built strong visions, and executed effective strategies. You will discover proven tactics for branding, online engagement, and business expansion, helping you avoid pitfalls and stay competitive in today's dynamic market.

Students and Aspiring Professionals

Students seeking to understand how theoretical business concepts play out in real life will benefit from contextualized lessons in leadership, marketing, and productivity. The case studies reveal how success happens in practice, offering valuable insights for future careers. Additionally, the narratives encourage critical thinking and problem-solving, skills essential for academic and professional growth.

Professionals and Business Leaders

For established professionals, this volume provides fresh perspectives on branding, strategy, and time management. Whether you're looking to refine your leadership style, launch new initiatives, or develop a more impactful personal brand, these case studies offer inspiration and strategies that can be adapted to your needs. You'll find actionable insights to reinvigorate your career and build new opportunities for growth.

Flexible Use for Every Reader

You can use this volume in different ways:

- Read sequentially to build a strong foundation from vision creation to innovation.

- Select specific chapters relevant to your immediate goals, such as mastering social media or enhancing productivity.

- Engage in group discussions by sharing these stories with peers, creating a collaborative learning experience.

This volume is more than just a collection of success stories; it is a practical toolkit designed to equip you with ideas and strategies to achieve your personal and professional goals. No matter your role or industry, the insights within these pages will help you think strategically, act purposefully, and build a lasting impact.

Real-World Practicality

This volume focuses on real-world applications by offering 70 case studies that showcase how successful businesses and individuals have navigated challenges, seized opportunities, and built lasting success. Each case goes beyond theory, presenting concrete examples of strategies in action, highlighting both triumphs and setbacks. The goal is to provide practical insights that readers can immediately apply to their ventures or careers.

Learning from Success and Setbacks

Business is often a journey of trial and error, and these case studies provide valuable lessons from both successful outcomes and unexpected failures. Readers will explore how entrepreneurs have adapted to change, restructured their strategies, or innovated on the fly to overcome obstacles. These real-world stories are designed to inspire readers to think creatively and proactively approach challenges, using lessons learned from others' experiences.

Practical Strategies You Can Implement

Every case study is accompanied by actionable takeaways that you can apply to your business or personal brand. Whether it's learning time management techniques from high-performing entrepreneurs, developing impactful brand identities, or optimizing social media engagement, these cases are packed with practical advice. The goal is not only to inspire but to equip readers with strategies they can tailor to their unique situations.

Broad Applications Across Industries

The diversity of the case studies ensures relevance across industries. Whether you are in tech, retail, publishing, or services, the strategies presented—such as storytelling in marketing or planning for business expansion—offer versatile insights applicable to multiple fields. This broad scope allows readers to see patterns and apply best practices, no matter the specific market.

Action-Oriented Learning

Unlike abstract business theories, these case studies offer tangible lessons rooted in real-world scenarios. By presenting examples of successful entrepreneurs, businesses, and strategies, the volume aims to encourage readers to take immediate action. Whether you are refining your brand, building an online audience, or planning for future growth, you will find ready-to-implement strategies that fit your goals.

With a focus on practicality and actionable outcomes, this volume ensures readers can bridge the gap between knowledge and action, enabling them to navigate their journeys with greater confidence and insight.

Unique Methodology and Themes

This volume uses a structured and deliberate methodology to guide readers through key aspects of business growth and personal branding, ensuring that each case study offers relevant insights and practical lessons. The case studies are designed not only to inform but to inspire action, with each chapter presenting real-world scenarios and actionable takeaways that readers can apply immediately.

Problem-Solution Framework for Clear Learning

Each case study follows a problem-solution framework, beginning with a specific challenge, followed by the strategies implemented, and concluding with the outcomes. This structure helps readers understand how businesses overcome obstacles in real-life scenarios. It emphasizes the importance of critical thinking, adaptation, and execution, providing readers with a clear understanding of the decision-making processes involved.

Emphasis on Practical Themes for Business Success

This volume addresses fundamental themes essential for modern business success, including:

- Vision and strategy execution: How to create inspiring visions and develop actionable plans.

- Personal branding and marketing: Insights into building a distinctive personal identity in the marketplace.

- Productivity and time management: Practical tools to enhance efficiency and focus.

- Digital engagement and innovation: Strategies for building an online presence, mastering social media, and driving innovation for business growth.

These themes are interconnected, showing readers that success requires a combination of strategic thinking, personal development, and practical skills.

Encouraging Application and Reflection

The methodology encourages readers to reflect on their own challenges and aspirations as they move through the case studies. Each chapter provides guiding questions and practical exercises, enabling readers to apply what they've learned directly to their own situations. Whether focusing on goal-setting, marketing, or leadership development, this volume equips readers with the tools to craft a tailored approach to their business journey.

Adaptability Across Contexts

The case studies span multiple industries and business models, demonstrating that the principles of vision, strategy, and personal branding are adaptable to any field. This diversity ensures that readers from various industries and professional backgrounds will find relevant insights that they can customize to fit their specific contexts.

By blending real-world relevance with a structured learning approach, this volume offers a comprehensive guide that empowers readers to develop strategic plans, build strong brands, and master the art of storytelling and productivity—all while remaining adaptable to changing markets and opportunities.

Value Beyond Insights

This volume offers more than just business lessons and strategies—it provides inspiration, motivation, and a framework for personal and professional growth. Each case study is designed to equip readers with valuable insights, but the true power lies in how these lessons can transform mindsets and inspire action. The stories illustrate that success is not just about achieving goals but about overcoming challenges, learning from setbacks, and developing resilience.

Practical Inspiration for Immediate Action

The case studies go beyond sharing success stories by offering practical takeaways that readers can apply immediately to their own ventures. This volume encourages readers to reflect on their own circumstances, set actionable goals, and execute strategies that align with their vision. Whether through branding exercises, marketing techniques, or time management frameworks, these stories provide tools to empower personal growth and professional advancement.

Fostering Creativity and Innovation

Exposure to diverse perspectives and business models fosters creative thinking, encouraging readers to find innovative solutions to their challenges. The insights within these pages are intended to spark new ideas and push readers to reimagine their strategies. Innovation is presented not as a luxury but as a necessity for those looking to thrive in dynamic and competitive markets.

Building Resilience and Cultivating Growth Mindsets

The stories in this volume demonstrate that setbacks are not the end of the road but opportunities to grow and adapt. By learning how others have navigated obstacles and uncertainty, readers can develop a resilient mindset that will serve them through their own journeys. The emphasis on reflection and perseverance offers a blueprint for long-term growth and sustainability.

Motivating Personal and Professional Growth

Beyond practical applications, this volume serves as a source of personal motivation. The successes and lessons from these case studies inspire readers to set higher goals, take calculated risks, and remain committed to their vision. Whether readers are starting new ventures, scaling existing businesses, or advancing in their careers, the stories encourage them to strive for excellence and impact.

By offering value beyond mere insights, this volume becomes not just a business resource but a companion on the entrepreneurial journey, guiding readers toward success while inspiring them to think bigger, act boldly, and create lasting change.

Integration with Other Volumes and Series

This volume, "70 Case Studies in Vision, Strategy, and Personal Branding," serves as the first installment of the Empire Blueprint Series. However, it is also interwoven with themes and insights from other books within the AuthorsDoor Series, Masterclass Series, and Empire Builders Series. These interconnected works are part of a larger ecosystem, creating a comprehensive resource for entrepreneurs, students, and professionals.

Synergy Across the Empire Blueprint Series

The other volumes in the Empire Blueprint Series build on the foundation laid here by diving into leadership, resilience, technology, and growth strategies. Readers who find value in these case studies will benefit from exploring Volume 2 and Volume 3, which provide additional business insights focused on leadership, innovation, and creating a lasting legacy.

Each volume is designed to stand on its own while also working in tandem with others, allowing readers to customize their learning journey. Together, the three volumes form a comprehensive guide for anyone seeking to master the art of building a thriving business.

Connections to the AuthorsDoor Series

Many of the quotes and success stories featured in this volume have their origins in the AuthorsDoor Series: Publisher and Her World. These works emphasize the intersection of publishing, entrepreneurship, and business strategy, making them an ideal complement to the lessons shared in this volume. Readers with interests in publishing, personal branding, and storytelling will find deeper exploration of those topics in the AuthorsDoor Masterclass Series and Advanced Series.

Mastering Business and Law with the Empire Builders Series

The broader Empire Builders Series, where the original *From Idea to Empire* book resides, provides a strategic focus on business and law. Readers pursuing a deeper understanding of legal foundations and business models will benefit from cross-referencing these other titles. This case study volume provides practical applications that align with the strategic frameworks introduced in the larger series.

A Holistic Learning Experience

Together, these volumes and series offer a holistic learning path, empowering readers to develop a broad understanding of business concepts and strategies while also mastering the finer details of personal branding, leadership, and growth. By engaging with multiple volumes and series, readers can enhance their expertise and gain a well-rounded perspective, whether their focus is on entrepreneurship, publishing, leadership, or business expansion.

This integration across volumes creates a rich learning environment that ensures consistent growth and development, helping readers progress from foundational concepts to advanced mastery as they build their businesses and personal brands.

Tools and Resources for Readers

This volume, "70 Case Studies in Vision, Strategy, and Personal Branding," offers more than just insights—it provides practical tools and resources to help readers apply the lessons they learn and track their progress. Whether you are working through these case studies independently or with a team, the following resources will enhance your learning experience and ensure that knowledge transforms into action.

Self-Assessment and Reflection Exercises

Each chapter encourages readers to reflect on their personal or business challenges and apply the insights from the case studies. Use journals or dedicated worksheets to document your thoughts and track your progress as you implement new strategies. Reflective prompts such as:

- *What challenges am I facing in my business that align with this case study?*

- *How can I adapt these strategies to my unique goals?*

These exercises allow you to internalize lessons and build a customized action plan.

Actionable Checklists and Templates

To make it easier to translate insights into action, you can create checklists and templates based on the strategies discussed in the case studies. Examples might include:

- Brand-building worksheets to outline your personal or business brand identity.

- Marketing checklists for developing online campaigns or social media strategies.

- Goal-setting templates to break down your long-term vision into smaller, achievable steps.

These tools help you stay organized and measure your progress over time.

Group Learning and Peer Collaboration

Readers are encouraged to discuss these case studies in groups or professional settings. Book clubs, mastermind groups, or study sessions offer valuable opportunities for peer feedback and collaborative learning. Consider sharing your reflections, brainstorming solutions, or role-playing different business scenarios to gain fresh perspectives. Working through these case studies with others fosters accountability and encourages creative problem-solving.

Supplementary Digital Resources and Further Reading

Readers can further enhance their understanding by exploring related books, courses, and online resources from the broader Empire Builders and AuthorsDoor series. Use these supplementary materials to delve deeper into specific topics, such as leadership, time management, or digital marketing.

If available, consider using:

- Online workbooks or exercises tied to this volume.

- Author interviews, webinars, or podcasts that elaborate on themes from the case studies.

- Reading lists to continue exploring similar business concepts.

Progress Tracking and Long-Term Planning

As you implement the lessons from these case studies, use progress-tracking tools, such as monthly planners or task management apps, to monitor your growth. Set milestones and regularly revisit the lessons to adjust your strategies and maintain momentum.

By actively engaging with these tools and resources, you can ensure that the insights gained from this volume lead to tangible results. Whether you're a solo entrepreneur or working within a larger team, the right resources will help you apply what you've learned strategically and effectively, empowering you to take meaningful steps toward your personal and professional goals.

How to Use This Volume

Each case study is designed to offer insights and inspiration that readers can immediately apply to their own ventures. Whether you're focused on vision-setting, personal branding, or marketing, these stories will equip you with the tools and knowledge to overcome challenges and pursue success more confidently. The goal of this volume is not just to inform but to motivate action—encouraging you to take the next step in your business journey with clarity and purpose.

Throughout these chapters, you'll find examples of success from diverse industries, allowing you to draw lessons from different contexts. Some stories might resonate with your current challenges, while others may offer unexpected insights that lead to new strategies.

Conclusion: Building the Foundation
for Your Empire

This first volume of the Empire Blueprint Series is a comprehensive guide to the foundational elements of business success. It offers a rich tapestry of experiences, highlighting how vision, planning, branding, and innovation come together to create sustainable enterprises. The lessons within these pages will prepare you to craft a vision that inspires, execute strategies that drive results, and build a brand that stands the test of time.

No matter where you are on your journey—whether starting out, scaling a business, or honing your leadership skills—this volume provides invaluable insights to help you build and grow. These 70 case studies will not only inspire you but also serve as a practical resource to guide your decisions as you shape your own path toward success.

Welcome to Volume 1 of the Empire Blueprint Series—where your journey toward business mastery begins.

CHAPTER ONE

Crafting a Vision That Inspires

At the heart of every thriving business lies a vision that transcends spreadsheets and financial forecasts. Vision is the foundation of purpose—a reflection of what drives you as an entrepreneur and why your business exists beyond merely making a profit. A compelling vision doesn't just guide internal decision-making; it resonates with employees, customers, investors, and partners, acting as a unifying force that aligns all efforts toward a common goal. It provides clarity in times of uncertainty and motivates your team to go the extra mile, even when challenges arise. Crafting a vision that inspires is the first essential step in transforming an idea into an enduring enterprise.

The process of shaping a powerful vision begins with understanding your "why." As leadership expert Simon Sinek emphasizes, starting with "why" enables businesses to connect with audiences on an emotional level. Your vision should communicate not just what your business does, but why it matters. This deeper purpose becomes the spark that ignites passion in your team and fosters long-term customer loyalty. This principle is evident in the journeys of leaders like Oprah Winfrey and Indra Nooyi, who have built powerful brands around their core values, showing how meaningful visions can differentiate businesses in a crowded marketplace.

Once your vision is clear, the challenge is to turn it into a tangible strategy. A vision without action is merely a dream; it must guide your strategic decisions and influence every aspect of your operations, from product development to customer experience. Business icons like Philip Kotler and Richard Branson have demonstrated how a compelling vision not only directs business strategy but also becomes the cornerstone of brand identity. When your vision is woven into the fabric of your organization, every decision—big or small—becomes a step toward fulfilling that larger purpose.

However, a powerful vision must also be adaptable. The business world is dynamic, and market conditions can shift rapidly. Your vision should inspire without being rigid, leaving room for growth and evolution. We'll explore stories of visionary leaders like Walt Disney and Angela Duckworth, who remained committed to their core missions while adapting to changing environments. Effective leadership requires the ability to balance long-term focus with the flexibility to pivot when necessary.

This chapter will provide practical insights and tools to help you craft a vision that inspires action and fosters resilience. From brainstorming your core mission to crafting vision statements that resonate, we'll walk you through the process of developing a vision that guides and grows with your business. You'll also learn techniques for communicating your vision effectively to stakeholders—whether through storytelling, branding, or company culture.

By the end of this chapter, you'll be equipped to create a vision that not only motivates but also drives sustainable success. A well-crafted vision becomes the backbone of your business strategy, the source of your brand's strength, and the reason why your customers, employees, and partners will choose to align with you. When your vision inspires, it lays the groundwork for building something far greater than a business—it creates an empire.

Philip Kotler's Success Story: The Father of Modern Marketing

"A well-defined vision is the starting point for any successful marketing strategy. It gives your brand a voice and your actions a direction, ensuring every campaign resonates with your core mission."
— PHILIP KOTLER, DISTINGUISHED PROFESSOR OF INTERNATIONAL MARKETING

"Effective marketing doesn't just sell books; it creates a spectacle that captivates the audience, turning each campaign into a performance that leaves readers clamoring for an encore." — PHILIP KOTLER, MARKETING GURU

"Creating a comprehensive marketing plan is like drawing a map to treasure. It doesn't just guide you there, it ensures you navigate the marketing maze with confidence, avoiding pitfalls and seizing opportunities along the way." — PHILIP KOTLER, MARKETING EXPERT

"Adopting the mindset of a Sales Titan means planning not just to participate in the market, but to dominate it. Strategic advertising is your map; bold execution is your compass." — PHILIP KOTLER, MARKETING EXPERT

"Developing a PR roadmap is about more than charting a path to visibility—it's about steering your narrative through the complexities of public opinion to arrive at your destination of renown."
— PHILIP KOTLER, MARKETING GURU

"Every bestseller begins with a plan that understands its audience as well as it understands the story it wants to sell. Your marketing blueprint is the script of your success; make sure it's as compelling as your book."
— PHILIP KOTLER, MARKETING AUTHOR AND PROFESSOR

"Selecting your brand's mark isn't just about aesthetics; it's a strategic decision that encapsulates your mission, vision, and the unique promise you deliver to your customers." — PHILIP KOTLER, MARKETING AUTHOR AND PROFESSOR

Philip Kotler, widely regarded as the "Father of Modern Marketing," revolutionized the field by bringing academic rigor and strategic thinking to marketing. His journey from a young economist to a global thought leader shaped how businesses understand and engage with customers. Kotler's success stems from his groundbreaking theories, books, and teachings that elevated marketing from a functional activity to a vital driver of business success.

From Economics to Marketing: An Unconventional Start
Philip Kotler was born in Chicago in 1931 and pursued economics early in his academic career. He earned his master's degree in economics from the University of Chicago and went on to complete his PhD at the Massachusetts Institute of Technology (MIT) under Nobel Prize-winning economist Paul Samuelson. Kotler was initially passionate about economics, believing that it held the key to understanding human behavior and solving real-world problems.

However, he soon realized that while economics focused on demand and supply curves, it lacked depth in understanding why customers make decisions and how businesses could align their offerings to meet those needs. This curiosity led Kotler to shift his focus to marketing—a field largely ignored by economists at the time.

Joining Kellogg and Transforming Marketing Theory
Kotler began teaching at Northwestern University's Kellogg School of Management in 1962, where he embarked on his lifelong mission of redefining the discipline of marketing. At that time, marketing was often viewed as a tactical function—limited to advertising, sales, and promotions. Kotler believed that marketing should be elevated to a strategic, analytical discipline, integrating insights from economics, psychology, and sociology.

He pioneered the idea that marketing is not just about selling products but about creating, communicating, and delivering value to customers. Kotler's approach emphasized long-term relationships, brand loyalty, and customer satisfaction as the cornerstones of business success.

The Publication of 'Marketing Management' and Global Recognition
In 1967, Kotler published his landmark textbook, "Marketing Management: Analysis, Planning, and Control." The book was revolutionary. It introduced the

concept of segmentation, targeting, and positioning (STP) and advocated for a customer-centric business model. This textbook became the gold standard for marketing education worldwide, influencing generations of students, professors, and business leaders.

Unlike traditional marketing books that focused on practical tips, Kotler's work provided a strategic framework for marketing as a science. His analytical approach, rooted in his background in economics, made the book appealing to business schools and managers alike. Today, *Marketing Management* is in its 15th edition and remains one of the most widely used textbooks in the field.

Contributions to Marketing Thought and Practice
Kotler didn't stop at writing textbooks. Over his career, he authored more than 80 books on various facets of marketing, including international marketing, social marketing, digital marketing, and sustainable marketing. Some of his influential concepts include:

1. The 4 Ps of Marketing – Product, Price, Place, Promotion, which became a foundational model for marketing strategies.

2. Social Marketing – Applying marketing principles to promote social change, not just products.

3. Holistic Marketing – A view of marketing that emphasizes the interconnectedness of various business functions.

4. Marketing 3.0 and 4.0 – Exploring how marketing evolves with technological changes, focusing on customer empowerment and digital transformation.

Kotler's ability to adapt to changing times kept his work relevant as the world shifted toward digital platforms and customer-driven economies. His forward-thinking mindset ensured that his theories evolved with new trends, including the rise of big data, artificial intelligence, and sustainability.

Global Influence and Legacy
Beyond the classroom, Kotler became a sought-after consultant and advisor to corporations and governments worldwide. He has worked with companies like IBM, General Electric, and Coca-Cola, helping them develop strategies to

enhance their customer engagement and brand positioning. Kotler also advised public institutions on how to apply marketing principles to health campaigns, tourism, and economic development.

He frequently traveled around the globe, delivering keynote speeches and engaging with audiences across cultures, which further cemented his reputation as the world's leading marketing expert. Kotler's teachings went beyond textbooks—he actively shaped the marketing profession by fostering communities of practitioners, scholars, and thought leaders.

Awards, Honors, and Continuing Impact

Kotler's contributions have been recognized with numerous awards and accolades. He has received honorary degrees from over 20 universities and continues to be honored at marketing events worldwide. His influence extends to professional associations, where he helped develop thought leadership in organizations like the American Marketing Association (AMA).

Kotler's Marketing 3.0 and Marketing 4.0 frameworks also demonstrate his visionary thinking, addressing how businesses must adapt to changes in technology, customer expectations, and global challenges. Today, Kotler is still actively involved in research and public speaking, advocating for businesses to adopt sustainable marketing practices that benefit both companies and society.

Lessons from Philip Kotler's Success

1. **Curiosity Drives Innovation:** Kotler's shift from economics to marketing came from his willingness to question established norms and explore new ideas.

2. **Strategic Thinking Matters:** His focus on frameworks and models transformed marketing from a tactical activity into a strategic function.

3. **Adapt to Change:** Kotler's work on Marketing 4.0 and sustainable marketing demonstrates the importance of staying ahead of trends.

4. **Impact Beyond Profit:** Kotler believes that marketing is not just about driving sales but also about creating positive societal change.

5. **Lifelong Learning:** Even after decades in the field, Kotler continues to evolve his thinking, proving that success comes from continuous learning.

Conclusion: A Legacy that Shaped Modern Marketing

Philip Kotler's journey from economics to marketing redefined the way businesses operate. His work helped shape marketing into a science, moving beyond slogans and advertisements to become a strategic tool that drives business success. Kotler's ideas continue to inspire companies to create value for customers while promoting social good.

Through his books, speeches, and consultancy work, Kotler has influenced countless entrepreneurs, managers, and students. His contributions have left a lasting legacy, ensuring that marketing will always be at the heart of innovation and customer connection. Today, his name is synonymous with modern marketing, and his teachings continue to drive the next generation of business leaders toward a more customer-focused future.

———————

Simon Sinek's Success Story: A Journey to Purposeful Leadership

"Analyzing your competitors isn't about copying their moves, but about learning their strengths and weaknesses to find your unique edge. Success comes from seeing what they miss and delivering what the market truly wants."
— SIMON SINEK, AUTHOR AND MOTIVATIONAL SPEAKER

"Book sales soar not by chance, but through clever, targeted strategies that engage readers and spark their desire to buy." — SIMON SINEK, LEADERSHIP EXPERT AND AUTHOR

"In B2B advertising, it's not about selling products but about forging partnerships and solving problems that elevate businesses to new heights of success." — SIMON SINEK, AUTHOR AND INSPIRATIONAL SPEAKER

"Building a successful brand doesn't start with what you sell, but with what you stand for. Crafting a unique strategy is about aligning your mission with your market to create not just a business, but a legacy." — SIMON SINEK, AUTHOR AND INSPIRATIONAL SPEAKER

"Innovative leadership is about seeing beyond the horizon of current trends and crafting practices that not only respond to emerging challenges but redefine the playing field entirely." — SIMON SINEK, AUTHOR AND MOTIVATIONAL SPEAKER

"Every name in your database is more than a number; it's a doorway to a new relationship. Use your newsletter to open these doors wide." — SIMON SINEK, LEADERSHIP EXPERT AND AUTHOR

"People don't follow you for what you do; they follow you for why you do it. The goal is not to do business with everyone who needs what you have; the goal is to do business with people who believe what you believe." — SIMON SINEK, AUTHOR AND INSPIRATIONAL SPEAKER

"Leadership is not about being in charge. It's about taking care of those in your charge." — SIMON SINEK, AUTHOR AND MOTIVATIONAL SPEAKER

"Maintaining your brand's authentic voice isn't just about consistency; it's about ensuring every message resonates with truth and aligns with your core values." — SIMON SINEK, LEADERSHIP EXPERT AND AUTHOR

"Knowing your audience is the first step in selling anything effectively. Understand their desires, their pains, and their joys. Speak directly to them, and they will not only buy your book—they will champion it." — SIMON SINEK, AUTHOR AND MOTIVATIONAL SPEAKER

"Future-proofing your trademark isn't just about securing rights today; it's about strategic planning and continuous vigilance to protect and enhance your brand's value for years to come." — SIMON SINEK, LEADERSHIP EXPERT AND AUTHOR

"Every contract you sign is more than a document; it's a promise.
Understanding and upholding these commitments is fundamental
to maintaining trust and credibility in your business dealings."
— SIMON SINEK, LEADERSHIP EXPERT AND AUTHOR

Simon Sinek's journey to becoming a thought leader and bestselling author began with a question: *"Why?"* Born in Wimbledon, England, on October 9, 1973, Simon spent his early years moving between different countries, including South Africa and Hong Kong, before settling in the United States. This international upbringing exposed him to a variety of perspectives and cultures, shaping his worldview early on. After studying law at London's City University, Simon realized his passion lay not in law but in understanding human behavior. He later pursued a degree in cultural anthropology at Brandeis University in Massachusetts, laying the foundation for his fascination with leadership and motivation.

The Turning Point: Finding His "Why"

In the early 2000s, Simon worked in marketing and advertising for high-profile agencies such as Ogilvy & Mather and Euro RSCG. While these roles gave him valuable experience in branding and communication, Simon struggled with a personal crisis of motivation. Despite outward success, he found himself feeling unfulfilled and disengaged with his work. This period of soul-searching became a turning point. Simon realized that he needed to reconnect with a deeper purpose—a reason for what he was doing beyond just career advancement.

During this time, Simon began developing his idea of the Golden Circle, a simple yet profound concept that emphasizes the importance of starting with *Why*—the core purpose or belief that drives every successful person, company, or movement. This epiphany became the foundation of his philosophy: people and organizations that know *why* they do what they do are more innovative, influential, and successful than those who focus solely on *what* they do or *how* they do it.

Publishing Success: *Start with Why*

In 2009, Simon published his first book, *Start with Why: How Great Leaders Inspire Everyone to Take Action*. The book was initially met with moderate success but soon gained traction through word of mouth and Simon's growing reputation as a speaker. His central thesis—"People don't buy what you do; they buy why you do it"—resonated deeply with entrepreneurs, business leaders, and individuals seeking meaningful work. The book's success skyrocketed when Simon gave a TED Talk titled "How Great Leaders Inspire Action."

The TED Talk, released in 2009, became one of the most-watched TED videos of all time, with over 60 million views. This global exposure cemented Simon's reputation as a leading thinker in leadership, branding, and motivation. His message inspired countless companies to rethink how they communicate their mission, not only to customers but also to employees.

Becoming a Thought Leader

Following the success of *Start with Why*, Simon expanded his philosophy through books like *Leaders Eat Last* (2014), which explores the importance of creating environments where people feel safe, valued, and empowered. His next book, *Together Is Better* (2016), emphasized the significance of collaboration and building strong relationships. In 2019, Simon released *The Infinite Game*, a book that encourages readers to shift from short-term thinking to an infinite mindset, focusing on sustainability, adaptability, and long-term impact.

Beyond writing, Simon became a sought-after speaker, consultant, and mentor. He worked with organizations such as Microsoft, the United Nations, and the U.S. military, sharing his insights on leadership, teamwork, and motivation. His message wasn't just about making companies more profitable—it was about creating workplaces where people could thrive.

Building a Global Brand

Simon Sinek's approach to leadership emphasizes the human side of business. His philosophy resonates not just with executives but with anyone seeking a deeper sense of purpose in their work. His consulting firm, Sinek Partners, helps companies transform their culture by adopting the Golden Circle philosophy. Simon also launched an online community called The Optimists, offering courses, tools, and resources to help individuals and teams apply his ideas in everyday life.

Simon's influence extends beyond business—his insights have become guiding principles for educators, non-profits, and even governments seeking to inspire change. His engaging speaking style, combined with his knack for storytelling, makes him a charismatic and compelling presence on the global stage.

Legacy of Purpose and Impact
Simon's work has redefined how leaders approach business, marketing, and personal fulfillment. His emphasis on starting with *Why* has empowered millions to rediscover their passion and align their actions with a greater purpose. Whether inspiring corporate executives to lead with empathy or encouraging entrepreneurs to find deeper meaning in their ventures, Simon's message continues to spark a global movement toward more purposeful leadership.

Through books, public speaking, and his online platforms, Simon Sinek has built more than just a successful career—he has created a legacy centered on hope, inspiration, and positive change. His journey from struggling marketer to one of the most influential thinkers of our time exemplifies the power of knowing your *Why*. As Simon often reminds his audience: *"The goal is not to do business with everyone who needs what you have; the goal is to do business with people who believe what you believe."*

Sir Richard Branson's Success Story: The Maverick Entrepreneur Who Built the Virgin Empire

"LinkedIn is not just a resume on the internet; it is a bustling marketplace of ideas, ambitions, and opportunities. Treat it as your digital boardroom where every connection counts and every content piece is a pitch." — SIR RICHARD BRANSON, FOUNDER OF VIRGIN GROUP

"True brand visionaries don't just chase the market—they lead it, transforming what it means to be seen and remembered in an ever-evolving landscape." — SIR RICHARD BRANSON, FOUNDER OF VIRGIN GROUP

"Your life story is not just what you tell people, it's what they believe about you based on the evidence you present." — SIR RICHARD BRANSON, FOUNDER OF VIRGIN GROUP

"Publishing is evolving at a breakneck pace. Embracing the latest trends and innovations isn't just wise—it's essential to thrive in tomorrow's literary landscape." — SIR RICHARD BRANSON, ENTREPRENEUR AND BUSINESS MAGNATE

"Collaboration has no downside, only the power to amplify your reach and impact. The right partnerships can transform your book's journey from a solo venture to a shared success story." — SIR RICHARD BRANSON, FOUNDER OF VIRGIN GROUP

"Understanding the legal landscape isn't just about avoiding pitfalls; it's about finding opportunities where others see obstacles. The best entrepreneurs know that legal preparedness is a strategic asset." — SIR RICHARD BRANSON, FOUNDER OF VIRGIN GROUP

"A trademark does not just protect an asset, it projects your business's identity to the world, making it a cornerstone of your success." — SIR RICHARD BRANSON, FOUNDER OF VIRGIN GROUP

"Licensing is the art of monetizing your creativity without giving away your control. It's about building partnerships that respect your vision and reward your innovation." — SIR RICHARD BRANSON, FOUNDER OF VIRGIN GROUP

"Negotiation is the subtle art of getting the best deal without compromising the worth of your creation." — SIR RICHARD BRANSON, FOUNDER OF VIRGIN GROUP

Sir Richard Branson is one of the most recognizable and audacious entrepreneurs in the world. As the founder of Virgin Group, Branson built an empire that spans industries—from music and travel to telecoms, health, and space tourism. His journey is one of bold risks, unconventional thinking, and an unrelenting pursuit of adventure. Branson's story proves that innovation, persistence, and a willingness to fail can lead to remarkable success.

Early Life and Education: An Entrepreneurial Spirit Takes Root
Born on July 18, 1950, in Blackheath, London, Branson struggled with dyslexia as a child, making school a constant challenge. However, his entrepreneurial spark

ignited early. At the age of 16, he left school and launched his first venture—a magazine called *Student*, which featured interviews with celebrities and covered social issues. Branson financed the magazine by selling ads to local businesses, learning valuable lessons about business and marketing along the way.

Though *Student* didn't make Branson wealthy, it gave him his first taste of running a business—and he was hooked.

Enter the Virgin Brand: A Record-Breaking Beginning

In 1970, Branson identified a gap in the market: affordable mail-order records. He launched Virgin Mail-Order Records, selling discounted albums to students. The venture was a hit, and Branson used the profits to open his first Virgin Records store on London's Oxford Street in 1971.

Two years later, Branson took an even bigger risk—he started Virgin Records, a music label, to sign new and unconventional artists. The gamble paid off when Virgin signed Mike Oldfield, whose album "Tubular Bells" became a global success. The label went on to sign groundbreaking artists like The Sex Pistols and Culture Club, cementing Virgin's reputation as a rebellious, edgy brand willing to take risks on the unconventional.

Expanding the Virgin Empire: Planes, Trains, and Mobile Phones

Branson's appetite for adventure and innovation knew no limits. In the 1980s, he expanded Virgin into industries far beyond music. First, he launched Virgin Atlantic Airways in 1984 to compete with British Airways, aiming to provide better service and a more enjoyable flying experience. Branson's hands-on approach, including appearing in ads and serving drinks mid-flight, gave Virgin Atlantic a distinct personality that attracted loyal customers.

In the following years, Branson diversified the Virgin brand into a wide array of industries:

- **Virgin Trains**: Revolutionizing rail travel in the UK.

- **Virgin Mobile**: Entering the telecoms sector with an innovative business model.

- **Virgin Media**: Competing with giants in the broadband and entertainment space.

His ability to identify opportunities and disrupt industries was uncanny, and the Virgin name became synonymous with innovation, adventure, and bold risk-taking.

Surviving Crises: Challenges and Comebacks

Not every venture was smooth sailing. Branson faced multiple setbacks and failures throughout his career. In the 1990s, Virgin Atlantic was locked in a bitter rivalry with British Airways, which resorted to sabotage tactics to try and crush Virgin's success. Branson fought back with resilience and creativity, winning a libel lawsuit against British Airways and using the settlement to reward Virgin Atlantic staff with a bonus—a testament to his loyalty to his team.

Another tough decision came in 1992, when Branson sold Virgin Records to EMI for $1 billion to fund Virgin Atlantic's expansion. It was a heartbreaking sale for Branson, who reportedly cried after the deal was finalized. However, it allowed him to keep Virgin Atlantic afloat, proving his ability to pivot and make difficult decisions to safeguard the future of his empire.

Adventures Beyond Business: Setting World Records and Space Travel

Branson's life has been as much about adventure as entrepreneurship. He set world records for crossing the Atlantic and the Pacific in hot air balloons, epitomizing his fearless, larger-than-life persona. These daring feats weren't just stunts—they were part of his philosophy that life and business should be lived boldly.

In 2004, Branson announced his most ambitious venture yet: Virgin Galactic, a commercial space tourism company. Despite years of setbacks, technical challenges, and criticism, Virgin Galactic successfully launched its first passengers into space in 2021, with Branson himself onboard, fulfilling his lifelong dream of reaching the stars.

Leadership Style: Empowering Teams and Promoting Fun

Branson's leadership style is as unique as his businesses. He believes in delegating authority to trusted teams, giving them the freedom to innovate and take risks. His philosophy? "Train people well enough so they can leave, treat them well enough so they don't want to."

He fosters a work environment that emphasizes fun, creativity, and work-life balance, famously saying, "If it's not fun, it's not worth doing." This approach has made Virgin a magnet for talent and a model of employee empowerment.

Philanthropy and Social Impact

In recent years, Branson has focused more on philanthropy and social causes. He founded the Virgin Unite Foundation to address issues such as climate change, human rights, and poverty reduction. Branson is also a member of The Elders, a group of global leaders working to promote peace and human rights, alongside figures like Nelson Mandela.

His commitment to sustainable business practices has driven Virgin's efforts to reduce its environmental footprint, especially in industries like aviation and space travel.

Lessons from Branson's Success

Branson's journey offers several key lessons:

- **Take risks**: Every great opportunity comes with risks, but fortune favors the bold.

- **Embrace failure**: Setbacks are part of the journey—learn from them and move forward.

- **Stay curious**: Constantly seek new challenges and opportunities to innovate.

- **Build a strong brand identity**: Virgin's rebellious, fun persona sets it apart in every industry.

- **Lead with empathy**: Treat employees and customers with care, and success will follow.

Conclusion: A Legacy of Bold Innovation

Richard Branson's story is more than just the tale of an entrepreneur—it's a testament to the power of audacity, creativity, and resilience. From record stores to airlines, telecoms, and space travel, Branson has built an empire by embracing change, challenging the status quo, and having fun along the way. His fearless approach to life and business has made him a role model for dreamers and disruptors alike.

Branson's legacy will not just be the companies he built but the spirit of adventure, innovation, and possibility that he embodies. His story reminds us that success isn't just about building businesses—it's about living boldly and making a lasting impact on the world.

Oprah Winfrey's Success Story: How One Woman Changed the World

"To know what you value most is akin to finding your own North Star – a constant light by which to navigate your life's journeys." — OPRAH WINFREY, MEDIA EXECUTIVE AND PHILANTHROPIST

"The key to realizing a dream is to focus not on success, but on significance— and then even the small steps and little victories along your path will take on greater meaning." — OPRAH WINFREY, MEDIA EXECUTIVE AND PHILANTHROPIST

Oprah Winfrey's journey to becoming one of the most influential figures in media is a story of resilience, self-belief, and vision. Born on January 29, 1954, in Kosciusko, Mississippi, Oprah grew up in poverty, raised by her grandmother during her early years. Her childhood was marked by hardship, including abuse and neglect, but these challenges would later shape her empathetic, relatable, and inspiring public persona.

Overcoming Adversity

Oprah's early life was difficult—she moved between homes, living at times with her mother, father, and grandmother. Despite the instability, Oprah developed a passion for public speaking at a young age. She discovered her talent for storytelling when her grandmother taught her to read by the age of three, and she later found solace in books. At school, her eloquence and confidence stood out, and she quickly gained recognition as a gifted speaker.

After winning a local beauty pageant at age 17, Oprah caught the attention of radio station WVOL in Nashville, where she began working part-time while still in high school. This opportunity became her first step into the world of media, sparking a lifelong passion for broadcasting and storytelling.

Early Career in Television

Oprah's first significant break came when she was hired as the youngest and first Black female news anchor at WLAC-TV in Nashville. Her ability to connect emotionally with audiences set her apart, although her less conventional, compassionate approach didn't initially fit the rigid style of traditional news reporting. Recognizing her natural warmth and ability to engage viewers, Oprah transitioned into talk shows, where she found her true calling.

In 1976, Oprah moved to Baltimore to co-host *People Are Talking*, a local morning talk show. The show's ratings soared, and Oprah's genuine curiosity and empathy with guests made her a beloved figure in the city. But it was in 1983, when she moved to Chicago to host *A.M. Chicago*, that her career took a transformational turn.

The Oprah Winfrey Show: A Cultural Phenomenon

Oprah's charisma and ability to connect with diverse audiences quickly turned *A.M. Chicago* into the top-rated talk show in the city. Just a year later, the show was renamed *The Oprah Winfrey Show* and expanded to a national audience. Premiering in 1986, the show became an unprecedented success, running for 25 years and influencing millions of viewers across the globe.

Unlike other talk shows of the time, Oprah's program took a unique approach, blending entertainment with meaningful conversations about personal growth, relationships, spirituality, and mental health. Oprah tackled taboo topics—such as addiction, abuse, and trauma—with compassion and openness, creating a space for candid dialogue and emotional healing. Her ability to make every guest feel seen, heard, and valued resonated deeply with viewers.

Oprah's iconic "Oprah's Book Club," launched in 1996, became a cultural force in its own right, turning many titles into instant bestsellers. Her endorsement of books and products became known as "the Oprah Effect," demonstrating her unmatched influence over consumer behavior.

Expanding Her Empire

Oprah's media empire expanded far beyond her talk show. In 1988, she founded Harpo Productions, becoming one of the first women in entertainment to own a production company. Harpo not only produced *The Oprah Winfrey Show* but also other major films and TV shows, including the acclaimed movie *The Color Purple* (1985), in which Oprah starred.

Oprah's entrepreneurial ventures continued to grow, with Harpo Productions developing award-winning films, television series, and documentaries. She also ventured into publishing, launching *O, The Oprah Magazine* in 2000, which quickly became one of the most successful women's lifestyle magazines.

In 2011, Oprah took another bold step by launching her own television network, OWN: The Oprah Winfrey Network. Though it initially struggled with ratings, Oprah's perseverance and adaptability transformed the network into a thriving platform focused on storytelling, inspiration, and self-improvement.

A Philanthropic Legacy

Throughout her career, Oprah has remained committed to philanthropy and social causes, using her influence to create positive change. In 1998, she founded Oprah's Angel Network, which raised millions for charitable causes worldwide. She later established the Oprah Winfrey Leadership Academy for Girls in South Africa, providing education and mentorship to young women from disadvantaged backgrounds.

Oprah's giving spirit has touched countless lives, both through her personal philanthropy and the generosity she inspires in others. Whether donating cars to her studio audience or giving scholarships to students, Oprah has consistently used her platform to uplift and empower.

A Global Icon of Inspiration

Oprah's influence goes far beyond entertainment—she has become a symbol of hope, empowerment, and personal transformation. Her ability to connect authentically with people from all walks of life has made her a trusted voice on topics ranging from mental health to spirituality. Oprah's interviews with public figures, such as her groundbreaking 2021 conversation with Prince Harry and Meghan Markle, continue to shape public discourse.

She has earned numerous awards throughout her career, including the Presidential Medal of Freedom in 2013, awarded by President Barack Obama. Oprah's legacy as a trailblazer and role model for women, people of color, and anyone facing adversity is profound.

The Oprah Effect: Building a Lasting Legacy

Oprah's story is a testament to the power of perseverance, purpose, and authenticity. Her journey from a small-town girl in Mississippi to a global media icon was fueled by her unwavering belief in the power of storytelling and her desire to make a difference in the world.

Even after ending *The Oprah Winfrey Show* in 2011, Oprah's influence has only grown. She continues to inspire through her network, books, podcast appearances, and motivational speeches. Her commitment to fostering personal growth, advocating for mental health, and promoting lifelong learning ensures that her legacy will endure for generations.

Conclusion

Oprah Winfrey's journey to success is not just a story of fame—it is a story of impact. She turned her pain into purpose, built an empire on authenticity, and used her platform to make the world a better place. Today, Oprah stands as a beacon of inspiration for anyone striving to overcome challenges, find their purpose, and live a life of meaning. As Oprah herself often says:

Indra Nooyi's Success Story: A Trailblazer's Journey to the Top of Corporate Leadership

"Keeping score in business means continuously monitoring and managing performance to not only meet targets but to exceed them, ensuring strategic growth and operational excellence." — INDRA NOOYI, FORMER CEO OF PEPSICO AND INFLUENTIAL BUSINESS EXECUTIVE

"Being a CEO is about more than leading a company; it's about setting a course that others will follow, not because they have to, but because they believe in the vision you've charted." — INDRA NOOYI, FORMER CEO OF PEPSICO

"As a Chief Brand Officer, your job isn't just to oversee the brand's image but to be its biggest advocate and visionary, transforming every challenge into a stepping stone towards unprecedented brand elevation." — INDRA NOOYI, FORMER CEO OF PEPSICO

"Understanding and adapting to regional compliance isn't just a legal duty; it's a competitive edge that allows your business to operate smoothly and expand confidently into new territories." — INDRA NOOYI, FORMER CEO OF PEPSICO

"Maintaining your trademark involves consistent vigilance and strategic foresight. Utilizing detailed checklists ensures that no aspect of your brand's protection is overlooked, securing its integrity and value in a competitive market." — INDRA NOOYI, FORMER CEO OF PEPSICO AND INFLUENTIAL BUSINESS EXECUTIVE

"Drafting a contract is like drawing a map. It guides the journey of a business relationship, ensuring all parties know the route and the destination clearly." — INDRA NOOYI, FORMER CEO OF PEPSICO

"Resolving financial disputes is an art—approach it with the right mix of facts, diplomacy, and firmness, and you can turn potential conflicts into opportunities for mutual gain." — INDRA NOOYI, FORMER CEO OF PEPSICO

Indra Nooyi, the former CEO and Chairperson of PepsiCo, is celebrated as one of the most influential business leaders of her generation. Nooyi's rise to success is a story of perseverance, bold decisions, and transformative leadership. Throughout her career, she broke barriers, redefined corporate strategy, and inspired countless women and aspiring leaders around the globe.

Early Life and Education: Foundations of Excellence

Indra Nooyi was born on October 28, 1955, in Chennai, India (then Madras). Raised in a middle-class family, Nooyi credits her upbringing for shaping her confidence and ambition. Her mother encouraged her to dream big and often had Nooyi and her sister debate on what they would do if they became prime ministers or presidents—early exercises that nurtured her leadership mindset.

Nooyi pursued her undergraduate degree in Physics, Chemistry, and Mathematics at Madras Christian College and went on to earn an MBA from the Indian Institute of Management (IIM) in Calcutta, one of the most prestigious business schools in India. Eager to further her education, she moved to the United States and enrolled at Yale School of Management, where she earned a master's degree in Public and Private Management in 1980.

Early Career: Gaining Experience Across Industries

After graduating from Yale, Nooyi worked for major companies across various industries, including The Boston Consulting Group (BCG), Motorola, and Asea Brown Boveri (ABB). These roles gave her broad exposure to business strategy, technology, and leadership in competitive industries. Nooyi's ability to navigate complex challenges and craft forward-thinking strategies earned her a reputation as a rising star in corporate America.

However, balancing cultural adaptation in the U.S. while advancing her career was not easy. Nooyi often reflected on her journey, sharing that she had to work twice as hard to be recognized as both a woman and an immigrant. But it was precisely her diverse perspective—influenced by both Indian and American cultures—that set her apart in the corporate world.

Joining PepsiCo: The Start of a Remarkable Journey

In 1994, Nooyi joined PepsiCo as Senior Vice President of Corporate Strategy and Development. Her analytical skills and strategic thinking quickly propelled her to higher roles within the company. Nooyi played a pivotal role in shaping PepsiCo's long-term vision, focusing on sustainable growth and preparing the company for future challenges.

Her most notable early contribution came in the acquisition of Tropicana in 1998 and the merger with Quaker Oats in 2001—two major deals that significantly expanded PepsiCo's product portfolio. The Quaker Oats deal also brought Gatorade into PepsiCo's fold, giving the company a stronger foothold in the health and wellness market.

Becoming CEO: A Vision for Transformation

In 2006, Nooyi was named CEO of PepsiCo, becoming one of the few women and the first woman of color to lead a Fortune 500 company. Her leadership style was marked by bold vision, empathy, and long-term strategic thinking. One of her defining initiatives was the introduction of "Performance with Purpose," a strategy that sought to balance business growth with environmental and social responsibility.

Under Nooyi's leadership, PepsiCo shifted its focus from sugary sodas to healthier food and beverage options, anticipating changing consumer preferences. She emphasized the importance of sustainability, nutrition, and environmental stewardship, transforming the company's operations and product lines.

Strategic Shifts and Bold Decisions

Nooyi's tenure as CEO was marked by several bold decisions:

1. **Diversification into Healthier Products:** She restructured PepsiCo to focus on health-conscious brands like Quaker, Tropicana, and Gatorade, reducing the company's reliance on sugary beverages.

2. **Environmental Sustainability:** Nooyi spearheaded initiatives to reduce PepsiCo's environmental footprint, including **water conservation and sustainable packaging** efforts.

3. **Global Expansion:** Under her leadership, PepsiCo expanded aggressively into international markets, especially China and India, further solidifying its position as a global powerhouse.

Her ability to balance short-term profitability with long-term sustainability set PepsiCo apart in the highly competitive food and beverage industry. Despite skepticism from some shareholders over the shift toward healthier products, Nooyi stayed committed to her vision, ensuring PepsiCo's growth remained aligned with evolving market trends.

Challenges and Legacy

Nooyi's journey was not without challenges. Navigating internal resistance to change while keeping shareholders happy required both resilience and tact. Additionally, leading a company with global operations demanded navigating complex geopolitical and economic challenges.

However, her unwavering focus on innovation, sustainability, and inclusive leadership paid off. Under her 12-year tenure as CEO, PepsiCo's revenue grew by 80%, and the company consistently outperformed many of its competitors. Nooyi stepped down as CEO in 2018 but continued as Chairperson of the Board until early 2019.

Life After PepsiCo: New Chapters and Giving Back

After leaving PepsiCo, Nooyi continued to inspire leaders and entrepreneurs globally. She published her memoir, "My Life in Full: Work, Family, and Our Future" in 2021, reflecting on her journey, leadership lessons, and the challenges of balancing career and family life.

Nooyi also joined the boards of several prominent companies, including Amazon, and remains actively involved in initiatives supporting diversity in leadership and women's empowerment. Her advocacy for policies that support working mothers and families reflects her belief that corporate success must go hand-in-hand with societal progress.

Personal Life: Balancing Work and Family

Throughout her career, Nooyi has been candid about the challenges of balancing work and family life. She credits much of her success to her family's support, particularly her husband Raj and their two daughters. Nooyi often speaks about the need for better policies and support systems for working parents, drawing from her personal experiences juggling career and family responsibilities.

Key Lessons from Indra Nooyi's Success

1. **Think Long-Term:** Nooyi's focus on sustainability and future trends allowed PepsiCo to stay ahead of market changes.

2. **Lead with Empathy:** Her "Performance with Purpose" strategy emphasized the importance of balancing business goals with social responsibility.

3. **Embrace Change:** Nooyi's ability to pivot PepsiCo toward healthier products demonstrated her agility and foresight.

4. **Diversity is Strength:** As a woman and immigrant leader, Nooyi proved that diverse perspectives drive innovation.

5. **Balance and Support:** Nooyi's advocacy for work-life integration highlights the importance of supportive environments for working parents.

Conclusion: A Legacy of Bold Leadership and Impact

Indra Nooyi's journey from Chennai to the top of PepsiCo is a powerful testament to the importance of visionary leadership, resilience, and purpose-driven success. She redefined what it means to be a global business leader, demonstrating that companies can thrive while contributing positively to society.

Her story continues to inspire leaders worldwide, proving that success is not just about financial results but about leaving a lasting impact—on businesses, people, and the world. Nooyi's legacy as a trailblazing leader will endure, as she continues to advocate for more inclusive, sustainable, and compassionate leadership for generations to come.

Walt Disney's Success Story: From dreams to Global Magic

"Copyright ensures that your creative labor isn't just for today—it's a legacy that extends well beyond your lifetime. It's about making sure your voice, your vision, remains alive and well for generations."
— WALT DISNEY, FOUNDER OF THE
WALT DISNEY COMPANY

Walt Disney, a visionary in entertainment and innovation, transformed childhood dreams and storytelling into a global empire. Born in 1901, Disney's passion for art and animation was evident from a young age, though his early career was marked by setbacks and financial struggles. Refusing to give up, he revolutionized the entertainment industry with the creation of Mickey Mouse and later redefined animation with the release of *Snow White and the Seven Dwarfs*. Disney's relentless pursuit of creativity extended beyond film, leading to the creation of Disneyland and inspiring the birth of theme parks worldwide. His story is one of imagination, persistence, and the belief that with hard work, even the most ambitious dreams can become reality.

Early Life and Passion for Art

Walter Elias Disney was born on December 5, 1901, in Chicago, Illinois. Raised in a family with modest means, Walt developed an early passion for drawing and storytelling. As a child, he sold sketches to neighbors and experimented with cartooning while attending school. His family moved to Kansas City, where Disney's fascination with entertainment and performance grew as he attended vaudeville shows and read comic strips. Despite struggling academically, his artistic ambition persisted, laying the foundation for his future career.

The First Steps: From Laugh-O-Grams to Hollywood

After serving briefly in World War I as an ambulance driver, Disney returned to Kansas City, where he pursued a career in commercial art. He founded his first venture, Laugh-O-Gram Studios, producing animated shorts based on fairy tales. Although creative, the studio lacked financial success and eventually went bankrupt. Undeterred, Disney moved to Hollywood in 1923 with just $40 and a suitcase filled with dreams.

In Los Angeles, Walt and his brother, Roy Disney, established the Disney Brothers Studio. They began producing a successful series called Alice Comedies, blending live action with animation. But it wasn't until they created Oswald the Lucky Rabbit that they found widespread recognition. However, Disney lost the rights to Oswald due to a legal dispute, an experience that taught him valuable lessons about business control and intellectual property.

The Creation of Mickey Mouse: A Cultural Icon is Born

Determined to recover from the loss of Oswald, Disney and animator Ub Iwerks developed a new character: Mickey Mouse. Mickey's first two silent cartoons failed to attract interest, but the third attempt, Steamboat Willie (1928), became the first synchronized sound cartoon, a pioneering achievement. Mickey Mouse quickly became an international sensation, cementing Walt Disney's reputation as a leader in the entertainment industry.

The success of Mickey Mouse allowed Disney to expand his creative ambitions, introducing other beloved characters such as Donald Duck, Goofy, and Pluto. In 1932, Walt Disney received an honorary Academy Award for the creation of Mickey, the first of many accolades throughout his career.

Innovation with Feature-Length Films

Disney's drive to innovate led him to pursue a project that most people deemed impossible: the first-ever feature-length animated film, Snow White and the Seven Dwarfs. Released in 1937, the film was a groundbreaking success, both financially and critically, and demonstrated the power of animation to tell deep, emotional stories. This triumph provided the funds for Disney to expand his studio and develop additional classics, including Pinocchio (1940), Fantasia (1940), Dumbo (1941), and Bambi (1942).

However, Disney's path was not without obstacles. World War II interrupted film production, and the studio faced financial difficulties. Yet, Walt remained committed to his vision, constantly searching for new ways to captivate audiences.

Building Disneyland: A World of Imagination

In the early 1950s, Walt Disney turned his attention to an even grander dream: Disneyland, a theme park where children and adults could experience the magic of his creations firsthand. Disneyland opened in Anaheim, California, in 1955 and was an instant success, redefining the amusement park industry with its attention to detail, immersive storytelling, and innovative attractions.

Walt's vision extended beyond the boundaries of a single park. He envisioned Walt Disney World in Florida as a utopian city blending entertainment with urban innovation, though he did not live to see its completion. Walt Disney World opened in 1971, five years after his death, fulfilling his dream of creating a place where magic, creativity, and innovation coexisted.

The Legacy of Disney Studios

Under Walt Disney's leadership, the company continued to break new ground, launching The Wonderful World of Disney television series and acquiring rights to beloved stories such as Mary Poppins. Beyond films and parks, Disney cultivated a culture of imagination that extended into merchandising, music, and entertainment ventures. His relentless pursuit of creativity and excellence laid the foundation for what is today one of the most influential entertainment companies in the world.

Challenges and Triumphs

Throughout his career, Disney faced numerous challenges, from financial setbacks to skeptics who doubted his ambitious projects. Yet, he persisted, driven by an unshakable belief in the power of imagination. Walt's ability to balance business acumen with creative storytelling set him apart. Despite health struggles later in life, he never stopped working, constantly dreaming of new possibilities.

Impact and Lasting Legacy

Walt Disney passed away in 1966 from complications related to lung cancer, but his legacy continues to thrive. The Walt Disney Company has grown into a global empire encompassing film, television, theme parks, and media networks. His creations—from Mickey Mouse to Disneyland—remain cherished symbols of joy, nostalgia, and wonder.

Disney's impact transcends generations, teaching people that dreams can become reality through perseverance, creativity, and bold thinking. His life is a testament to the power of storytelling and the importance of believing in one's vision, no matter the obstacles. As Disney once said, "All our dreams can come true, if we have the courage to pursue them."

===

Angela Duckworth's Success Story: The Science of Grit and Success

"Post-launch marketing is like stoking a fire; you must keep feeding it fresh material to maintain its warmth and light, ensuring your book continues to illuminate in the minds of readers." — ANGELA DUCKWORTH, PSYCHOLOGIST AND AUTHOR

Angela Duckworth, a psychologist, researcher, and bestselling author, has redefined how the world views success. Known for her groundbreaking concept of *grit*, Duckworth emphasizes that passion and perseverance—not talent alone—are the key drivers of achievement. From her early career as a teacher to becoming an acclaimed author and academic, Duckworth's journey reflects the very principles she champions: persistence, growth, and relentless dedication. Through her research, book, and nonprofit initiatives, she has empowered countless individuals and institutions to embrace grit, transforming the way people approach challenges and long-term goals.

Early Life: Curiosity and Academic Pursuits

Angela Duckworth, born in 1970 to Chinese immigrant parents, grew up in a household that emphasized the importance of hard work and education. Her father often reminded her that she wasn't a "genius," a label that would later inspire her to question traditional ideas about talent. Duckworth's childhood was filled with challenges and expectations, instilling in her a drive to understand what truly leads to success.

Shifting Career Paths: From Consulting to Education

Initially, Duckworth pursued a corporate career, working as a management consultant at McKinsey & Company. However, she found herself drawn to deeper, more meaningful work. Leaving behind the corporate world, she became a public school teacher, where she observed that students' success wasn't determined by IQ alone. This experience sparked her curiosity about the traits that influence achievement beyond innate talent.

Academic Pursuits and Breakthrough Research

Driven by her desire to understand human potential, Duckworth returned to academia to earn her Ph.D. in psychology at the University of Pennsylvania. It was during her research that she identified a crucial concept: *grit*. Duckworth defined grit as the combination of passion and perseverance in the pursuit of long-term goals, suggesting that persistence is just as vital as talent for success.

Writing *Grit: The Power of Passion and Perseverance*

In 2016, Duckworth published her groundbreaking book, *Grit: The Power of Passion and Perseverance*. Drawing on both personal experience and years of research, the book argues that sustained effort and resilience are more critical than intelligence or talent in achieving success. *Grit* became an instant bestseller, resonating with readers across industries and education systems, and igniting conversations about the importance of character and effort.

Impact and Influence

Duckworth's research and book have influenced fields ranging from education to business and athletics. She co-founded the Character Lab, an organization dedicated to promoting research-based practices for character development in children, and her ideas have been widely embraced by schools and institutions worldwide. Duckworth's TED Talk on grit has garnered millions of views, further cementing her influence in shaping how society thinks about success.

Legacy and Continuing Work

Angela Duckworth's career is a testament to her belief in the power of perseverance. From corporate offices to classrooms, she has continuously sought deeper understanding and made meaningful contributions to education, psychology, and personal development. Today, Duckworth continues to teach, research, and speak globally, inspiring individuals to adopt a mindset focused on grit, determination, and lifelong learning.

―――――――

CHAPTER TWO

Planning for Success

Success in business is rarely an accident—it's the result of meticulous planning, strategic thinking, and consistent execution. While vision serves as the guiding star, a well-thought-out plan acts as the map, transforming ideas into actionable steps. A solid business plan provides the structure needed to navigate uncertainty, anticipate challenges, and chart a path forward. Planning for success means more than just setting goals—it requires the ability to translate dreams into concrete strategies that cover every aspect of your business, from operations to marketing, finance, and growth.

This chapter explores how effective planning acts as both a safeguard against risks and a tool for seizing opportunities. As Michael Porter, a leading authority on business strategy, emphasizes, "Strategy is about making choices, trade-offs; it's about deliberately choosing to be different." Every business plan should reflect these deliberate choices—clearly identifying the market you will serve, the customers you will reach, and the competitive edge that will set you apart. Planning for success involves pinpointing the specific steps that will transform your concept into a sustainable business model. We'll dive into examples from entrepreneurs like Phil Knight, who leveraged strategic planning to outmaneuver competitors and achieve lasting growth.

A key component of planning is flexibility. While detailed plans are essential, business environments are fluid, requiring continuous adaptation. The most successful entrepreneurs, such as Eric Ries, author of *The Lean Startup*, recognize that success often necessitates multiple iterations of a business model before finding the perfect fit. This chapter will guide you in constructing a plan that is both detailed and adaptable, providing your business with a strong foundation while allowing room to pivot when necessary.

Planning for success also involves mastering financial projections and risk management. We'll cover essential tools like break-even analysis, cash flow projections, and budgeting techniques to ensure your business can survive and thrive through unexpected challenges. Warren Buffett wisely stated, "Risk comes from not knowing what you're doing." Understanding the financial side of your business equips you to make informed decisions and minimizes uncertainty. Whether you're seeking investors, managing daily operations, or planning for long-term growth, clear financial planning gives you the insight and confidence to act decisively.

Additionally, this chapter will explore the importance of setting measurable goals. From defining key performance indicators (KPIs) to developing timelines and milestones, we'll help you create a framework that keeps your business on track. Effective planning doesn't conclude with writing a plan—it requires continuous monitoring and refinement. Influential thinkers like Daniel Pink and Seth Godin advocate for data-driven approaches, so we'll introduce practical methods for tracking progress and making informed adjustments along the way, ensuring your business stays aligned with both its short-term objectives and long-term vision.

By the end of this chapter, you'll understand the key elements of planning that lead to success. You'll be equipped with tools to create a comprehensive business plan, strategies for managing risks, and techniques for setting realistic goals that drive performance. Planning for success means preparing for the unexpected while remaining focused on your larger mission, giving your business the best chance to grow, evolve, and thrive. With the right plan in place, you won't just launch a business—you'll build an enterprise ready to succeed in any market conditions.

Michael Porter's Success Story: The Father of Competitive Strategy and Modern Business Thinking

"Strategic business planning is about setting a course for your company that not only anticipates market changes but also aligns every action and decision with your core mission and long-term goals."
— MICHAEL PORTER, ECONOMIST AND PROFESSOR
AT HARVARD BUSINESS SCHOOL

"Strategy is about making choices, trade-offs; it's about deliberately choosing to be different." — MICHAEL PORTER,
ECONOMIST AND RESEARCHER

"Filing for a trademark isn't just a procedural step; it's a strategic move that protects your brand's core identity and paves the way for long-term success in the marketplace." — MICHAEL PORTER, PROFESSOR
AND AUTHORITY ON CORPORATE STRATEGY AND
THE COMPETITIVENESS OF NATIONS

Michael Porter is widely regarded as the pioneer of modern competitive strategy and one of the most influential thinkers in the fields of business, economics, and public policy. His groundbreaking work on competitive advantage, industry analysis, and strategic frameworks has shaped the way companies, governments, and non-profits think about competition, innovation, and growth. Porter's journey from an ambitious student to a world-renowned strategist and professor at Harvard Business School is a story of intellectual rigor, visionary thinking, and lasting impact.

Early Life and Education
Michael Eugene Porter was born on May 23, 1947, in Ann Arbor, Michigan. Growing up in a family that valued education, Porter excelled in academics and was a gifted athlete, particularly in golf. His passion for learning and problem-

solving led him to Princeton University, where he studied mechanical and aerospace engineering and graduated in 1969.

Despite his technical background, Porter developed an interest in the intersection between economics and business strategy. This fascination motivated him to pursue a Master's in Business Administration (MBA) from Harvard Business School (HBS) and later a Ph.D. in Business Economics from Harvard University.

Breaking New Ground at Harvard Business School
Porter began his academic career at Harvard Business School in the mid-1970s as a professor of business strategy. It was here that he would make a groundbreaking contribution to the world of business with the development of his Five Forces Framework—a tool that revolutionized the way businesses think about industry competition and profitability.

Porter's Five Forces model, published in his seminal book "Competitive Strategy: Techniques for Analyzing Industries and Competitors" (1980), introduced a simple but profound idea: the success of any business is determined not just by internal factors, but by external competitive forces. The Five Forces are:

1. **Industry Rivalry**

2. **Threat of New Entrants**

3. **Bargaining Power of Suppliers**

4. **Bargaining Power of Customers**

5. **Threat of Substitutes**

This framework provided companies with a systematic way to analyze competition and develop strategies to achieve competitive advantage. The book became an instant classic, cementing Porter's reputation as a leading thinker in strategic management.

Defining Competitive Advantage
In 1985, Porter further expanded his work with the publication of "Competitive Advantage: Creating and Sustaining Superior Performance." This book introduced the concept of the value chain, a tool that helps companies identify the activities that contribute to competitive advantage. Porter argued that companies

could gain an edge by either pursuing cost leadership or differentiation, laying the foundation for what is now known as competitive positioning.

The book's influence extended beyond corporations to consultants, policymakers, and business schools, making Porter a sought-after expert in the field of strategic management. His work redefined how companies compete in dynamic markets and maintain profitability over time.

Expanding His Influence into Public Policy
Porter's expertise didn't stop at the corporate level—he extended his research into economic development and public policy. His 1990 book, "The Competitive Advantage of Nations," introduced a framework for understanding how nations and regions achieve economic success. Porter's Diamond Model identified four key factors that contribute to national competitive advantage:

1. **Factor Conditions** (e.g., resources, infrastructure)

2. **Demand Conditions** (e.g., local market demand)

3. **Related and Supporting Industries**

4. **Firm Strategy, Structure, and Rivalry**

Porter's work in this area had a significant impact on governments and policymakers, guiding economic development strategies around the world. His insights into the role of clusters—geographical concentrations of interconnected businesses—became instrumental in shaping regional economic policy.

Founding the Institute for Strategy and Competitiveness
In 2001, Porter founded the Institute for Strategy and Competitiveness at Harvard Business School. The Institute became a hub for research on topics ranging from healthcare innovation to corporate social responsibility (CSR). Porter's later work focused on the concept of "shared value"—the idea that businesses can create both economic value and social value by addressing societal challenges.

This groundbreaking work redefined how companies think about their role in society and provided a new framework for sustainable business practices. Porter became a thought leader on the intersection of business and social impact, influencing a generation of executives and policymakers.

Global Recognition and Thought Leadership

Over the years, Porter's contributions have earned him numerous awards and accolades. He has been recognized as one of the most influential thinkers in business and economics by publications like Harvard Business Review and Fortune. His Five Forces model remains a core part of MBA programs around the world, and his work continues to shape how businesses and governments develop strategies for growth.

Porter has also served as an advisor to heads of state, CEOs, and major organizations, influencing economic development in countries like Singapore, Rwanda, and Colombia. His ability to bridge the gap between theory and practice has made him a respected figure in both academia and the business world.

Legacy and Impact

Today, Michael Porter's theories on strategy, competition, and economic development are more relevant than ever. His frameworks have become essential tools for businesses, helping leaders navigate complex markets, achieve sustainable growth, and gain a competitive edge. His influence extends far beyond business strategy—Porter's work has redefined how companies, regions, and nations create value in an interconnected world.

Porter's ability to think deeply, act strategically, and communicate clearly has made him one of the most influential thought leaders of our time. His legacy lies not just in the books he has written or the awards he has won, but in the millions of businesses and individuals who have applied his ideas to solve real-world challenges.

Conclusion

Michael Porter's journey from a young scholar to the father of competitive strategy is a testament to the power of intellectual curiosity and relentless pursuit of excellence. His work has not only transformed how companies compete but has also reshaped the way economies grow and societies thrive. Through his groundbreaking research, Porter has left an indelible mark on business, economics, and public policy, ensuring his influence will be felt for generations to come.

Eric Ries's Success Story: The Lean Journey to Success

"Mastering the art of the pivot in business is about recognizing when the path you're on isn't leading you towards your goals and having the courage to take a new direction for better outcomes." — ERIC RIES, ENTREPRENEUR AND AUTHOR OF THE LEAN STARTUP

Eric Ries, best known as the author of *The Lean Startup*, carved a unique path from aspiring software engineer to entrepreneurial thought leader, transforming the way startups approach innovation and growth. His journey is a testament to the value of persistence, learning from failure, and questioning traditional business models.

Early Beginnings and First Ventures

Eric Ries graduated from Yale University in 2001 with a degree in computer science. After graduation, he plunged into the tech world, fueled by the dot-com boom. His early ventures, however, were not without challenges. One of his first startups, Catalyst Recruiting, which aimed to connect students with companies, failed. This experience taught Ries valuable lessons about execution, the unpredictability of customer behavior, and the importance of adaptability.

Still determined, Ries took a role as a software engineer at There.com, a virtual world startup. The platform was ambitious, but after raising over $40 million, it ultimately shut down. The painful closure of There.com reinforced Ries's growing belief: excessive reliance on assumptions about users and lengthy product development cycles often spell doom for startups.

IMVU: Where Theory Meets Reality

Ries's pivotal moment came when he co-founded IMVU, a 3D social networking service, in 2004. IMVU was a platform where users could create avatars and purchase virtual goods to interact socially. This project became the breeding ground for the ideas that would later shape his philosophy of *lean entrepreneurship*.

At IMVU, the founders initially believed that users wanted product features like avatar interoperability across platforms. They spent six months building these features without any customer feedback, only to discover that users were uninterested. The realization hit hard: time and money had been wasted building something customers didn't need.

To avoid future missteps, Ries and his team adopted an iterative approach. They launched incomplete versions of the product—Minimum Viable Products (MVPs)—to test customer response. They learned directly from user feedback, discarding unnecessary features and focusing on what worked. This new strategy led to IMVU's success, with the company growing steadily and reaching profitability.

The Birth of the Lean Startup Methodology
Through the highs and lows of IMVU, Ries crystallized a new framework for building companies. He realized the old-school mentality of writing a full-fledged business plan and following it religiously no longer worked in the fast-paced world of tech startups. Instead, companies needed to adopt an agile, experimental mindset.

This led to the birth of the Lean Startup methodology, which revolves around three core principles:

1. **Build-Measure-Learn:** Start with a small experiment (an MVP), measure customer response, and learn what works.

2. **Validated Learning:** Use feedback from real customers to guide further development.

3. **Pivot or Persevere:** If an idea isn't working, change direction (pivot) without hesitation.

By focusing on validated learning rather than assumptions, companies could move faster, make fewer mistakes, and increase their odds of success.

The Lean Startup Movement
After IMVU, Ries dedicated himself to refining and sharing the *Lean Startup* philosophy. His approach was initially met with skepticism—many business leaders were reluctant to embrace the idea of releasing unfinished products. But Ries's method resonated with entrepreneurs frustrated by outdated practices.

In 2011, Ries published The Lean Startup: How Today's Entrepreneurs Use Continuous Innovation to Create Radically Successful Businesses. The book became a global sensation, providing a blueprint for startups, large corporations, and even non-profits. It quickly became a must-read in the startup world and was hailed for giving practical tools to entrepreneurs navigating uncertainty.

Beyond Lean Startup: Scaling the Impact

Ries didn't stop with writing the book. He became a sought-after speaker and consultant, working with companies like GE and Toyota to implement lean principles at scale. His philosophy extended beyond startups to established corporations through the Lean Startup Labs, helping organizations innovate from within by creating internal entrepreneurial teams.

Ries also founded the Long-Term Stock Exchange (LTSE), a public market aimed at promoting long-term thinking among companies and investors. LTSE aligns with his vision of sustainable innovation by encouraging businesses to focus on lasting impact rather than quarterly profits.

The Legacy of Eric Ries

Eric Ries's journey is not just a story of personal success—it's about reshaping the way people think about building businesses. By advocating for small, rapid iterations and customer-centric development, Ries has empowered countless entrepreneurs to pursue innovation without fear of failure. His philosophy challenges the status quo, teaching that failure is not a dead end but a stepping stone to learning.

Today, Ries's legacy lives on in the thriving global *Lean Startup* community. From Silicon Valley to corporate boardrooms, his ideas continue to inspire new generations of entrepreneurs to embrace uncertainty, experiment boldly, and build better, faster, and more resilient companies.

Key Takeaways from Eric Ries's Story

1. **Learn from Failure:** Every failure contains valuable lessons if you reflect on what went wrong.

2. **Test Ideas Early:** Launch small experiments to learn what works before committing resources.

3. **Customer-Centric Approach:** Build what your customers want, not what you assume they need.

4. **Embrace Change:** Be prepared to pivot when your initial assumptions prove wrong.

5. **Focus on Long-Term Success:** Sustainable innovation requires long-term thinking.

Eric Ries's story exemplifies how persistence, learning from mistakes, and a willingness to challenge traditional thinking can pave the way to extraordinary success. His *Lean Startup* methodology has not only transformed how startups operate but also made an indelible mark on the business world at large.

―――――

Warren Buffett's Success Story: From Young Investor to the Oracle of Omaha

"Crafting realistic financial projections isn't just a numbers game; it's a critical exercise in forecasting the future health and potential of your business."
— WARREN BUFFETT, INVESTOR AND PHILANTHROPIST

"Risk comes from not knowing what you're doing." — WARREN BUFFETT, INVESTOR AND PHILANTHROPIST

"Evaluating the economic viability of your business idea is the cornerstone of entrepreneurial success. It's not just about having capital; it's about knowing how, when, and where to allocate it to maximize your return." — WARREN BUFFETT, CEO OF BERKSHIRE HATHAWAY

"Each trademark success or setback teaches a critical lesson in brand protection. By studying these cases, we sharpen our strategies and strengthen our defenses." — WARREN BUFFETT, CHAIRMAN AND CEO OF BERKSHIRE HATHAWAY

"Adhering to legal agreements isn't just about following rules—it's about establishing a reputation of reliability and trust in a world where your word is your bond." — WARREN BUFFETT, CEO OF BERKSHIRE HATHAWAY

Warren Buffett, one of the most successful investors of all time, didn't build his fortune overnight. His rise to success is a story of discipline, patience, and long-term vision. Often referred to as the "Oracle of Omaha," Buffett is known for his simple yet profound investment principles and his unparalleled ability to create wealth over decades. Here's how Warren Buffett became one of the richest and most respected businessmen in the world.

Early Life and Business Acumen

Born in 1930 in Omaha, Nebraska, Warren Buffett demonstrated his knack for business and finance at a young age. By the time he was 11, he made his first stock purchase, buying three shares of Cities Service Preferred at $38 per share. While the price dropped to $27 soon after his purchase, Buffett held onto his investment until it rebounded to $40. The lesson he learned from this experience—to be patient and think long-term—would shape his investment philosophy for life.

Buffett's entrepreneurial spirit was evident from his childhood. He sold Coca-Cola and magazines door to door and operated a pinball machine business with a friend, reinvesting profits to purchase additional machines.

Education and Mentorship

Buffett attended the University of Nebraska at age 16 and graduated with a degree in business. He then applied to Harvard Business School but was rejected. Instead, he enrolled at Columbia Business School, where he studied under Benjamin Graham, the father of value investing and author of the highly influential book, "The Intelligent Investor."

Graham's teachings on value investing—focusing on companies that are undervalued by the market but have strong potential—deeply influenced Buffett's investment style. After graduation, Buffett worked at Graham's firm, Graham-Newman Corp, learning firsthand the principles of value investing.

The Creation of Buffett's Empire: Berkshire Hathaway

In 1956, Warren Buffett returned to Omaha and started Buffett Partnership Ltd. His early investment partnerships were highly successful, growing exponentially over the years. By the late 1960s, Buffett had amassed significant wealth, and in 1965, he took control of Berkshire Hathaway, a struggling textile company.

While the textile business didn't thrive, Buffett transformed Berkshire Hathaway into a holding company, using it as a vehicle for investing in other businesses. His early acquisitions included companies like National Indemnity (insurance) and GEICO (auto insurance). Insurance became a cornerstone of Buffett's strategy because it provided significant cash reserves, called "float," that he could invest elsewhere.

Investment Philosophy and Key Successes

Buffett's investment strategy has always been simple but effective: invest in companies with strong fundamentals, durable competitive advantages, and capable management, but only when they are available at attractive prices. He looks for businesses that he understands and believes in, typically holding investments for the long term, reflecting his famous quote: "Our favorite holding period is forever."

Some of Buffett's most famous investments include:

- **Coca-Cola**: Buffett began buying shares in Coca-Cola in 1988, eventually becoming its largest shareholder.

- **American Express**: After a financial scandal in the 1960s, Buffett saw long-term potential in the company and invested heavily.

- **Apple**: Although initially averse to tech stocks, Buffett's company, Berkshire Hathaway, invested in Apple in 2016, which became one of his most profitable holdings.

Buffett is also known for shunning risky trends and speculative markets like dot-com stocks in the 1990s, sticking to his philosophy of investing in stable, profitable companies.

Personal Wealth and Philanthropy

Despite his incredible wealth—Buffett's net worth regularly ranks among the top 10 richest people in the world—he is known for his frugality and modest lifestyle. He still lives in the same house in Omaha that he purchased in 1958 for $31,500, and he famously drives a Cadillac rather than expensive luxury cars.

Buffett's success has not just been financial. His commitment to philanthropy is equally impressive. In 2006, he pledged to give away the majority of his wealth to charitable causes, primarily through the Bill & Melinda Gates Foundation. Buffett is also one of the co-founders of The Giving Pledge, an initiative that encourages the world's wealthiest individuals to give away at least half of their fortunes to charity.

Legacy: The Oracle of Omaha

Warren Buffett's long-term approach to investing, his refusal to follow trends, and his unwavering belief in the value of fundamental analysis have made him one of the most successful and admired investors in history. Today, Berkshire Hathaway is a multibillion-dollar conglomerate with interests in everything from insurance and energy to retail and railroads.

Buffett's enduring success serves as a powerful lesson for investors around the world: patience, discipline, and a deep understanding of the companies you invest in are the keys to building long-term wealth.

Seth Godin's Success Story: From Marketing Maverick to Thought Leader

"Great marketing isn't about pushing products; it's about pulling people in. The key is to understand your audience so well that your message feels like a personal invitation they can't resist." — SETH GODIN, MARKETING EXPERT AND BEST-SELLING AUTHOR

"Don't find customers for your products, find products for your customers." — SETH GODIN, MARKETING GURU AND BESTSELLING AUTHOR

"Effective marketing and promotion go beyond spreading the word; they involve crafting messages that resonate deeply, creating meaningful connections with your audience and turning interest into action." — SETH GODIN, AUTHOR AND MARKETING EXPERT

"If your website doesn't grow your audience, it's not an asset; it's a liability." — SETH GODIN, MARKETING GURU AND BEST-SELLING AUTHOR

"Turn your blog into a business where every word you write can open a door to a new revenue stream. It's not just about building an audience; it's about building a marketplace." — SETH GODIN, AUTHOR AND ENTREPRENEUR

"Building a community is about more than just gathering an audience. It's about creating an environment where every interaction adds value and every member feels like they belong. When you achieve that, you turn your followers into advocates." — SETH GODIN, MARKETING EXPERT AND BESTSELLING AUTHOR

"Pre-marketing is like setting the stage before the curtain rises. It's your chance to ensure that by the time the spotlight hits, the audience is not just present, but excited." — SETH GODIN, MARKETING EXPERT

"Adopting a market leader's mindset is about seeing the invisible and doing the impossible. It's not just about leading in sales, but leading in innovation, influence, and insight." — SETH GODIN, MARKETING GURU

"Crafting dynamic ad campaigns goes beyond flashy visuals; it's about building connections and driving conversions with every click." — SETH GODIN, AUTHOR, ENTREPRENEUR, AND MARKETING EXPERT

"Turning interest into revenue is an art form where each strategy is a brushstroke that paints a compelling picture for your customers, drawing them irresistibly into the narrative of your brand." — SETH GODIN, MARKETING EXPERT

"Strategic PR for authors isn't just about selling books; it's about crafting a narrative around your work that captivates and engages, turning each release into a must-read event." — SETH GODIN, AUTHOR AND MARKETING EXPERT

"Marketing is no longer about the stuff that you make, but about the stories you tell and the worlds you create around your brand."
— SETH GODIN, MARKETING EXPERT

"Being on trend is a safe place to be; starting a trend is where true leaders thrive." — SETH GODIN, AUTHOR AND MARKETING EXPERT

"Hosting book signings and launch events is not just about publicity—it's about creating memorable experiences that forge lasting connections with your readers." — SETH GODIN, AUTHOR, ENTREPRENEUR, AND MARKETING EXPERT

"Going beyond the basics with service marks and promotional strategies is about creating a distinct identity that communicates value and builds lasting connections with your audience." — SETH GODIN, AUTHOR, ENTREPRENEUR, AND MARKETING EXPERT

Seth Godin is widely recognized as one of the most influential minds in marketing, entrepreneurship, and personal development. He has reshaped how people think about marketing by focusing on creativity, empathy, and breaking away from traditional methods. His journey to success is marked by bold thinking, innovation, and an unrelenting passion for challenging the status quo.

Early Life and Entrepreneurial Beginnings

Seth Godin was born in 1960 in Mount Vernon, New York. He attended Tufts University, where he earned a degree in computer science and philosophy. He then went on to earn an MBA from Stanford Graduate School of Business. His educational background gave him a solid foundation in both analytical thinking and creativity, a combination that would become key in his later success.

After completing his education, Godin worked at Spinnaker Software, a computer software company, where he honed his marketing skills. In 1986, he founded Seth Godin Productions, a book packaging business, where he developed a deep understanding of publishing and content creation. However, it wasn't until his next venture that Godin truly began to disrupt the marketing landscape.

Yoyodyne and the Birth of Permission Marketing

In 1995, Godin founded Yoyodyne, an innovative internet-based direct marketing company. Yoyodyne specialized in using online contests and games to promote businesses and build customer engagement. It was through Yoyodyne that Godin first began exploring the concept of permission marketing, a revolutionary idea at the time.

Permission marketing was based on the idea that businesses should ask for customers' permission before marketing to them, rather than bombarding them with unsolicited ads. This approach recognized the importance of building trust and relationships with customers and was a stark contrast to the interruptive advertising methods that dominated the industry.

Godin's ideas about permission marketing gained significant traction, and in 1998, Yahoo! purchased Yoyodyne for $30 million, making Godin a recognized figure in the marketing world. His work at Yoyodyne helped lay the foundation for many of the personalized, customer-focused marketing strategies that are common in today's digital age.

Thought Leadership and Bestselling Books

After selling Yoyodyne, Seth Godin shifted his focus to writing and public speaking, becoming one of the most prominent voices in marketing. In 1999, he published *Permission Marketing: Turning Strangers into Friends and Friends into Customers*, a book that solidified his status as a thought leader. The book outlined his philosophy that marketing should be about earning the trust and attention of customers rather than intruding on it.

Godin went on to write several more bestselling books that challenged conventional wisdom and offered innovative ways to approach business, marketing, and personal development. Some of his most notable books include:

- *Purple Cow* (2003): This book encourages businesses to be remarkable in a world filled with ordinary products. Godin emphasizes that in order to stand out, companies need to create products that are truly different, much like a purple cow would stand out in a field of brown cows.

- *Tribes* (2008): Godin talks about the power of leadership and community in this book. He explores how people are looking for leaders to guide

45

them and how businesses can thrive by building a tribe of loyal followers who believe in their mission.

- *Linchpin* **(2010)**: In this book, Godin challenges individuals to become indispensable by embracing creativity, taking initiative, and becoming "linchpins" in their organizations.

- *The Dip* **(2007)**: Godin addresses the idea that quitting at the right time is just as important as persevering through challenges. This book encourages readers to focus their energy on areas where they can truly excel and let go of pursuits that aren't yielding results.

Blogging and Public Speaking

Seth Godin's influence extends far beyond his books. He is also known for his highly popular blog, which offers daily insights on business, marketing, and personal development. Godin's blog, considered one of the most-read in the world, reflects his straightforward and impactful style. His short, thought-provoking posts resonate with millions of readers, consistently delivering fresh perspectives on marketing, leadership, and innovation.

In addition to his writing, Godin is a prolific public speaker. He has delivered talks and keynotes at countless conferences, including TED, where his talks on marketing, leadership, and creativity have garnered millions of views. His ability to communicate complex ideas with clarity and simplicity has made him one of the most sought-after speakers in the business world.

The AltMBA and Education Initiatives

In recent years, Godin has turned his attention to education. In 2015, he launched The altMBA, an intensive online leadership and management workshop designed to help people develop critical skills for the modern world. The altMBA focuses on collaboration, accountability, and hands-on projects rather than traditional lectures, embodying Godin's belief in transformational learning over rote memorization.

Godin has also expanded his education initiatives through The Akimbo Workshops, a series of online workshops that cover topics ranging from marketing to personal development. These initiatives reflect his dedication to empowering people to make a difference in their work and lives.

The Legacy of Seth Godin

Seth Godin's career has been defined by his ability to challenge the status quo and his relentless pursuit of better ways to do business. His ideas about permission marketing, leadership, and creativity have influenced countless entrepreneurs, marketers, and business leaders. Whether through his books, blog, or speaking engagements, Godin's impact on marketing and personal development is undeniable.

Godin's approach to marketing as storytelling, building authentic relationships with customers, and embracing remarkability continues to inspire new generations of marketers and leaders. Today, Seth Godin is more than a marketing expert—he is a mentor, philosopher, and visionary whose work has transformed the way people think about business and success.

Daniel Pink's Success Story: Redefining Motivation, Work, and the Human Mind

"Planning ahead for future works and options is about creating a roadmap for success, enabling strategic flexibility and readiness to capitalize on opportunities as they arise." — DANIEL PINK, AUTHOR AND BEHAVIORAL SCIENCE EXPERT

"Analyzing your launch outcomes isn't just about measuring success; it's about mining your data for the golden insights that will guide your next big move." — DANIEL PINK, AUTHOR AND BEHAVIORAL EXPERT

"In sales, success doesn't come from what you sell; it comes from how you sell it. Mastery lies in understanding the customer so well that the product or service fits them and sells itself." — DANIEL PINK, AUTHOR AND SALES EXPERT

Daniel H. Pink, a bestselling author and thought leader in business, psychology, and human behavior, is known for his groundbreaking insights on motivation, creativity, and the future of work. Pink's journey from a law student turned speechwriter to one of the most influential thinkers on the modern workplace

47

exemplifies the power of curiosity, reinvention, and deep inquiry into what drives human success. His books, including *Drive*, *To Sell Is Human*, and *When*, have reshaped how individuals and organizations approach work and performance.

Early Life and Education: The Foundation of Curiosity

Daniel Pink was born on July 23, 1964, in Bexley, Ohio, a suburb of Columbus. Growing up in a middle-class family, Pink was drawn to writing, public speaking, and understanding human behavior. He excelled in academics, and after graduating high school, he enrolled at Northwestern University, where he earned a degree in linguistics.

After Northwestern, Pink pursued a law degree at Yale Law School, following the traditional path toward a professional career. However, after completing his JD, Pink realized that a legal career wasn't his true passion. Instead, he sought a career that allowed him to explore human behavior, communication, and big ideas—all of which would later become central themes in his writing.

A Detour into Politics: Speechwriting and Communication

After law school, Pink shifted gears and entered the world of politics and public service. He worked as a speechwriter for Al Gore, the Vice President of the United States, in the mid-1990s. In this role, Pink honed his ability to craft messages that resonate with audiences and communicate complex ideas clearly—skills that would serve him well in his future writing career.

Despite his success in politics, Pink realized that he wanted more creative freedom. He left the political world to become a writer, pursuing his passion for exploring ideas at the intersection of business, psychology, and human behavior. The decision to leave a stable career behind was a risky move, but it allowed Pink to follow his curiosity and write about what truly fascinated him.

Breaking Through: 'Free Agent Nation' and the New World of Work

Pink's first major book, *Free Agent Nation: The Future of Working for Yourself*, was published in 2001. It explored the rise of freelancers, independent contractors, and self-employed individuals—a trend that was just beginning to reshape the economy. Based on extensive research and interviews, the book captured the early stages of the gig economy and offered insights into how people were finding freedom and fulfillment outside traditional employment.

Free Agent Nation resonated with many readers and established Pink as a forward-thinking voice in the business world. His ability to identify trends and articulate their impact on the workforce set the tone for his future work. The book gave Pink credibility as a thought leader and opened doors for speaking engagements and media appearances.

'A Whole New Mind': Creativity and the Conceptual Age

In 2005, Pink released "A Whole New Mind: Why Right-Brainers Will Rule the Future." The book argued that the future would belong to those who could think creatively, empathetically, and holistically—skills often associated with the right hemisphere of the brain. Pink suggested that as automation and outsourcing reduce the need for analytical and repetitive tasks, creative and emotional intelligence would become essential for success.

The book became a bestseller, particularly among educators, entrepreneurs, and innovators. Pink's message resonated with readers who saw the value of design, empathy, and storytelling in a rapidly changing economy. *A Whole New Mind* helped shift the conversation about the importance of creativity and set the stage for the rise of the creative economy.

'Drive': Transforming How We Think About Motivation

In 2009, Pink released his most influential book to date: *Drive: The Surprising Truth About What Motivates Us*. Drawing on research from psychology and behavioral economics, Pink challenged the traditional belief that rewards and punishments (the "carrot and stick" approach) are the best ways to motivate people.

Instead, Pink introduced the concept of intrinsic motivation, explaining that people are more motivated by three key factors:

1. **Autonomy:** The desire to direct one's own life.

2. **Mastery:** The urge to improve and excel at something meaningful.

3. **Purpose:** The need to feel that what you do has meaning and contributes to something larger than yourself.

Drive became a New York Times bestseller and sparked a revolution in management and leadership practices. Companies began rethinking their incentive structures, moving away from rigid performance metrics and embracing empowerment, learning, and purpose-driven work. The book remains a foundational text in organizational behavior and is widely used in business schools, leadership programs, and corporate training.

'To Sell Is Human': Redefining Sales in the Modern Era

In 2012, Pink turned his attention to sales with *To Sell Is Human: The Surprising Truth About Moving Others*. The book challenged the outdated stereotype of sales as manipulative and aggressive and argued that everyone engages in selling—whether convincing others to take action, share ideas, or adopt a new perspective.

Pink redefined sales as a human-centered activity based on understanding, empathy, and problem-solving. He provided readers with practical techniques for becoming better at persuasion and influence, drawing on insights from psychology and behavioral science.

To Sell Is Human was another bestseller, solidifying Pink's reputation as a thought leader in business psychology. His ability to combine research with practical advice made the book a favorite among entrepreneurs, marketers, and leaders seeking to improve their communication skills.

'When': The Science of Perfect Timing

In 2018, Pink released *When: The Scientific Secrets of Perfect Timing*, a book that explored the science behind timing and how it affects human performance. Pink delved into chronobiology (the study of natural rhythms) to explain how timing influences productivity, decision-making, and well-being.

The book provided readers with actionable strategies for making better decisions about when to start projects, take breaks, or tackle challenging tasks. Pink's ability to blend scientific research with practical applications made *When* another bestseller, helping people optimize their schedules and routines for peak performance.

Speaking, Podcasting, and Ongoing Influence

In addition to his books, Pink has become a sought-after speaker at conferences, companies, and universities around the world. His engaging presentations focus on motivation, behavior, and leadership, inspiring audiences to rethink how they work, lead, and live. Pink's TED Talk on the science of motivation has been viewed millions of times, further cementing his influence in the field of human behavior.

Pink also hosts "The Pinkcast," a short video series offering bite-sized insights and tips for improving work and personal life. His ability to communicate complex ideas with clarity and humor has made him a popular figure in both business and education.

Key Lessons from Daniel Pink's Success

1. **Follow Your Curiosity:** Pink's decision to leave law and politics allowed him to pursue ideas that fascinated him, leading to a more fulfilling career.

2. **Challenge Conventional Wisdom:** Each of Pink's books questions traditional beliefs about work, motivation, and performance, encouraging new ways of thinking.

3. **Make Research Accessible:** Pink's success lies in his ability to translate academic research into practical insights that people can use in their daily lives.

4. **Adapt to Change:** Pink has consistently explored emerging trends, positioning himself at the forefront of discussions about the future of work and human behavior.

5. **Focus on Purpose and Meaning:** His work emphasizes the importance of doing meaningful work that aligns with personal values.

Conclusion: A Thought Leader for the Modern World

Daniel Pink's journey from speechwriter to best-selling author demonstrates the power of following one's passion, embracing curiosity, and challenging the status quo. Through his books, speeches, and research, Pink has redefined how we think about motivation, creativity, and human performance.

His insights have helped companies transform their cultures, inspired individuals to seek purpose and autonomy in their work, and provided practical tools for navigating the challenges of modern life. Pink's legacy lies in his ability to bridge the gap between science and practical application, empowering people to live and work more intentionally in a fast-changing world.

====

Peter Drucker's Success Story: The Father of Modern Management

"Plans are only good intentions unless they immediately degenerate into hard work." — PETER DRUCKER, MANAGEMENT CONSULTANT AND AUTHOR

"Efficiency is doing things right; effectiveness is doing the right things." — PETER DRUCKER, MANAGEMENT CONSULTANT AND AUTHOR

Peter Drucker revolutionized the way we think about business and leadership, earning him the title of the *Father of Modern Management*. Born in Vienna, Austria, in 1909, Drucker's early exposure to economics, politics, and culture deeply shaped his worldview. Over the course of his life, he pioneered key management concepts that transformed businesses across the globe—ideas like decentralization, management by objectives, and the importance of people over profits. Drucker believed that management was not merely a business function but a societal responsibility, promoting ethical practices, innovation, and purpose-driven leadership. His prolific writing, influential consulting work, and decades of teaching shaped generations of leaders, leaving an enduring legacy that continues to inspire organizations to lead with integrity and impact.

Early Life and Influences

Peter Drucker was born on November 19, 1909, in Vienna, Austria, into a family that nurtured intellectual curiosity. His parents frequently hosted conversations with scholars, economists, and artists, exposing Drucker to a variety of ideas from an early age. This environment cultivated his fascination with economics, society, and business. After earning his law degree in Germany, Drucker started his career as a journalist, which provided him with firsthand exposure to political and economic shifts. However, the rise of the Nazi regime in the 1930s forced him to leave Europe, ultimately settling in England and later the United States.

Shaping His Philosophy

Drucker's early experiences witnessing the collapse of governments and economic systems in Europe profoundly shaped his thinking. He understood that

52

effective management—whether of institutions, companies, or governments—was essential for stability and progress. Drucker pursued a career that combined academia, writing, and consulting, allowing him to explore these ideas further. His belief that management is not just about profits but also about human capital became the bedrock of his philosophy.

The Breakthrough: Inventing Management as a Discipline

In 1943, Drucker accepted a consulting assignment at General Motors, which resulted in his seminal book, *Concept of the Corporation*. This book examined how large organizations function and introduced groundbreaking ideas about decentralization, management by objectives (MBO), and leadership structures. It laid the foundation for what would become the discipline of management.

Over the following decades, Drucker developed principles that shifted management from mere administration to a strategic, people-centered practice. He emphasized that businesses should focus not only on profits but also on innovation, customer satisfaction, and employee development. His insights turned management into a profession and redefined leadership in modern organizations.

Legacy Through Books and Teaching

Drucker wrote over 35 books on management, economics, and society, including classics like *The Practice of Management* and *The Effective Executive*. These works became essential reading for managers, entrepreneurs, and CEOs, influencing generations of business leaders. Drucker also taught management at Claremont Graduate University, where he mentored students who would go on to become leaders in their own fields.

Through his teaching and writing, Drucker revolutionized how businesses operate. He was among the first to advocate for treating employees as assets rather than costs, and he believed that companies have a responsibility not just to shareholders but to society at large. His ideas on corporate responsibility remain relevant in today's conversations about ethical business practices and sustainability.

Consulting and Global Impact

Throughout his career, Drucker advised major corporations, governments, and nonprofit organizations. He worked with companies such as IBM, Procter &

Gamble, and Toyota, helping them develop strategies based on his management theories. His consulting extended to the public sector and the nonprofit world, where he believed effective management was equally essential.

Lessons from Drucker's Success

- **People First:** Drucker was ahead of his time in recognizing that the key to a thriving business lies in investing in people.

- **Purpose-Driven Leadership:** He argued that leadership is not about rank but about responsibility, focusing on purpose and results.

- **Continuous Learning:** Drucker's life was a testament to the importance of lifelong learning and curiosity. He continued writing and teaching into his 90s.

Conclusion: A Lasting Legacy

Peter Drucker's contributions to management transformed how companies and leaders operate, and his principles continue to guide businesses today. His focus on purpose, innovation, and human capital laid the groundwork for modern management practices, earning him the title of the *Father of Modern Management*. Drucker's influence transcended industries and generations, making his teachings a vital part of the global business landscape. His legacy serves as a reminder that successful leadership is about more than profits—it's about people, purpose, and creating a positive impact.

Phil Knight's Success Story: Building Nike into a Global Empire

"Protecting a trademark from becoming generic is an ongoing battle of education and enforcement. It's about ensuring your brand doesn't become a victim of its own success." — PHIL KNIGHT, CO-FOUNDER OF NIKE

Phil Knight, the co-founder of Nike, transformed a small shoe-distribution business into one of the most iconic and influential sports brands in the world. With a blend of visionary thinking, relentless determination, and a passion for

54

athletics, Knight revolutionized the way people view sportswear. His journey from selling shoes out of the trunk of his car to leading a global empire is a story of grit, creativity, and calculated risks. Through innovative marketing campaigns, groundbreaking athlete endorsements, and a commitment to performance and style, Knight redefined the athletic industry and built a legacy that continues to inspire entrepreneurs and athletes alike.

Early Life and the Seed of an Idea

Born in Portland, Oregon, in 1938, Phil Knight's love for sports started at an early age. As a student-athlete, Knight ran track at the University of Oregon, where he trained under legendary coach Bill Bowerman. This relationship would later play a crucial role in Knight's entrepreneurial journey. After earning a degree in journalism, Knight pursued an MBA from Stanford University. It was during his time at Stanford that the idea for what would become Nike took shape. For a class project, Knight proposed importing inexpensive, high-quality running shoes from Japan to disrupt the U.S. athletic shoe market, which was then dominated by German brands.

Launching Blue Ribbon Sports

In 1964, Knight teamed up with Bowerman to launch *Blue Ribbon Sports*, starting with a mere $50 investment. Bowerman's expertise in sports innovation and Knight's business acumen were a perfect combination. Initially, Knight sold shoes out of the trunk of his car at local track meets, building personal relationships with athletes. The company imported Japanese running shoes from Onitsuka (later known as ASICS) and gained traction by word-of-mouth among runners who appreciated the superior quality and affordability of the footwear.

The Birth of Nike and the Iconic Swoosh

In 1971, after parting ways with Onitsuka, Knight and Bowerman rebranded their company as *Nike*, named after the Greek goddess of victory. That same year, Knight commissioned a design student to create the company's logo—what would become the iconic swoosh—for just $35. Nike released its first original product, the Cortez running shoe, which became an instant success. Knight's strategy of combining high-performance shoes with innovative marketing campaigns laid the foundation for Nike's future growth.

Endorsements and the Rise to Global Dominance

One of Knight's most strategic moves was signing endorsement deals with rising athletes, the most notable being basketball legend Michael Jordan in 1984. The launch of the Air Jordan line revolutionized both sports marketing and sneaker culture, turning Nike into a global powerhouse. Knight also emphasized the importance of brand identity, introducing the "Just Do It" campaign in 1988—a slogan that continues to inspire athletes worldwide.

Challenges and Triumphs

The journey to success wasn't without setbacks. Nike faced financial difficulties in the early years, including cash flow issues and legal battles. However, Knight's ability to pivot, take risks, and embrace unconventional strategies helped Nike weather these challenges. His leadership philosophy was rooted in persistence, innovation, and a willingness to learn from failure—qualities that are woven into the brand's DNA today.

Legacy and Lasting Impact

Knight stepped down as CEO of Nike in 2004 but remained actively involved with the company for years. His memoir, *Shoe Dog*, provides an intimate look at the triumphs and struggles that shaped Nike's journey. Today, Nike is one of the most valuable brands in the world, symbolizing athletic excellence and innovation. Knight's story continues to inspire entrepreneurs, reminding them that success often comes through resilience, bold vision, and a commitment to doing things differently.

═══════════

CHAPTER THREE

Business Structure and Strategy Execution

Choosing the right business structure is one of the most crucial decisions an entrepreneur will make, as it forms the foundation for how your business operates, grows, and interacts with stakeholders. A carefully selected structure not only defines legal and financial frameworks but also impacts everything from taxation to ownership rights, liability, and decision-making processes. As Mark Cuban, renowned entrepreneur and investor, states, "Choosing the right business structure is the first critical decision of many that shape the future of your enterprise. It's not just paperwork; it's the architecture of your ambition." This chapter focuses on aligning your business structure with your strategic goals, ensuring that every part of your enterprise is designed to function efficiently and effectively.

Whether you decide on a sole proprietorship, partnership, LLC, or corporation, each structure carries unique advantages and challenges. This chapter will help you evaluate your business needs and select a structure that supports both your current operations and future growth. We'll explore how the right structure provides not only legal protection but also operational flexibility, allowing you to adapt to evolving market demands. You'll also learn how to navigate the complex landscape of compliance, ensuring your business adheres to regulations and avoids costly mistakes.

But structure alone isn't enough—execution is where strategy becomes reality. As Jack Welch, former CEO of General Electric, noted, "Good business structure is not just about the hierarchy; it's about creating an environment where every piece and every person knows exactly where they fit in the puzzle of success." Strategy execution involves translating plans into actions by ensuring that your team, processes, and resources are aligned. This chapter will delve into the importance of defining roles, responsibilities, and workflows that empower your team to move in unison toward shared goals.

Successful execution also requires a culture of accountability and performance tracking. We'll cover strategies for creating effective communication channels and establishing clear performance metrics to ensure that your business stays on course. You'll learn how to build feedback loops, refine workflows, and empower employees, fostering an environment where every team member understands how their contribution drives success. Drawing inspiration from leaders like Jim Collins, who emphasized that greatness is achieved through conscious choice and discipline, we'll explore ways to instill these values into your business operations.

Another key element of strategy execution is financial alignment. We'll examine how your business structure affects capital flow, taxation, and investor relationships. From setting up efficient financial reporting systems to managing profit distribution and equity, you'll gain insights into optimizing financial performance while ensuring compliance with legal obligations. Insights from industry giants like Steve Jobs and Reid Hoffman will illustrate how clear financial strategies are critical to sustaining growth and fostering innovation.

Strategy execution isn't a one-time event—it's an ongoing process that requires constant monitoring and refinement. This chapter will introduce tools and frameworks to help you assess progress, identify gaps, and pivot when necessary. Whether you're executing a new marketing campaign, launching a product, or expanding into new markets, strategic agility ensures you stay competitive. As

Ginni Rometty has highlighted, the ability to pivot quickly can mean the difference between failure and sustainable success.

By the end of this chapter, you'll have a comprehensive understanding of how to select the right business structure and effectively execute your strategy. You'll learn to align processes with goals, empower your team, and establish a performance-driven culture. With the right structure and execution strategy in place, your business will not only be built on a solid foundation but also primed to thrive in an ever-changing marketplace.

Mark Cuban's Success Story: The Hustler-Turned-Billionaire Who Mastered Business and Innovation

"Choosing the right business structure is the first critical decision of many that shape the future of your enterprise. It's not just paperwork; it's the architecture of your ambition." — MARK CUBAN, ENTREPRENEUR AND INVESTOR

Mark Cuban is a billionaire entrepreneur, investor, and owner of the Dallas Mavericks, known for his unapologetic hustle, bold bets, and media-savvy personality. His rise from humble beginnings to tech mogul is a story of relentless ambition, risk-taking, and unconventional thinking. Cuban's journey shows that hard work, a little grit, and strategic foresight can turn dreams into billion-dollar realities.

Early Life: The Entrepreneurial Spirit Begins
Mark Cuban was born on July 31, 1958, in Pittsburgh, Pennsylvania, to a working-class Jewish family. His father was an auto upholstery installer, and his mother held various jobs. From a young age, Cuban demonstrated a knack for hustling and business. At 12 years old, he sold garbage bags door-to-door to save money for basketball shoes. This early venture would be a preview of Cuban's entrepreneurial spirit.

Throughout his teenage years, Cuban continued to explore business opportunities, whether it was selling stamps or coins. His curiosity for learning and making money was unstoppable, even leading him to skip his senior year of high school and enroll at the University of Pittsburgh. After a year, he transferred to Indiana University, where he chose to study business—mostly because it was the least expensive business school he could afford.

First Ventures: Lessons in Hustle and Risk

After graduating in 1981, Cuban moved to Dallas, Texas, where he worked as a bartender and computer software salesman. However, Cuban's knack for entrepreneurship soon got him into trouble—he was fired from his sales job after closing a deal without his boss's permission. Rather than viewing the firing as a setback, Cuban saw it as an opportunity to strike out on his own.

In 1983, Cuban launched MicroSolutions, a company that resold software and computer systems. With limited technical experience, Cuban taught himself everything he needed to know about networking and software. His hard work and customer-first mentality helped MicroSolutions grow quickly, and by 1990, Cuban sold the company to CompuServe for $6 million. This sale marked Cuban's first major success—but he was just getting started.

Betting Big on the Internet: The Birth of Broadcast.com

In 1995, Cuban saw the future potential of the internet. Alongside his college friend Todd Wagner, he co-founded AudioNet (later renamed Broadcast.com), an early streaming platform designed to broadcast audio and video content over the internet. Their idea was simple but ahead of its time: enable users to stream live sports games, radio shows, and corporate events online.

Broadcast.com grew rapidly as streaming technology gained traction. The timing was perfect—businesses and consumers were just beginning to explore the power of the internet. In 1999, Cuban and Wagner took the company public, and within months, they sold it to Yahoo! for $5.7 billion in stock.

This deal catapulted Cuban into billionaire status, marking one of the largest tech acquisitions of the dot-com era. Cuban's ability to recognize trends and act quickly proved to be a defining trait in his career.

Life After Broadcast.com: Living the Dream

After the Yahoo! sale, Cuban decided to enjoy his wealth—but in true Cuban style, he did so with flair. In 2000, he fulfilled a lifelong dream by purchasing the

Dallas Mavericks for $285 million. At the time, the team was struggling both on and off the court. Cuban brought a hands-on management approach, often sitting courtside and engaging directly with players and fans. His energetic leadership helped turn the Mavericks into a championship-winning franchise, culminating in an NBA title in 2011.

Cuban's ownership style broke the mold, but it also made him one of the most beloved and recognizable team owners in sports. His philosophy of creating a fun, winning culture not only boosted the team's performance but also enhanced the fan experience.

Shark Tank Fame and Expanding His Empire

In 2011, Cuban joined ABC's reality TV show "Shark Tank" as one of the investors, or "sharks." His candid, no-nonsense approach made him an instant fan favorite. Cuban invested in numerous startups on the show, many of which became successful businesses. His involvement in Shark Tank introduced him to millions of viewers and gave him a platform to mentor young entrepreneurs.

Cuban's role on Shark Tank also showcased his versatility as an investor, backing ventures ranging from tech companies to lifestyle brands. His philosophy is simple: invest in people, not just products. Cuban's willingness to mentor entrepreneurs reflects his belief that success comes from helping others succeed.

Expanding His Portfolio: Tech, Media, and Cryptocurrency

Over the years, Cuban has continued to diversify his investments. He has backed companies in tech, healthcare, AI, and entertainment. Cuban has also been a strong advocate for cryptocurrency and blockchain technology, calling Bitcoin and Ethereum game-changers. He invested in several blockchain startups and became a vocal proponent of decentralized finance (DeFi).

In addition to business ventures, Cuban is involved in philanthropy, donating millions to causes related to education, healthcare, and social justice. His entrepreneurial success has allowed him to give back, using both his wealth and influence to create positive change.

Key Lessons from Mark Cuban's Success

- **Hustle is non-negotiable:** Cuban's early ventures—selling garbage bags, bartending, and launching startups—showcase the importance of hard work and persistence.

- **Spot trends early:** Cuban recognized the potential of the internet and streaming before most people, leading to the creation and success of Broadcast.com.

- **Be hands-on:** His active involvement in the Dallas Mavericks demonstrates that personal commitment and leadership make a difference.

- **Take risks:** Cuban isn't afraid to take bold bets—whether investing in startups, cryptocurrency, or unconventional business ideas.

- **Invest in people:** Cuban's success on Shark Tank reflects his belief that great teams build great companies.

Conclusion: A Legacy of Bold Moves and Big Wins

Mark Cuban's story is one of tenacity, innovation, and fearless risk-taking. From selling garbage bags door-to-door to becoming a tech billionaire and NBA champion, Cuban has shown that success comes to those who work hard, adapt quickly, and aren't afraid to take risks.

Today, Cuban is not only known as an entrepreneur and investor but also as a mentor and public figure, inspiring countless people to pursue their dreams. His ability to spot trends early, embrace change, and lead with passion has cemented his place as one of the most influential figures in business. Cuban's story proves that with the right combination of hustle, vision, and a little luck, anyone can build an empire from scratch.

Jack Welch's Success Story: The Legendary CEO Who Transformed General Electric

"Good business structure is not just about the hierarchy; it's about creating an environment where every piece and every person knows exactly where they fit in the puzzle of success." — JACK WELCH, FORMER CEO OF GENERAL ELECTRIC

"Renegotiating contracts is a strategic opportunity to ensure that the terms continue to serve your business interests and adapt to new challenges and opportunities." — JACK WELCH, FORMER CEO OF GENERAL ELECTRIC

"Effective business development doesn't just fill gaps in the market—it anticipates them, turning foresight into financial might through strategic expansion and bold partnerships." — JACK WELCH, FORMER CEO OF GENERAL ELECTRIC

Jack Welch, one of the most influential business leaders of the 20th century, revolutionized corporate management during his tenure as the CEO of General Electric (GE). Known for his dynamic leadership style and relentless focus on performance and efficiency, Welch's journey from humble beginnings to the pinnacle of corporate success offers valuable lessons in ambition, innovation, and strategic thinking.

Early Life and Education: Building a Competitive Spirit

John Francis "Jack" Welch Jr. was born on November 19, 1935, in Peabody, Massachusetts, into a working-class family. His father worked as a conductor for the Boston and Maine Railroad, and his mother, a homemaker, played a pivotal role in shaping his competitive drive and work ethic. Welch often credited his mother for fostering his determination to succeed, instilling in him the belief that no obstacle was insurmountable.

Welch excelled in school and sports, developing a passion for competition that would later define his leadership style. He attended the University of Massachusetts Amherst, earning a degree in chemical engineering. Afterward, he pursued a master's and PhD in chemical engineering at the University of Illinois, where he honed his analytical thinking and problem-solving skills.

Starting at General Electric: The Early Years

In 1960, Welch joined General Electric (GE) as a junior chemical engineer in its plastics division. Despite working at a company with a legacy of industrial success, Welch quickly grew frustrated with the bureaucracy and slow decision-making that plagued large corporations. In fact, in his first year at GE, Welch came close to quitting, feeling stifled by the company's rigid structure.

However, Welch's innovative thinking and focus on results earned him early recognition. In 1963, he led a team to develop a breakthrough plastic product, polyphenylene oxide (PPO), which became a commercial success. Welch's ability to deliver results in a competitive environment caught the attention of GE's senior leadership.

Climbing the Ranks: A Star on the Rise

Welch's combination of technical expertise, innovation, and managerial skill propelled him up the ranks at GE. By the early 1970s, he had earned a reputation as an aggressive leader who was not afraid to take risks. He demonstrated a sharp focus on profitability, demanding accountability from his teams and eliminating underperforming operations.

In 1979, after holding several senior positions across different divisions, Welch was named the youngest vice-chairman in GE's history, positioning him as a contender for the company's top job. His leadership philosophy—centered on lean operations, decentralization, and relentless efficiency—set him apart from the more conservative managers of the time.

Becoming CEO: A Bold Vision for Change

In 1981, at the age of 45, Welch became CEO of GE, succeeding Reginald Jones. At the time, GE was already one of the largest companies in the world, with interests in everything from appliances to industrial products. However, Welch believed the company was bloated with bureaucracy and needed radical change to remain competitive in a rapidly evolving global market.

Welch's first priority was to streamline GE's operations. He introduced a rigorous performance management system, evaluating businesses and employees based on their contribution to the company's profitability and growth. Welch was famous for his "fix it, sell it, or close it" approach, meaning that underperforming businesses were either turned around, divested, or shut down.

Reshaping GE: The 'Neutron Jack' Era

One of Welch's most controversial strategies was downsizing, which earned him the nickname "Neutron Jack"—a reference to the neutron bomb, which destroys people but leaves buildings standing. Over the course of the 1980s, Welch cut more than 100,000 jobs from GE's workforce, eliminating redundant layers of management and flattening the organizational structure. His goal was to create a more agile and competitive organization that could respond quickly to market changes.

While the downsizing efforts were painful, they reduced costs and increased profitability, setting GE on a trajectory of unprecedented growth. Welch also decentralized decision-making, empowering business unit leaders to run their operations like independent businesses. This move fostered a culture of accountability and entrepreneurship within the company.

The 'Number 1 or 2' Strategy and Acquisitions

Welch's strategy for growth was simple: GE would either be number 1 or number 2 in every market it operated in, or it would exit the business. This philosophy forced business units to compete fiercely, constantly innovating to maintain their market leadership. Under Welch's leadership, GE exited over 100 businesses and acquired dozens of companies, expanding into new industries such as financial services and healthcare.

Some of the most notable acquisitions included the purchase of RCA (the parent company of NBC) and investments in GE Capital, transforming GE into a diversified global conglomerate. By the 1990s, GE had evolved from an industrial manufacturing company into a powerhouse in finance, media, and technology, with global operations spanning more than 100 countries.

Leadership Development and the GE Way

Welch was deeply committed to developing future leaders. He believed that strong leadership was the key to long-term success and invested heavily in training programs at GE's Crotonville leadership development center. Welch's management principles became known as "The GE Way," emphasizing:

1. **Candor and Transparency:** Welch encouraged open dialogue and honest feedback.

2. **Meritocracy:** He rewarded top performers and managed out underperformers.

3. **Boundaryless Organization:** Welch promoted collaboration across departments, fostering innovation and agility.

4. **Stretch Goals:** Welch pushed teams to aim for ambitious targets beyond their comfort zones.

GE became known as a training ground for world-class executives, with many of its leaders going on to become CEOs of other major corporations.

Unprecedented Growth and Success

Under Welch's leadership, GE's market value grew from $14 billion in 1981 to over $410 billion by 2001, making it one of the most valuable companies in the world. The company's earnings per share grew 11% annually during his tenure, and shareholders enjoyed massive returns on their investments. Welch's success transformed him into a business icon, and his leadership style became a model for CEOs around the world.

Retirement and Legacy

In 2001, Welch retired after 20 years as CEO, handing the reins to Jeff Immelt. His leadership style, often described as brutally effective, earned him both admiration and criticism. While Welch's focus on performance and efficiency drove extraordinary growth, some critics argued that his aggressive cost-cutting strategies contributed to short-termism in corporate culture.

Following his retirement, Welch remained active as a public speaker, author, and consultant. He published several best-selling books, including "Jack: Straight from the Gut" and "Winning," sharing his leadership insights with a broader audience.

Challenges to His Legacy

While Welch's achievements were remarkable, GE struggled in the years following his retirement. Some analysts argue that Welch's emphasis on acquisitions and financial engineering left the company vulnerable in a changing market. GE's decline in the 2010s, coupled with management challenges under his successors, raised questions about the long-term sustainability of Welch's leadership model.

Despite these challenges, Welch's influence on corporate leadership remains undeniable. Many of the principles he championed—such as accountability, candor, and meritocracy—continue to shape management practices today.

Key Lessons from Jack Welch's Success

1. **Embrace Change:** Welch believed that staying ahead of market trends was essential to survival.

2. **Demand Accountability:** He held employees and business units accountable for delivering results.

3. **Invest in Leadership:** Welch understood that great leaders drive great companies and prioritized leadership development.

4. **Be Decisive:** Welch's willingness to make tough decisions, such as downsizing, was crucial to GE's success.

5. **Focus on Winning:** His "Number 1 or Number 2" strategy pushed GE to excel in every market it entered.

Conclusion: A Legacy of Bold Leadership

Jack Welch's story is one of transformation, discipline, and bold leadership. Through a combination of strategic vision, relentless execution, and a focus on results, Welch turned GE into one of the most valuable companies in the world. His no-nonsense management style and commitment to leadership development left an indelible mark on the business world.

While his tenure was not without controversy, Welch's principles continue to inspire leaders striving to build high-performing organizations. His legacy serves as a reminder that leadership is not just about maintaining success but about transforming challenges into opportunities for growth.

———

Jim Collins' Success Story: From Researcher to Leadership Guru

"Greatness is not a function of circumstance. Greatness, it turns out, is largely a matter of conscious choice, and discipline." — JIM COLLINS, BUSINESS CONSULTANT AND AUTHOR

Jim Collins is a thought leader whose work has shaped the way businesses and leaders think about long-term success and sustainability. As the author of bestselling books like *Good to Great* and *Built to Last*, Collins has dedicated his career to understanding what separates high-performing companies from mediocre ones. His rigorous research, analytical insights, and passion for leadership have made him a trusted authority in business strategy and management.

Early Life and Academic Foundations

Born in Boulder, Colorado, in 1958, Jim Collins grew up with a natural curiosity about the world. He attended Stanford University, where he earned a degree in mathematical sciences. Collins initially set out on a conventional corporate career, working for the technology giant Hewlett-Packard after graduation. However, he soon discovered that his true passion lay in understanding leadership, business strategy, and the dynamics that foster long-term success.

Collins returned to Stanford to pursue an MBA, and it was during this period that he was introduced to management theory and research. The academic environment, combined with his own interest in organizational behavior, laid the foundation for his future work. He remained at Stanford after earning his MBA, joining the university's Graduate School of Business faculty, where he honed his skills in teaching and research.

A Transformative Shift into Research

Collins began to gain recognition not only as an insightful teacher but also as a meticulous researcher. His time at Stanford introduced him to several influential business thinkers, including **John Gardner**, a former U.S. Secretary of Health, Education, and Welfare, and an advocate for public leadership. Gardner's mentorship had a profound impact on Collins, fostering his belief in disciplined thinking and the power of leadership to shape institutions.

In 1992, Collins co-authored *Beyond Entrepreneurship* with his mentor, Bill Lazier, a Stanford professor. This work emphasized how companies could move from start-up mode to long-term, sustainable success. This was Collins' first significant venture into the world of business publishing and marked the beginning of a lifelong focus on identifying what distinguishes exceptional companies from the rest.

The Birth of *Built to Last*

In 1994, Collins collaborated with Jerry I. Porras, another Stanford faculty member, to write *Built to Last: Successful Habits of Visionary Companies*. The book was a game-changer, offering in-depth insights into companies that had not only achieved success but sustained it over decades. Rather than focusing on charismatic leaders or momentary success, the book explored the enduring practices that helped companies like Disney, Hewlett-Packard, and 3M thrive through generations.

Built to Last became an instant bestseller and established Collins as a leading thinker in the world of business literature. The book was hailed for its data-driven approach, offering a blueprint for organizations seeking to build a lasting legacy. This success allowed Collins to leave the world of academia and focus entirely on his research and writing.

Founding a Research Lab

In the mid-1990s, Collins made a bold move—he left Stanford and established his own research lab in Boulder, Colorado. His goal was to explore business dynamics without the constraints of traditional academic settings. Operating independently, Collins dedicated himself to studying the factors that distinguish great companies from merely good ones.

Collins and his research team embarked on extensive studies, analyzing data across industries to determine patterns of success. The hallmark of Collins' approach was his commitment to rigorous research and deep analysis. He didn't just look at what successful companies did right; he sought to understand why they succeeded where others failed.

Good to Great: A Defining Masterpiece

In 2001, Collins released *Good to Great: Why Some Companies Make the Leap…and Others Don't*, a book that would become one of the most influential business titles of all time. The book presented Collins' groundbreaking "Level 5 Leadership" concept, which described leaders who exhibit a blend of personal humility and fierce determination. These leaders, Collins argued, were essential to companies that achieved sustained excellence.

Collins also introduced ideas like the Hedgehog Concept, The Flywheel Effect, and First Who, Then What, all of which became essential principles in the field of business management. *Good to Great* resonated with readers across industries, offering actionable insights for leaders and companies aspiring to achieve exceptional results. It became a bestseller, selling millions of copies worldwide, and is still widely referenced in business schools and boardrooms.

Consulting, Speaking, and Influence

Following the success of *Good to Great*, Collins became a sought-after consultant and speaker, working with companies, nonprofits, and government organizations. His ability to distill complex research into practical insights made him a favorite among CEOs and business leaders. Companies ranging from technology firms like Amazon to social organizations like the Girl Scouts of America have applied his principles to enhance their performance.

Collins also expanded his research to explore the challenges of leadership in turbulent times. His 2009 book, *How the Mighty Fall: And Why Some Companies Never Give In*, examined why once-great companies decline and how they can avoid collapse. This work reinforced his reputation as a thought leader capable of offering both strategic foresight and practical guidance.

A Lifelong Commitment to Learning and Teaching

Collins has never stopped learning. In recent years, he has continued to publish influential works, such as *Great by Choice*(2011), which focuses on how companies succeed in unpredictable and chaotic environments. His research consistently emphasizes discipline, curiosity, and continuous improvement—qualities that Collins himself embodies.

Despite his success, Collins remains deeply committed to his original mission: helping leaders build organizations that make a positive impact and endure over time. His passion for research and teaching is evident in his workshops and public speaking engagements, where he challenges leaders to think beyond short-term goals and focus on long-term impact.

Conclusion

Jim Collins' journey from a math major to one of the most respected voices in business leadership is a story of intellectual curiosity, rigorous research, and a relentless commitment to understanding what makes organizations great. Through his bestselling books, consulting work, and public speaking, Collins has influenced countless leaders, guiding them toward disciplined thinking and sustainable success.

His work continues to resonate with readers across the globe, offering insights that apply not only to businesses but to personal growth and leadership as well. Collins' legacy lies in his ability to inspire individuals and organizations to strive for greatness—not through shortcuts, but through discipline, humility, and relentless improvement. As Collins himself often says:

———

Steve Jobs' Success Story: Visionary Innovator Behind Apple

"Your brand is the single most important investment you can make in your business." — STEVE JOBS, CO-FOUNDER OF APPLE INC.

"Design is not just what it looks like and feels like. Design is how it works."
— STEVE JOBS, CO-FOUNDER OF APPLE INC. AND
TECHNOLOGY INNOVATOR

"Sometimes when you innovate, you make mistakes. It is best to admit them quickly, and get on with improving your other innovations."
— STEVE JOBS, CO-FOUNDER OF APPLE INC.

"The people who are crazy enough to think they can change the world are the ones who do." — STEVE JOBS, CO-FOUNDER OF APPLE INC.

Steve Jobs, co-founder of Apple Inc., was a genius entrepreneur whose relentless pursuit of innovation and perfection revolutionized technology, design, and business. Known for transforming multiple industries—from personal computing to mobile phones, digital publishing, and entertainment—Jobs' journey from a rebellious college dropout to one of the most influential figures in history is a remarkable tale of vision, resilience, and groundbreaking success.

Humble Beginnings and Early Curiosity
Steve Jobs was born on February 24, 1955, in San Francisco, California, to parents who gave him up for adoption. Raised by Paul and Clara Jobs, Steve grew up in Mountain View, a region that would later become the heart of Silicon Valley. From a young age, Jobs exhibited a curious mind and a rebellious spirit. His father, a mechanic, nurtured his interest in electronics by teaching him how to repair cars and build gadgets from spare parts.

Jobs' early education was marked by both brilliance and frustration—he was known to be intelligent but resistant to traditional school structures. This restless nature led him to Reed College in Oregon, but he dropped out after one semester, finding the rigid curriculum uninspiring. Despite leaving formal education behind, Jobs continued to audit classes, including a calligraphy course, which would later inspire his focus on typography and design in Apple products.

The Birth of Apple in a Garage
In 1976, Jobs teamed up with Steve Wozniak, a brilliant engineer and friend, to start Apple Computer. Wozniak had created a prototype for a personal computer, and Jobs, recognizing its potential, convinced him to bring it to market. With minimal resources, they started the company in Jobs' parents' garage, selling

Wozniak's hand-built computers. Their first product, the Apple I, was a bare-bones computer sold to hobbyists.

The turning point came with the Apple II, launched in 1977, one of the first personal computers with a color display. Its user-friendly design and innovative features made it a commercial success, cementing Apple's place in the nascent personal computer industry. By 1980, Apple had gone public, and Jobs became a multimillionaire at just 25 years old.

Success, Setbacks, and the Power of Resilience
However, the rapid success of Apple was not without challenges. As the company grew, Jobs' ambitious vision and uncompromising nature often clashed with other executives. In 1983, he hired John Sculley, a seasoned executive from Pepsi, to help manage the business side of Apple. But their relationship soon deteriorated. In 1985, amid internal conflicts, Jobs was forced out of the company he had founded.

Despite this devastating setback, Jobs didn't give up. He went on to create NeXT Computer, a company focused on high-end computers for education and business. Although NeXT never achieved mainstream success, its technology—especially its operating system—would later play a crucial role in Apple's revival.

Jobs also acquired Pixar Animation Studios from filmmaker George Lucas for $5 million. Under Jobs' leadership, Pixar revolutionized animation with Toy Story (1995), the world's first fully computer-animated film. Pixar's success made Jobs a billionaire and positioned him as a visionary leader in the entertainment industry.

A Triumphant Return to Apple
Apple struggled during Jobs' absence, facing declining sales and leadership challenges. By the mid-1990s, the company was on the verge of bankruptcy. In 1996, Apple acquired NeXT, bringing Jobs back into the company as an advisor. In 1997, he officially returned as **CEO**, and what followed was one of the greatest corporate turnarounds in history.

Jobs wasted no time in streamlining Apple's product line, cutting unprofitable projects, and focusing on simplicity and innovation. His philosophy—"Think different"—became the foundation for Apple's resurgence. In 1998, Apple introduced the **iMac**, a sleek, colorful computer that redefined design standards and was an instant success.

Revolutionizing Industries

With Jobs back at the helm, Apple embarked on a series of product launches that changed the world. In 2001, the company unveiled the iPod, a portable music player that transformed the way people consumed music. Jobs also introduced iTunes, which became a revolutionary digital marketplace, allowing users to purchase individual songs instead of entire albums.

In 2007, Apple introduced the iPhone, combining a phone, iPod, and internet browser into one device. The iPhone not only revolutionized the mobile phone industry but also became the cornerstone of the smartphone revolution. Following this, Apple launched the App Store, creating an ecosystem that empowered developers and offered consumers endless possibilities through apps.

The innovation continued with the iPad in 2010, establishing a new category of devices between laptops and smartphones. Jobs' focus on elegant design, seamless user experience, and cutting-edge technology made Apple the most valuable company in the world.

Leadership Style and Legacy

Jobs was known for his intense leadership style, characterized by perfectionism, high expectations, and a relentless drive for innovation. He was a master storyteller, captivating audiences with product launches that felt like theatrical performances. His visionary mindset allowed him to see opportunities that others missed, and he had an uncanny ability to anticipate what consumers wanted before they knew it themselves.

Jobs believed in the intersection of technology and the humanities—that great products should not only function well but also evoke emotion and beauty. This philosophy shaped Apple's products, making them not just tools but works of art.

Health Struggles and Final Years

In 2003, Jobs was diagnosed with a rare form of pancreatic cancer. Despite undergoing surgery and treatments, his health deteriorated over the years. Jobs continued to work through his illness, overseeing the development of groundbreaking products like the iPhone 4 and iPad 2. In 2011, with his health rapidly declining, Jobs resigned as Apple's CEO, passing the torch to Tim Cook.

On October 5, 2011, Steve Jobs passed away at the age of 56. His death was met with an outpouring of grief from around the world, with millions mourning the loss of a man who had changed their lives through his inventions.

A Lasting Legacy
Steve Jobs' influence extends far beyond the products he created. His work transformed personal computing, music, telecommunications, and entertainment, leaving an indelible mark on multiple industries. Apple continues to thrive, building on the foundation Jobs laid, with products that remain synonymous with innovation and elegance.

Jobs' story is a testament to the power of vision, resilience, and an unyielding commitment to excellence. His journey from a college dropout working in a garage to one of the most celebrated entrepreneurs in history serves as an inspiration to dreamers and innovators worldwide. As Jobs famously said:

================

Reid Hoffman's Success Story: From Social Network Visionary to Silicon Valley Powerhouse

"Scaling new heights in business requires not just vision but also a robust strategy that includes scalability from the start, turning small wins into major growth opportunities." — REID HOFFMAN, ENTREPRENEUR AND CO-FOUNDER OF LINKEDIN

"Expanding networks through strategic collaborations isn't just about growing your contacts—it's about multiplying your opportunities and broadening your horizons." — REID HOFFMAN, ENTREPRENEUR AND CO-FOUNDER OF LINKEDIN

Reid Hoffman, co-founder of LinkedIn and one of the most successful investors in Silicon Valley, built his career on the idea of connecting people to unlock opportunity. Known as a serial entrepreneur, venture capitalist, and author, Hoffman's journey is marked by innovation, strategic thinking, and a passion for helping others succeed. His path from academic aspirations to becoming a social media pioneer showcases how a blend of vision, perseverance, and risk-taking can lead to extraordinary success.

Early Life and Education: Foundations of Ambition

Reid Hoffman was born on August 5, 1967, in Palo Alto, California—the heart of Silicon Valley. From a young age, he displayed an intellectual curiosity and a love for strategy games and problem-solving. Hoffman initially planned to pursue a career in academia, believing he could make a significant impact by teaching philosophy and helping people think more critically.

He earned a bachelor's degree in Symbolic Systems from Stanford University and went on to pursue graduate studies in Philosophy at Oxford University as a Marshall Scholar. However, during his time at Oxford, Hoffman realized that academia moved too slowly for the impact he wanted to make. He decided to pivot toward entrepreneurship, where he saw opportunities to change the world more quickly through technology and business.

Early Career: From Apple to PayPal

After leaving Oxford, Hoffman returned to Silicon Valley and took on various roles in tech companies. His first major job was at Apple, where he worked on eWorld, an early attempt at an online social network. Though the product was eventually discontinued, the experience gave Hoffman crucial insights into the power of online communities.

Hoffman also worked at Fujitsu before deciding to start his own company. In 1997, he co-founded SocialNet, an early social networking site focused on connecting people for dating, professional networking, and shared interests. Although SocialNet was ahead of its time, it failed to gain traction. However, the lessons Hoffman learned from this failure were invaluable.

In 2000, Hoffman joined PayPal as one of the company's earliest employees. At PayPal, he served as Executive Vice President, helping the company navigate rapid growth and its eventual acquisition by eBay. PayPal's success also connected Hoffman with a powerful network of future entrepreneurs, including Elon Musk, Peter Thiel, and Max Levchin, all of whom would go on to build influential companies.

Founding LinkedIn: The Birth of a Professional Network

After PayPal was acquired in 2002, Hoffman returned to his passion for building online communities. In 2003, he co-founded LinkedIn with the goal of creating a platform that would allow professionals to connect, share knowledge, and unlock career opportunities. At the time, the idea of using social networks for professional purposes was still novel—most online platforms were focused on personal connections and entertainment.

Hoffman's vision for LinkedIn was to redefine networking for the digital age. He believed that opportunities are often unlocked through personal and professional connections, and LinkedIn could become the go-to platform for creating these opportunities at scale.

In its early days, growth was slow, and many people didn't immediately understand the value of a professional networking site. But Hoffman and his team persisted, focusing on building a critical mass of users and adding features like job listings and recommendations. As more professionals joined, LinkedIn's value as a career tool became clear.

By 2011, LinkedIn had grown exponentially, reaching over 100 million users and going public with a successful IPO. Under Hoffman's leadership, LinkedIn became the world's largest professional networking platform, fundamentally transforming the way people manage their careers and connect with opportunities.

A Strategic Investor and Mentor

After LinkedIn's IPO, Hoffman transitioned from CEO to Executive Chairman, focusing on expanding the company's partnerships and long-term vision. In 2016, Microsoft acquired LinkedIn for a staggering $26.2 billion, solidifying the platform's place as an essential tool for professionals worldwide.

Beyond LinkedIn, Hoffman became a prolific angel investor and venture capitalist. As a partner at Greylock Partners, one of Silicon Valley's top venture capital firms, Hoffman invested in companies that would go on to achieve massive success, including:

- **Facebook**

- **Airbnb**

- **Zynga**

- **Flickr**

Hoffman's investment strategy revolves around identifying companies that leverage networks, create value through connections, and scale rapidly. His ability to spot emerging trends early has made him one of the most respected investors in the tech industry.

Thought Leadership: Writing and Podcasting

Hoffman is not only an entrepreneur and investor but also a respected author and thought leader. In 2012, he co-authored "The Start-up of You" with Ben Casnocha, advocating for individuals to think of their careers like startups—adapting, innovating, and embracing change to stay competitive. The book became a bestseller, helping professionals navigate the complexities of the modern job market.

In 2018, Hoffman published *Blitzscaling: The Lightning-Fast Path to Building Massively Valuable Companies*, where he outlined strategies for companies to scale rapidly in competitive markets. The book draws from his experiences at LinkedIn and PayPal, as well as insights from other high-growth companies.

Hoffman also hosts the podcast "Masters of Scale," where he interviews some of the world's top entrepreneurs, including Mark Zuckerberg, Reed Hastings, and Sara Blakely. The podcast explores how businesses grow, adapt, and succeed, offering practical lessons for entrepreneurs at every stage.

Mentorship and Social Impact

Hoffman is known for his generosity as a mentor, often sharing advice with entrepreneurs and young professionals. His commitment to using technology for good is evident in his philanthropic efforts as well. Hoffman has donated millions to causes related to education, economic opportunity, and civic engagement. He believes that entrepreneurship can solve some of the world's biggest challenges by empowering individuals to create opportunities for themselves and others.

Key Lessons from Reid Hoffman's Success

1. **Embrace Failure as a Learning Tool:** Hoffman's early setbacks with SocialNet taught him valuable lessons that he applied to LinkedIn.

2. **Leverage Networks for Growth:** Hoffman's success at PayPal and LinkedIn demonstrates the power of building and using networks strategically.

3. **Think Long-Term:** Hoffman's focus on creating lasting value helped LinkedIn weather slow initial growth and emerge as a global platform.

4. **Invest in Relationships:** Hoffman's investments in companies like Airbnb and Facebook reflect his belief in the importance of personal connections.

5. **Adapt and Evolve:** Whether writing, investing, or building companies, Hoffman's ability to spot trends and adapt quickly has been central to his success.

Conclusion: A Legacy of Connection and Innovation

Reid Hoffman's journey from academic aspirations to Silicon Valley legend is a powerful testament to the value of connecting people, embracing risk, and thinking boldly. Through LinkedIn, Hoffman revolutionized how professionals manage their careers and unlock opportunities. His work as an investor, mentor, and author continues to shape the future of entrepreneurship, creating ripple effects across the tech industry and beyond.

Hoffman's story reminds us that success is not a solo journey—it is built through collaboration, community, and meaningful relationships. His commitment to empowering others ensures that his influence will endure for generations, inspiring the next wave of entrepreneurs to dream big, take risks, and build the future together.

===========

Bob Iger's Success Story: From Humble Beginnings to Global Icon

"Protecting your interests isn't just a defensive measure; it's an essential aspect of nurturing and preserving the integrity of your work." — BOB IGER, FORMER CEO OF THE WALT DISNEY COMPANY

Bob Iger is one of the most influential business leaders of the 21st century, known for his transformative leadership at The Walt Disney Company. From humble beginnings in television production at ABC to leading one of the world's most beloved entertainment giants, Iger's journey is a masterclass in vision, strategy, and resilience. As Disney's CEO from 2005 to 2020, he spearheaded some of the most successful acquisitions in media history, including Pixar, Marvel, and Lucasfilm, revitalizing Disney's creative legacy. Iger's ability to balance bold innovation with strategic foresight not only expanded Disney's global reach but also reshaped the entertainment landscape, leaving a lasting impact on the industry.

Early Life and Career Beginnings

Bob Iger was born on February 10, 1951, in Oceanside, New York. His father was a World War II Navy veteran and advertising executive, while his mother worked at a local school. Growing up in a modest household, Iger developed a love for television and entertainment from a young age. His passion for storytelling guided his decision to pursue a career in media and entertainment.

After graduating from Ithaca College with a degree in television and radio, Iger began his career in the early 1970s at ABC as a low-level studio supervisor. Though he started at the bottom, Iger's work ethic and commitment to learning every aspect of the business helped him climb the corporate ladder steadily.

Rising Through the Ranks at ABC

At ABC, Iger gained valuable experience across multiple departments, from sports production to programming. In 1989, he played a key role in the network's coverage of major events like the Olympics, which showcased his ability to lead and manage large-scale projects under pressure. His talent for innovative thinking and problem-solving earned him higher responsibilities, and by 1994, Iger had become president of the ABC Network.

When The Walt Disney Company acquired ABC in 1996, Iger's leadership impressed Disney executives. He was appointed chairman of ABC's parent company, Capital Cities/ABC, continuing to refine his management skills while navigating the challenges of merging the two companies' cultures.

Becoming CEO of Disney

In 2005, Bob Iger succeeded Michael Eisner as the CEO of The Walt Disney Company. Disney at the time was facing declining profits, creative stagnation, and strained relationships with partners like Pixar. Iger understood that in order to restore Disney's magic, bold decisions were needed—especially in an era of rapidly changing technology and consumer behavior.

One of Iger's first moves as CEO was mending Disney's relationship with Pixar. His negotiation skills and respect for creative talent led to Disney acquiring Pixar in 2006 for $7.4 billion. This acquisition not only revitalized Disney's animation division but also paved the way for more strategic acquisitions under Iger's leadership.

Strategic Acquisitions That Transformed Disney

Iger's tenure as CEO is best known for a series of transformative acquisitions that turned Disney into a global entertainment powerhouse. After Pixar, Iger orchestrated the acquisition of Marvel Entertainment in 2009 for $4 billion, giving Disney access to an extensive library of beloved superhero characters. In 2012, Disney acquired Lucasfilm, bringing the *Star Wars* franchise under its umbrella. Iger's ability to identify and acquire valuable intellectual properties positioned Disney as the leader in blockbuster entertainment.

One of Iger's final major acquisitions was the purchase of 21st Century Fox in 2019. This acquisition expanded Disney's content library and paved the way for the launch of Disney+, a streaming platform that allowed Disney to compete in the evolving digital landscape. Disney+ became a massive success, attracting millions of subscribers worldwide within months of its release.

Leadership Philosophy and Legacy

Iger is widely recognized for his leadership style, which emphasizes creativity, innovation, and long-term vision. He cultivated a culture that balanced business acumen with creative freedom, empowering Disney's storytellers and creators to push boundaries. Iger's calm demeanor and thoughtful decision-making, even during times of uncertainty, earned him the respect of his peers and employees.

His tenure at Disney was also marked by the company's commitment to diversity, sustainability, and technological innovation. Iger believed in creating an inclusive environment where bold ideas could flourish. His ability to stay ahead of industry trends allowed Disney to adapt to changing markets, ensuring its relevance across generations.

Stepping Down and Ongoing Influence

In 2020, Iger stepped down as Disney's CEO, passing the torch to Bob Chapek. However, Iger remained with the company as executive chairman, helping Disney navigate the early challenges of the COVID-19 pandemic and continuing to provide strategic guidance. His memoir, *The Ride of a Lifetime*, offers insights into his career journey and the leadership principles that guided his success.

Bob Iger's story is a testament to the power of vision, perseverance, and smart risk-taking. Through innovative acquisitions, strong partnerships, and a commitment to storytelling, he transformed Disney into a global leader in entertainment. Iger's legacy is one of reinvention, growth, and creative excellence—a shining example of how business and imagination can merge to shape the future of an industry.

Ginni Rometty's Success Story: A Trailblazer in Transformational Leadership

"In the digital age, a CIO doesn't just manage IT infrastructure; they architect the digital transformations that drive future business success and innovation." — GINNI ROMETTY, FORMER CEO OF IBM

"Managing your trademark portfolio with regular renewals is akin to navigating a ship through ever-changing waters; it requires constant vigilance and strategic foresight to ensure your brand remains protected and powerful." — GINNI ROMETTY, FORMER CEO OF IBM

"Digital rights management is not just about control; it's about ensuring your content's integrity while maintaining trust with your audience."
— GINNI ROMETTY, FORMER CEO OF IBM

Ginni Rometty, the first female CEO of IBM, is a powerful example of how vision, resilience, and innovation can drive meaningful change. From humble beginnings in Chicago to leading one of the world's most iconic tech companies, Rometty's journey is a testament to the importance of adaptability in a fast-evolving industry. Her tenure at IBM was marked by bold pivots into artificial intelligence, cloud computing, and hybrid solutions, redefining the company's future. Beyond technology, Rometty also championed diversity and lifelong learning, believing that a more inclusive workforce leads to greater innovation. Her ability to navigate challenges and transform IBM during turbulent times cemented her legacy as a pioneering leader in business.

Early Life and Education
Virginia "Ginni" Rometty was born on July 29, 1957, in Chicago, Illinois. Raised in a middle-class family, she learned the value of hard work early on. After her parents divorced, Rometty saw her mother juggle jobs to support the family, inspiring her determination and resilience. She attended Northwestern University on a scholarship, earning a degree in computer science and electrical engineering in 1979—fields where few women ventured at the time.

Climbing the Ranks at IBM
Rometty began her career at General Motors but soon joined IBM in 1981 as a systems engineer. She steadily rose through the company's ranks, gaining experience in sales, consulting, and management roles. Known for her ability to lead complex projects, she spearheaded IBM's acquisition of PricewaterhouseCoopers' consulting arm in 2002, a move that expanded IBM's consulting capabilities and paved the way for its evolution beyond hardware.

Her work in business strategy, combined with her knack for spotting future trends, positioned Rometty as a visionary leader within the company. She became IBM's first female CEO in 2012, marking a significant milestone for women in tech leadership.

Transforming IBM's Future
When Rometty took the helm, IBM faced declining revenues in its traditional hardware business. To reinvent the company, she made bold moves, pivoting IBM toward cloud computing, artificial intelligence, and data analytics. Under her

leadership, IBM launched the Watson platform, focusing on AI-powered solutions for industries such as healthcare, finance, and retail.

Rometty emphasized the importance of cognitive computing, recognizing that AI would define the future of technology. She also shifted IBM's focus to hybrid cloud infrastructure, acquiring Red Hat in 2018 for $34 billion, the largest acquisition in IBM's history. This move positioned IBM as a leader in cloud services, allowing it to compete with tech giants like Amazon and Microsoft.

Commitment to Diversity and Inclusion

Throughout her tenure, Rometty championed diversity and inclusion in the workplace. She introduced programs that prioritized hiring and promoting women and underrepresented groups, believing that a diverse workforce fosters innovation. She also focused on retraining IBM employees for the digital age, introducing initiatives like P-TECH (Pathways in Technology Early College High Schools) to equip students with the skills needed for tech careers.

Legacy and Impact

After stepping down as CEO in 2020, Rometty's legacy as a transformative leader remains evident. She steered IBM through one of the most challenging periods in its history, transitioning the company from legacy systems to cutting-edge technologies. Her focus on AI, cloud computing, and inclusion set IBM on a path for sustainable growth.

Lessons from Ginni Rometty's Journey

- **Bold Vision:** Rometty's willingness to pivot IBM into emerging technologies demonstrates the power of embracing change.

- **Resilience:** Facing both personal and professional challenges, Rometty's career is a testament to persistence.

- **Diversity as Strategy:** She showed that inclusivity is not just a social cause but a business imperative that drives innovation.

- **Continuous Learning:** Her emphasis on lifelong learning reflects the need to evolve in an ever-changing digital world.

Ginni Rometty's journey from systems engineer to IBM's first female CEO is an inspiring story of vision, leadership, and perseverance. Through bold decisions and strategic foresight, she not only transformed IBM but also set a new standard for tech leadership, leaving a lasting mark on the industry.

CHAPTER FOUR

The Power of Personal Branding

In today's competitive landscape, personal branding has evolved from a mere buzzword to a vital tool for entrepreneurs, business leaders, and creatives. A well-defined personal brand goes beyond titles or qualifications—it reflects who you are, what you stand for, and the unique value you bring to the world. Your personal brand serves as your reputation, your identity, and your story, creating a bridge between you and your audience. As Jason Hartman, real estate expert and entrepreneur, puts it: "Your personal brand is a promise to your clients . . . a promise of quality, consistency, competency, and reliability." In this chapter, we explore how harnessing the power of personal branding can transform not only your business but also your life and career trajectory.

Successful entrepreneurs like Beyoncé have shown that personal branding is deeply intertwined with authenticity. Beyoncé's ability to connect with her audience on a personal level, embracing vulnerability and empowerment, has turned her into a global icon. Personal branding is not about creating a persona but about presenting the most genuine version of yourself—one that resonates with your audience and leaves a lasting impression. We'll explore how self-awareness and understanding your core values are the starting points for crafting an authentic brand that aligns with both your personal and professional goals.

Your personal brand can also serve as a competitive advantage, especially in industries saturated with products and services that often seem indistinguishable. Guy Kawasaki, renowned author and entrepreneur, emphasizes that "Your life story is not just what you tell people, it's what they believe about you based on the evidence you present." In this chapter, you'll learn how to leverage your personal narrative to connect emotionally with customers, partners, and investors. Whether through social media, public speaking, or writing, every interaction is an opportunity to shape perceptions and establish trust.

With the rise of digital platforms, personal branding has become more accessible—and more necessary—than ever before. Amy Jo Martin, founder of Digital Royalty, explains: "In the digital age, your personal brand is your new resume. What you publish online becomes your public persona, and your social media networks are just extensions of your brand." This chapter will guide you through building a consistent online presence, ensuring that your brand message remains unified across platforms like LinkedIn, Instagram, and personal websites. We'll explore best practices for engaging with your audience, creating meaningful content, and maintaining professional authenticity in every post.

Moreover, personal branding isn't just a tool for external visibility—it's also a pathway to personal growth. Tony Robbins, the renowned motivational speaker, notes that "The only limit to your impact is your imagination and commitment." Defining your brand forces you to reflect on your strengths, areas for improvement, and long-term vision. This chapter will challenge you to align your personal goals with your business mission, helping you create a brand identity that not only reflects your purpose but also inspires others to follow your journey.

Throughout this chapter, we'll provide actionable strategies to help you build and enhance your personal brand. You'll learn how to develop a compelling elevator pitch, manage your online reputation, and cultivate relationships that elevate your personal brand to new heights. We'll also explore real-world examples of entrepreneurs like Arianna Huffington and Marie Forleo, who successfully leveraged their personal brands to create impactful legacies. Their stories will inspire you to embrace your uniqueness and use it as a foundation for professional growth.

Whether you're just starting out or looking to refine your existing brand, this chapter offers practical tools and insights to help you create a personal brand that opens doors to new opportunities. As Marie Forleo reminds us: "Consistency is one of the biggest factors in success and brand loyalty. It breeds familiarity, and familiarity breeds trust." By the end of this chapter, you'll understand how to harness the power of personal branding to stand out in a crowded marketplace, build meaningful connections, and position yourself as an authority in your field. With a strong personal brand, you'll not only attract opportunities but also inspire others, becoming the architect of your own legacy.

Jason Hartman's Success Story: From Real Estate Novice to Investment Thought Leader

"Your personal brand is a promise to your clients . . . a promise of quality, consistency, competency, and reliability." — JASON HARTMAN, REAL ESTATE EXPERT AND ENTREPRENEUR

Jason Hartman's journey to success began in humble surroundings. Raised in Southern California, he grew up with a fascination for entrepreneurship. Inspired by early experiences with personal finance and the idea of passive income, Hartman was determined to break away from the traditional 9-to-5 lifestyle. His story is one of resilience, experimentation, and eventually becoming a leading voice in real estate investing.

Early Career: Starting in Sales

Hartman's professional journey began in the world of real estate sales. At the age of 19, he obtained his real estate license and worked as an agent, selling homes and gaining firsthand experience in the complexities of property transactions. Despite his initial success in sales, Hartman quickly realized that being a traditional real estate agent was not the path to long-term wealth. He sought to shift from earning active income through commissions to creating streams of passive income through property ownership.

Pivot to Property Investment

Hartman saw real estate not just as a job, but as a powerful vehicle for financial freedom. In his twenties, he made the leap from agent to investor, purchasing rental properties with a focus on generating positive cash flow. Over time, he accumulated a substantial portfolio of single-family homes across several U.S. markets, developing a strategic approach to real estate investing. His philosophy centered on the concept of "buy and hold," targeting income-producing properties in growing markets to build lasting wealth.

Expanding Influence and Education

Through trial and error, Hartman refined his investment strategies, becoming a recognized expert in the field. But his vision extended beyond personal success—he wanted to educate others. In 2003, he founded The Hartman Media Company and began producing educational content about real estate, personal finance, and wealth creation. He launched podcasts and hosted seminars, using his growing platform to share insights about inflation, tax strategies, and market cycles.

Hartman's "Creating Wealth Podcast" became a flagship show, drawing an audience of aspiring investors from around the world. With more than a thousand episodes, his podcast features interviews with industry experts, economists, and thought leaders, empowering listeners to make informed decisions and build financial independence.

The Rise of the Hartman Network

Building on his success as an educator, Hartman expanded his brand by founding The Jason Hartman Network, which offers clients turnkey real estate investment solutions. His services guide investors through every stage of the investment process, from market selection to property management. Hartman also emphasizes the importance of leverage, teaching clients how to use mortgages as tools to grow wealth strategically.

Philosophy for Success

Hartman's approach to wealth-building goes beyond real estate. He emphasizes the importance of "location-independent income," where financial freedom allows individuals to live life on their terms, free from geographic constraints. His motto—"Your personal brand is a promise of quality, consistency, and reliability"—encapsulates his belief that success is built on trust, education, and providing value to others.

Legacy and Impact

Today, Jason Hartman is more than a successful real estate investor. He is a prominent speaker, educator, and thought leader, helping thousands of people achieve financial independence through strategic real estate investments. His ability to distill complex economic principles into actionable insights has made him a respected figure in the wealth-building community.

Hartman's journey from a young real estate agent to an international investment coach exemplifies how knowledge, strategy, and persistence can turn ambition into long-term success. His legacy lies not only in his personal achievements but also in the countless individuals he has empowered to transform their financial futures.

———

Amy Jo Martin's Success Story: Pioneering the Intersection of Social Media and Personal Branding

"In the digital age, your personal brand is your new resume. What you publish online becomes your public persona and your social media networks are just extensions of your brand." — AMY JO MARTIN, FOUNDER AND CEO OF DIGITAL ROYALTY

"Mastering social media PR isn't just about broadcasting your message; it's about engaging in a way that makes each follower feel like part of your brand's ongoing story." — AMY JO MARTIN, DIGITAL MEDIA STRATEGIST AND AUTHOR

Amy Jo Martin's rise to success is the story of a trailblazer who saw the potential of social media before it became mainstream. From working in corporate environments to becoming a trusted digital strategist for major celebrities, athletes, and Fortune 500 companies, Martin's career demonstrates how foresight, authenticity, and innovation can shape an entire industry.

The Early Years: From Sports Marketing to Social Media

Born and raised in the Midwest, Amy Jo Martin initially pursued a degree in marketing at Arizona State University. After graduating, she began her career in sports marketing, working with the Phoenix Suns of the NBA. It was during her time with the Suns that she discovered the immense potential of social media. Platforms like Twitter were in their infancy, but Martin quickly recognized that these tools could build personal brands, engage fans, and enhance connections between athletes and audiences.

At the Suns, she led early efforts to integrate social media into the team's marketing strategy. Her innovative ideas increased the team's online following and brought fans closer to the players. Recognizing that social media was more than a fad, Martin saw an opportunity to help organizations and individuals embrace these platforms strategically.

The Birth of Digital Royalty

In 2009, Martin decided to step out on her own and founded Digital Royalty, a social media agency focused on helping brands and public figures build meaningful relationships with their audiences. Early in her entrepreneurial journey, she landed a groundbreaking opportunity to work with NBA star Shaquille O'Neal, managing his personal social media presence. Through playful and authentic engagement, Shaq's online following skyrocketed, making him one of the most popular athletes on Twitter at the time.

Martin's partnership with O'Neal validated her approach to social media and launched her into the spotlight. Soon, high-profile brands and celebrities—including companies like Nike, Hilton Worldwide, and the UFC—sought her expertise. Her ability to humanize large brands and public figures through authentic storytelling became her signature strategy.

Redefining Personal Branding in the Digital Era

As social media became central to marketing strategies, Martin emphasized the importance of "personal branding"—the idea that individuals must craft an intentional, authentic online presence. For Martin, personal branding was about more than marketing; it was about creating real connections with audiences by sharing stories, values, and behind-the-scenes moments.

Her mantra, "Be your authentic self and share your journey," resonated with her clients and followers alike. Through Digital Royalty, she provided social media training to corporate leaders and entrepreneurs, equipping them with the tools and confidence to grow their influence online.

The Power of Social Influence and Community Building

Martin didn't just focus on helping clients build influence—she also created Digital Royalty University, an online education platform offering courses in social media strategy, branding, and engagement. Her courses empowered students and entrepreneurs around the globe to harness the power of social platforms to grow their businesses and personal brands.

Throughout her career, Martin emphasized the importance of community building. She believed that social media should be used not just for self-promotion, but to foster genuine conversations and collaborations. Her work showcased how businesses could transform their relationships with customers by shifting from broadcasting to engaging.

Transition to Speaker and Author

After successfully running Digital Royalty, Martin shifted gears to focus on speaking engagements and writing. She authored the bestselling book, "Renegades Write the Rules," where she outlined the principles that helped her build Digital Royalty and drive digital transformation for her clients. In her book, Martin shared insights into how the most successful brands—whether personal or corporate—embrace risk, challenge norms, and connect authentically.

Martin's journey also included a personal transformation. After years of relentless work, she realized the importance of balancing her professional success with mental and emotional well-being. This led her to advocate for mindfulness and intentional living, inspiring others to pursue both personal and professional fulfillment.

Legacy and Impact

Amy Jo Martin's pioneering work in social media and personal branding has left a lasting legacy. She was among the first to recognize that social platforms were not just marketing tools but powerful connectors between individuals, brands, and communities. Her ability to merge storytelling with technology set a standard that many marketing professionals follow today.

Martin's story is one of vision, authenticity, and adaptability—qualities that enabled her to thrive in an ever-changing digital landscape. As a speaker, educator, and thought leader, she continues to inspire entrepreneurs to embrace their unique journeys, build meaningful brands, and use social media as a force for positive change. Her influence on the world of personal branding and digital engagement remains a testament to her innovative spirit and commitment to empowering others.

Marie Forleo's Success Story: The Multi-Passionate Entrepreneur Who Built a Business Empire

"Consistency is one of the biggest factors to success and brand loyalty. It breeds familiarity, and familiarity breeds trust." — MARIE FORLEO, ENTREPRENEUR AND AUTHOR

Marie Forleo's journey to success is an inspiring story of resilience, creativity, and the power of embracing multiple passions. From working odd jobs to founding a globally renowned business coaching platform, Forleo has transformed her love for dance, marketing, and personal development into a career that empowers millions. Her ability to blend diverse interests into a thriving business has made her a role model for entrepreneurs, particularly those who don't fit into traditional career molds.

From Wall Street to Dancing Shoes

Marie Forleo began her career in a place many would find surprising—Wall Street. After graduating from Seton Hall University with a business degree, she landed a job at the New York Stock Exchange. Despite the prestige, Forleo quickly realized that the corporate environment didn't align with her passion for creative expression. She felt unfulfilled and knew deep down that she wasn't living her purpose.

Determined to find a career she truly loved, Forleo left Wall Street and explored different paths. She worked as a bartender, fitness instructor, and dance teacher while juggling freelance writing assignments. Her passion for dance led her to train professionally, eventually performing with top artists, including Jennifer Lopez. However, she still felt pulled toward something bigger—a way to integrate her love for creativity, business, and personal development.

Discovering Coaching and Entrepreneurship

Forleo's turning point came when she stumbled upon the concept of life coaching. Intrigued by the idea of helping people achieve their goals, she pursued a coaching certification in her early 20s. At that time, life coaching was a relatively new field, and Forleo faced skepticism from both peers and mentors who doubted her ability to build a sustainable career in such an unconventional profession.

Undeterred, Forleo took a leap of faith and launched her coaching business. She started with no email list, no investors, and no marketing budget, relying solely on her passion, creativity, and willingness to learn. To make ends meet, she continued working side jobs while building her coaching practice, often writing newsletters and coaching clients during her lunch breaks.

Building the Marie Forleo Brand

Determined to stand out in a crowded market, Forleo embraced authenticity and infused her personality into everything she did. She combined personal development principles with practical business advice, creating a unique coaching style that resonated with aspiring entrepreneurs. As her client base grew, Forleo began sharing her insights through an email newsletter, laying the foundation for her personal brand.

In 2009, Forleo launched MarieTV, a free online show where she answered viewer questions about business, life, and everything in between. Her approachable, fun, and insightful style quickly attracted a global audience. The show's success helped position her as a thought leader in personal development and entrepreneurship, with followers drawn to her mantra, "Everything is figureoutable."

Creating B-School: A Business Education Revolution

In 2010, Forleo took her business to the next level with the launch of B-School, an online program designed to teach entrepreneurs how to build businesses that align with their values. B-School became an instant hit, attracting thousands of students from around the world. Unlike traditional business courses, B-School emphasized heart-centered marketing, mindset mastery, and personal growth.

Through B-School, Forleo built a thriving community of entrepreneurs, creatives, and changemakers. The program's success cemented her status as one of the leading voices in online business education, and many graduates credit B-School with helping them launch and grow their businesses.

The Global Impact of "Everything is Figureoutable"

Forleo's career reached new heights with the release of her New York Times bestselling book, *Everything is Figureoutable* (2019). In the book, Forleo shares her philosophy that no challenge is insurmountable and that with the right mindset, anyone can achieve their goals. The book resonated with readers worldwide, earning praise from thought leaders like Oprah Winfrey and Sir Richard Branson.

Forleo's message struck a chord with individuals facing personal and professional challenges, inspiring them to adopt a problem-solving mindset. She also expanded her reach through public speaking, appearing on major stages and platforms, including Oprah's SuperSoul Sessions.

Balancing Success with Purpose and Joy

Despite her business success, Forleo has always emphasized the importance of joy, self-care, and balance. She encourages her audience to build businesses that serve their lives, rather than sacrificing their lives for business. Her transparency about the ups and downs of entrepreneurship has made her a relatable figure, inspiring others to pursue their dreams without fear of failure.

Forleo also channels her success into philanthropy. She donates a portion of B-School's profits to charities supporting education, health, and empowerment for women and girls. Her commitment to giving back underscores her belief that entrepreneurship is not just about personal success but about making a positive impact on the world.

Legacy and Influence

Marie Forleo's journey from juggling side jobs to building a global business empire reflects the power of creativity, resilience, and authenticity. She has paved the way for a new generation of entrepreneurs who reject conventional paths and embrace their unique talents and passions. Through MarieTV, B-School, and her bestselling book, she has empowered millions to create meaningful businesses and lives they love.

Today, Forleo continues to inspire through her coaching programs, media content, and public speaking. Her philosophy—"Everything is figureoutable"—remains a guiding principle for those seeking to overcome obstacles and achieve success on their own terms. With her blend of business savvy, creative flair, and commitment to purpose, Marie Forleo stands as a shining example of what's possible when you pursue your passions fearlessly and authentically.

———————

Guy Kawasaki's Success Story: The Evangelist of Innovation and Technology

"Instagram is not just a tool for showing, it's a platform for storytelling. Every image you post should open a window into your world, inviting followers to step inside." — GUY KAWASAKI, MARKETING SPECIALIST AND AUTHOR

"Create something people want to belong to." — GUY KAWASAKI, MARKETING SPECIALIST AND VENTURE CAPITALIST

"Social media is not just an activity; it is an investment of valuable time and resources. Surround yourself with people who not just support you and stay with you, but inform your thinking about ways to WOW your online presence." — GUY KAWASAKI, MARKETING SPECIALIST AND AUTHOR

"Mastering social media isn't just about broadcasting your message; it's about crafting content so compelling that it begs to be bookmarked and shared, turning every post into a stepping stone towards greater brand impact."
— GUY KAWASAKI, MARKETING SPECIALIST AND AUTHOR

Guy Kawasaki's story is one of entrepreneurial spirit, innovation, and a relentless passion for making complex ideas accessible. Best known for popularizing the concept of evangelism in the tech world, Kawasaki rose to prominence as a marketing maverick at Apple and has since built a remarkable career as an author, entrepreneur, and venture capitalist. His journey showcases the power of creative thinking and staying ahead of technological trends.

From Honolulu to Silicon Valley

Born in Honolulu, Hawaii in 1954, Guy Kawasaki's early life was shaped by strong family values and a love for learning. His parents emphasized the importance of education, which led him to Stanford University, where he earned a degree in psychology. Though his major wasn't in technology, Kawasaki's curiosity and love for problem-solving set the foundation for his future career.

After Stanford, he pursued an MBA at UCLA's Anderson School of Management. It was here that Kawasaki first realized the importance of understanding both the creative and business sides of innovation—a skill that would later prove essential. His early career took him into the world of jewelry sales, where he learned firsthand about customer psychology and marketing tactics. While unconventional, this experience honed his ability to understand how to connect with consumers—a talent that would become a signature part of his career.

Joining Apple and Becoming the Chief Evangelist

Kawasaki's big break came when he joined Apple in 1983 as part of the original Macintosh team. At the time, Apple was still a young company with an ambitious vision to revolutionize personal computing. Kawasaki's job was to serve as the "software evangelist"—a term he coined to describe his mission of convincing developers to create software for the Mac platform.

Kawasaki's approach was revolutionary. Rather than using traditional sales techniques, he focused on storytelling and building emotional connections between people and the Macintosh. He wasn't just selling software—he was inspiring developers to become part of a movement. Kawasaki believed that technology had the power to change lives, and his enthusiasm was contagious. His ability to communicate complex ideas in simple, compelling ways became his hallmark.

The Macintosh became an icon in personal computing, and Kawasaki's work laid the foundation for the role of evangelism marketing—inspiring customers and partners to become advocates for a product or brand. This philosophy would later shape how tech companies approach brand loyalty and product promotion.

Transitioning to Entrepreneurship and Writing

After his initial stint at Apple, Kawasaki shifted gears to explore his passion for entrepreneurship. He co-founded several startups, including Aciqra, a database software company, and Garage Technology Ventures, a venture capital firm that funded early-stage tech companies. Through these ventures, Kawasaki became deeply embedded in Silicon Valley's startup ecosystem, helping to launch and mentor a new generation of entrepreneurs.

Kawasaki's experiences in both marketing and entrepreneurship inspired him to share his knowledge through writing. In 1990, he published "The Macintosh Way," which detailed his insights on business, marketing, and technology. The book's success led Kawasaki to a career as a prolific author. Over the years, he has written numerous bestsellers, including "Art of the Start," "Enchantment," and "Wise Guy," cementing his reputation as a thought leader.

Return to Apple and the Rise of Social Media

In the late 1990s, Kawasaki returned to Apple during Steve Jobs's second tenure, once again taking on the role of chief evangelist. This time, Kawasaki's focus was on the company's resurgence with products like the iMac and the iPod, which would soon transform Apple into the world's most valuable company. His ability to foster excitement and loyalty around Apple's brand was crucial during this pivotal moment in the company's history.

As social media began to reshape the business landscape, Kawasaki recognized its potential early on. He became one of the first advocates for using platforms like Twitter, LinkedIn, and Facebook to build personal brands and connect with customers. Kawasaki's forward-thinking approach made him one of the most influential voices in the digital marketing space, and he leveraged social media to amplify his message to a global audience.

Empowering Entrepreneurs Through Education

In addition to his roles as a marketer and author, Kawasaki has dedicated much of his career to educating entrepreneurs. His work at Garage Technology Ventures gave him firsthand insight into the challenges faced by startups, and he became a mentor to many aspiring business leaders. Kawasaki frequently speaks at conferences and business schools, sharing his philosophy that entrepreneurship is not just about making money, but about creating value.

In 2013, Kawasaki joined Canva, a then-up-and-coming design platform, as their chief evangelist. He played a crucial role in helping Canva grow into one of the most popular and accessible design tools on the market. His involvement with Canva exemplifies Kawasaki's belief in democratizing technology—making powerful tools accessible to everyone, regardless of their technical expertise.

Legacy and Impact

Throughout his career, Guy Kawasaki has been a pioneer in innovation and marketing. His unique blend of enthusiasm, creativity, and business acumen has made him a revered figure in the tech world. Kawasaki's work has inspired countless entrepreneurs to pursue their passions, build meaningful brands, and embrace the power of storytelling. His ability to foresee trends and adapt to new technologies has kept him at the forefront of the industry for decades.

Kawasaki's influence extends far beyond his role at Apple. As an author, entrepreneur, and evangelist, he continues to inspire people around the world to think differently, take risks, and create products that make a difference. His message is simple: Success comes not from following a rigid formula but from being authentic, passionate, and committed to serving others.

Guy Kawasaki's Philosophy on Success

Kawasaki believes that the key to success lies in helping others succeed. His career exemplifies the power of building meaningful relationships, creating value, and embracing innovation. As he puts it:

> *"Don't worry, be crappy. Revolutionary means you ship and then make it better."*

This philosophy captures the essence of Kawasaki's journey—embrace imperfection, stay curious, and keep moving forward. With a career spanning decades and industries, Guy Kawasaki remains a guiding force in entrepreneurship, innovation, and marketing, inspiring the next generation to dream big and create boldly.

Tony Robbins' Success Story: From Struggles to Self-Made Success

"Setting goals is the first step in turning the invisible into the visible."
— TONY ROBBINS, MOTIVATIONAL SPEAKER AND AUTHOR

"Public speaking is more than delivering a message; it's an opportunity to engage, inspire, and sell your vision directly through the power of your voice." — TONY ROBBINS, MOTIVATIONAL SPEAKER AND AUTHOR

Tony Robbins is one of the world's most famous motivational speakers, authors, and life coaches. Known for his boundless energy, larger-than-life presence, and transformative seminars, Robbins' journey to the top was far from easy. His story is one of overcoming hardships, self-discovery, and a relentless desire to help others achieve their fullest potential.

Early Life: Overcoming Adversity
Tony Robbins was born Anthony J. Mahavoric on February 29, 1960, in North Hollywood, California. His childhood was marked by instability and financial hardship. Raised by a single mother who struggled with substance abuse, Robbins took on responsibilities beyond his years. He left home at 17 after a turbulent relationship with his mother and set out to make a name for himself with little to no resources.

During this time, Robbins worked as a janitor to make ends meet, but he was determined to rise above his circumstances. His early struggles played a crucial role in shaping his future philosophy of personal growth and empowerment. His own experiences with hardship instilled in him a desire to help others break free from the limitations of their environments.

The Beginning: Mentorship and Breakthrough

Tony's big break came when he started working as a promoter for motivational speaker Jim Rohn, a successful personal development coach. Rohn taught Robbins the principles of personal responsibility, success psychology, and the power of goal-setting, all of which deeply influenced Tony's future work. Rohn's teachings helped Robbins transform his own life and gave him the tools to develop his signature approach to personal development.

Robbins began conducting his own seminars, and at the age of 22, he started offering NLP (Neuro-Linguistic Programming) seminars, which focused on understanding human behavior and reprogramming the mind for success. He studied NLP under John Grinder, co-creator of the discipline, and this became a key foundation for Robbins' early work.

Unleashing the Power Within

In 1986, Tony Robbins created his first personal development seminar, Unleash the Power Within (UPW), which would become one of his most famous programs. The event focuses on helping people break through mental and emotional barriers, tap into their true potential, and take immediate, massive action toward their goals. Robbins introduced techniques such as the firewalk, where participants walk barefoot over hot coals, as a metaphor for overcoming fear and limitations.

UPW became a life-changing event for thousands of attendees, and Robbins quickly gained a following as a high-energy, results-oriented coach. His engaging and immersive style, combined with practical tools for transforming lives, made him a standout in the self-help industry.

Bestselling Author and Media Personality

In 1987, Robbins published his first book, "Unlimited Power," which laid out his personal development philosophy and strategies for achieving success in all areas of life—health, finances, relationships, and more. The book became an instant bestseller and established him as a thought leader in the personal development space. Robbins followed it up with "Awaken the Giant Within" in 1991, which further cemented his status as a bestselling author.

Throughout the 1990s and 2000s, Robbins became a media personality, making frequent appearances on television and radio, including interviews on The Oprah Winfrey Show, Larry King Live, and 60 Minutes. His media exposure helped him reach millions of people around the world, expanding his influence beyond the seminar room.

Business Ventures and Philanthropy

Tony Robbins is not just a life coach; he is also a successful entrepreneur and business strategist. Over the years, he has built a multi-faceted business empire that includes coaching, seminars, and consulting. He has worked with high-profile clients, including Bill Clinton, Serena Williams, and Oprah Winfrey, among others.

Robbins co-founded The Tony Robbins Foundation, a nonprofit organization dedicated to improving the quality of life for people in need. His philanthropy focuses on feeding millions of people, providing clean water to underserved communities, and supporting education initiatives globally.

In addition to his personal development work, Robbins has a vast portfolio of business interests. He is involved in more than 50 companies across various industries, including hospitality, education, sports, and finance. He also became a part-owner of Team Liquid, a successful eSports organization, further demonstrating his diverse business acumen.

Net Worth and Legacy

As of 2024, Tony Robbins' net worth is estimated to be over $600 million, thanks to his wide range of business ventures, bestselling books, and world-renowned seminars. He has impacted millions of people worldwide, helping them overcome personal struggles, achieve financial freedom, and live fulfilling lives.

Robbins' legacy is one of empowerment. He continues to inspire millions through his speaking engagements, digital content, and live events. His philosophy—rooted in the belief that we all have the power to change our lives—remains as powerful today as it was when he first started.

Conclusion: The Power of Transformation

Tony Robbins' success story is a testament to the power of transformation and resilience. From a difficult childhood to becoming one of the most successful life coaches in the world, Robbins has never stopped pushing the boundaries of personal growth. Through his work, Robbins has proven that with the right mindset and strategies, anyone can achieve greatness, no matter where they start.

Arianna Huffington's Success Story: The Dual Focus on Success and Well-Being

"Embracing digital news isn't just about reaching a wider audience; it's about strategically placing your brand in the current of global conversations, ensuring your message not only spreads but resonates."
— ARIANNA HUFFINGTON, CO-FOUNDER OF
THE HUFFINGTON POST

"Getting featured in print media isn't just about broadcasting your work—it's about crafting a story so compelling that editors feel they're missing out if they don't share it." — ARIANNA HUFFINGTON, FOUNDER OF THE HUFFINGTON POST AND THRIVE GLOBAL

Arianna Huffington is a trailblazing entrepreneur, author, and media mogul whose career has spanned journalism, politics, and wellness. Best known as the co-founder of *The Huffington Post*, she transformed the digital media landscape by merging traditional reporting with blogging and opinion-based content. Her journey reflects resilience and reinvention—from her early life in Greece to becoming one of the most influential women in media. In recent years, Arianna's focus on mental health and well-being through her venture, Thrive Global, has solidified her legacy as a leader who not only built empires but also championed sustainable success.

Early Life and Influences
Arianna Huffington, born Ariadni-Anna Stasinopoulou in Athens, Greece, grew up with a passion for literature, philosophy, and culture. Raised by a free-spirited mother who encouraged her to follow her dreams, Arianna's ambition took her to the University of Cambridge in England. There, she became president of the

Cambridge Union, one of the most prestigious debating societies, honing her skills in argument and public speaking.

An Early Writing Career and Personal Setbacks

After university, Arianna pursued a career in writing and published several books, including *The Female Woman*. She faced personal setbacks during her early years, including the end of a relationship with British journalist Bernard Levin. Still, her resilience kept her moving forward. Relocating to the United States, she married Michael Huffington, an oil heir and politician. Though the marriage didn't last, her time in American politics fueled her interest in public discourse and media.

The Launch of The Huffington Post

In 2005, Arianna co-founded *The Huffington Post*, originally conceived as a left-leaning online platform combining news aggregation and opinion blogs. Despite skepticism about its viability, the site quickly grew in popularity, blending traditional journalism with user-generated content. Under her leadership, *The Huffington Post* became a pioneer of online media, attracting millions of readers. Its mix of news, culture, and politics redefined digital journalism and bridged the gap between blogging and mainstream media.

The Acquisition by AOL and Continued Success

In 2011, AOL acquired *The Huffington Post* for $315 million, a testament to the site's influence and commercial success. Arianna stayed on as editor-in-chief, continuing to build the brand globally. During this time, she expanded coverage into new topics like lifestyle, health, and wellness, ensuring the platform evolved with shifting audience interests.

A Shift Toward Wellness and New Ventures

After stepping down from *The Huffington Post* in 2016, Arianna turned her attention to a new passion: wellness and mental health. Inspired by her own experiences with burnout, she launched Thrive Global, a wellness-focused startup aimed at promoting sustainable well-being in the workplace. Thrive Global has since become a leader in mental health solutions, working with organizations worldwide to improve employee well-being and productivity.

Legacy and Influence

Arianna Huffington's journey from writer to media mogul exemplifies the power of adaptability and perseverance. Throughout her career, she has redefined what it means to succeed, demonstrating that personal well-being and professional ambition can coexist. Today, Arianna continues to inspire individuals to pursue success on their own terms, balancing achievement with mindfulness. Her influence extends beyond journalism and media, leaving a lasting mark on how society values mental health in business and personal life.

Beyonce's Success Story: From Destiny's Child to Global Icon

"Royalties are not just a revenue stream; they're a recognition of your creativity's worth. Mastering them ensures your art sustains both your soul and your livelihood." — BEYONCÉ, SINGER-SONGWRITER AND BUSINESSWOMAN

Beyoncé Knowles-Carter's journey from a young girl performing in talent shows to becoming one of the most influential artists and business moguls in the world is a story of unmatched talent, relentless work ethic, and fearless reinvention. As a singer, songwriter, actress, and entrepreneur, Beyoncé has transcended the music industry to shape culture and inspire generations. From her early days with the iconic group Destiny's Child to her groundbreaking solo career, she has continuously pushed boundaries, blending art, activism, and business. With a legacy rooted in empowerment, creativity, and social impact, Beyoncé is not just a global superstar—she is a symbol of excellence, resilience, and unapologetic self-expression.

Early Life and the Beginnings of Destiny's Child

Born on September 4, 1981, in Houston, Texas, Beyoncé Giselle Knowles was destined for stardom. Raised by a supportive family, her mother, Tina Knowles, owned a hair salon and later designed costumes for Beyoncé's performances, while her father, Mathew Knowles, managed her early career. From a young age, Beyoncé displayed immense talent in singing and dancing, participating in school talent shows and local competitions. Her parents recognized her potential and began shaping her career, laying the foundation for what would become a groundbreaking journey in music and entertainment.

At just nine years old, Beyoncé formed a girl group, later known as *Destiny's Child*, with childhood friends Kelly Rowland and Michelle Williams. Managed by her father, the group initially struggled, going through name changes and rejections. However, their persistence paid off when they signed with Columbia Records in the late 1990s.

Breakout Success with Destiny's Child
Destiny's Child became one of the best-selling female groups of all time, releasing hits like "Say My Name," "Survivor," and "Independent Women." Their music was celebrated for empowering messages that resonated with women across the globe. Despite lineup changes and personal challenges, the group's chemistry, distinctive harmonies, and stage presence propelled them to international fame.

As the group achieved commercial success, Beyoncé emerged as the standout star. Her leadership within the group was evident, not only as a performer but also as a creative force behind their music and branding. In 2001, the group took a hiatus, allowing Beyoncé and her bandmates to pursue solo projects—a move that would mark a significant turning point in her career.

A Solo Career That Redefined Pop Music
Beyoncé's debut solo album, *Dangerously in Love* (2003), was a commercial and critical triumph, winning five Grammy Awards and producing chart-topping hits like "Crazy in Love" and "Baby Boy." With this album, she demonstrated her versatility by blending R&B, hip-hop, and pop, setting the tone for her solo career. The combination of her vocal talent, dance skills, and visionary artistry distinguished her from other pop artists.

Over the years, Beyoncé released a series of albums that showcased her growth as an artist and cultural force. Albums like *B'Day* (2006), *I Am . . . Sasha Fierce* (2008), and *4* (2011) continued to dominate the charts and cemented her status as a global superstar. But it was her self-titled visual album *Beyoncé* (2013) and *Lemonade* (2016) that redefined the boundaries of music, combining deeply personal storytelling with visual art and political commentary.

Empowerment and Business Ventures

Beyoncé's influence extends beyond music. She has become a cultural icon and a business mogul, venturing into fashion, film, and philanthropy. She co-founded *Parkwood Entertainment*, a multifaceted entertainment company involved in music, film, and event production. Her partnership with Adidas to launch *Ivy Park*, an activewear brand, further solidified her presence in the business world.

As a fierce advocate for women's empowerment, racial equality, and humanitarian causes, Beyoncé uses her platform to inspire social change. Her performances and visual projects often celebrate Black culture, womanhood, and resilience, such as her *Homecoming* performance at Coachella 2018, which paid homage to historically Black colleges and universities.

Family Life and Legacy

Beyoncé has managed to balance the pressures of fame with her personal life, especially after marrying rapper and businessman Jay-Z in 2008. Together, they have built a musical empire and welcomed three children, Blue Ivy, Rumi, and Sir. The couple's collaborative works, including their joint album *Everything Is Love* (2018), reflect their ability to blend artistry with personal experiences.

A Legacy That Transcends Music

Beyoncé's journey from a young girl in Houston to a global phenomenon is a testament to her relentless work ethic, talent, and ability to evolve. She has sold over 200 million records worldwide, won numerous awards, and become the most-awarded artist in Grammy history. But her legacy is more than just statistics—it's about inspiring others to embrace their power, creativity, and individuality.

Whether through her music, activism, or business ventures, Beyoncé continues to push boundaries and challenge norms, proving that success is not only about talent but also about vision, resilience, and a commitment to empowering others.

———————

CHAPTER FIVE

Time Management and Productivity

Time is the most precious resource for any entrepreneur or business leader, and mastering time management is essential for achieving both personal and professional success. Unlike money or physical assets, time cannot be replenished once spent. In today's fast-paced, constantly connected world, the ability to manage time effectively is what separates high achievers from those who struggle to meet their goals. Jim Rohn, entrepreneur and motivational speaker, famously said, "Time is more valuable than money. You can get more money, but you cannot get more time." This chapter explores how developing practical strategies for time management and boosting productivity can unlock your full potential and help you take control of your busy schedule.

Effective time management goes beyond creating to-do lists or filling calendars with meetings—it's about aligning your daily tasks with your most important goals. Diana Scharf, author and speaker, reminds us that "Goals are dreams with deadlines." In this chapter, we'll explore how setting priorities ensures that your time is spent on what matters most, whether it's growing your business, nurturing relationships, or taking care of your health. You'll learn how to break down big-picture goals into manageable tasks and integrate them into your daily routine.

The concept of balance also plays a crucial role in productivity. Jana Kingsford, motivational speaker, emphasizes, "Balance is not something you find; it's something you create." We'll explore practical ways to balance the demands of work, family, and personal life by scheduling with intention. You'll discover how to create structured routines while leaving room for flexibility, allowing you to respond effectively to unexpected challenges without feeling overwhelmed.

A critical element of productivity is identifying and overcoming distractions. In an era where technology often pulls us in multiple directions, staying focused has become more challenging than ever. Steven Pressfield, author of *The War of Art*, explains that mastering time management involves "aligning with your most productive periods." This chapter will guide you through strategies for blocking distractions, using tools such as time-blocking, and creating an environment conducive to deep work. We'll also cover the importance of rest and how breaks can enhance productivity rather than hinder it.

Another key component of effective time management is learning how to delegate. Morten T. Hansen, management professor and author, advises, "Do less, but obsess." We'll explore how to identify tasks that can be outsourced or assigned to team members, freeing up your time to focus on high-priority initiatives. Whether you're working solo or managing a team, knowing when and how to delegate is essential for scaling your business and avoiding burnout.

Technology also plays a vital role in productivity, with tools that can automate repetitive tasks and optimize workflow. Matt Goulart, a productivity expert, illustrates how effective use of technology can transform operations and save precious time. This chapter will introduce you to time-saving apps and techniques, from project management software to productivity hacks, that help streamline processes and reduce time spent on administrative tasks.

Managing time effectively is not just about squeezing more tasks into your day—it's about making deliberate choices about how you spend your time. Sierra Bailey, a leadership coach, emphasizes the importance of focusing on the few things that truly matter. This chapter encourages you to adopt a quality-over-quantity mindset, executing the essential tasks to the best of your ability.

Finally, we'll explore real-world examples of individuals and businesses that have mastered time management and used it to achieve remarkable success. These stories will highlight how even the most accomplished people face challenges with time management, but with the right strategies, they are able to remain productive and maintain a healthy work-life balance.

By the end of this chapter, you'll have a toolkit of practical strategies and insights to improve your time management and productivity. Whether you're striving to hit ambitious deadlines, scale your business, or simply reclaim more personal time, the principles outlined here will help you make the most of each day. As Aristotle wisely noted, "We are what we repeatedly do. Excellence, then, is not an act, but a habit." With disciplined time management, you'll create habits that support long-term success and unlock your full potential.

Jim Rohn's Success Story: The Philosopher of Personal Development

"Time is more valuable than money. You can get more money, but you cannot get more time." — JIM ROHN, ENTREPRENEUR AND MOTIVATIONAL SPEAKER

Jim Rohn's story is one of humble beginnings, transformative mentorship, and a relentless pursuit of personal growth. Known as the "father of personal development," Rohn built a career that spanned over four decades, influencing millions of people, including world-renowned figures like Tony Robbins, Brian Tracy, and Jack Canfield. His teachings on self-discipline, goal setting, and success principles continue to inspire generations long after his passing.

From Small-Town Beginnings to Big Dreams
Jim Rohn was born on September 17, 1930, in Yakima, Washington, and grew up on a small farm in Idaho. His parents instilled in him traditional values—honesty, hard work, and responsibility—which shaped his early outlook on life. However,

as a young man, Rohn struggled with direction. He dropped out of college after just one year and found himself working a series of dead-end jobs, uncertain of what he wanted to achieve.

By his mid-20s, Rohn was stuck in a routine, living paycheck to paycheck. He was married, raising a family, and frustrated by the lack of progress in his life. Financial struggles and a sense of unfulfilled potential weighed heavily on him. Despite his upbringing, he had not yet developed the habits or mindset necessary to achieve the success he desired.

A Life-Changing Encounter with a Mentor

Rohn's life changed forever when he met Earl Shoaff, a successful entrepreneur who became his mentor. Rohn was drawn to Shoaff's charisma, wisdom, and success, and the two quickly formed a mentor-student relationship. Shoaff challenged Rohn to rethink his approach to life. He taught him that success wasn't about luck or circumstance—it was about personal development, discipline, and setting clear goals.

One of Shoaff's most profound lessons was, "Success is something you attract by the person you become." This principle became the cornerstone of Rohn's philosophy and the foundation for his teachings throughout his career. Shoaff's mentorship helped Rohn develop a new mindset, one focused on taking ownership of his life and creating opportunities through intentional actions.

The Path to Financial Success and Personal Growth

Inspired by Shoaff's teachings, Rohn began applying the principles of personal development to his own life. He joined Shoaff's direct selling business, and within a few years, Rohn had achieved financial independence. By the age of 31, he was a self-made millionaire, transforming his life from one of struggle to one of abundance. However, more than financial success, Rohn experienced a profound personal transformation—he became more disciplined, confident, and purposeful.

After the death of Earl Shoaff, Rohn reflected on the importance of passing on what he had learned. He realized that success wasn't just about wealth—it was about becoming the best version of yourself and helping others do the same.

Becoming a Speaker and Influencing Millions

In the 1960s, Rohn was invited to speak at a Rotary Club meeting in California, where he shared the story of his transformation and the principles that had guided his success. His speech was a hit, and soon, he was receiving invitations to speak at seminars, workshops, and conferences. Word of his unique philosophy spread, and Rohn transitioned into motivational speaking and coaching, which would become his life's mission.

Rohn's style was simple yet profound. He used personal stories, witty anecdotes, and practical advice to inspire audiences. His ability to connect deeply with people, regardless of their background, set him apart from other speakers. Over the next four decades, Rohn traveled the world, delivering talks on topics such as goal setting, time management, financial literacy, and self-discipline.

The Mentor to the Mentors

Throughout his career, Rohn became a mentor to some of the most successful individuals in the personal development and business world. His teachings shaped the lives of influential figures such as Tony Robbins, who credits Rohn as the most important mentor in his early career. Robbins often recalls that attending a Jim Rohn seminar at the age of 17 changed the course of his life, leading him to pursue his passion for personal development.

In addition to Robbins, Rohn influenced leaders like Jack Canfield (author of *Chicken Soup for the Soul*), Darren Hardy(publisher of *SUCCESS Magazine*), and Brian Tracy (motivational speaker and author). His wisdom became the backbone of the personal development industry, with his principles integrated into countless programs, books, and seminars.

Books, Legacy, and Impact

Rohn's teachings reached an even wider audience through his books and audio programs. His most popular works include "The Five Major Pieces to the Life Puzzle," "Leading an Inspired Life," and "The Art of Exceptional Living." His timeless principles on personal growth, goal setting, and financial freedom continue to resonate with readers and listeners worldwide.

One of Rohn's core philosophies was the importance of personal responsibility. He famously said, "Don't wish it were easier, wish you were better." This idea of focusing on self-improvement rather than external circumstances became a guiding principle for many of his followers.

Rohn's seminars and books emphasized the importance of daily habits, such as reading, journaling, and practicing gratitude. He believed that small, consistent actions were the key to achieving long-term success, and his teachings encouraged individuals to cultivate these habits in their own lives.

Later Life and Ongoing Influence

Jim Rohn continued speaking, writing, and coaching until his retirement in the early 2000s. Even after stepping away from the public eye, his influence remained strong. Rohn passed away on December 5, 2009, at the age of 79, leaving behind a profound legacy that continues to shape the personal development industry.

Today, his principles live on through the thousands of entrepreneurs, authors, and speakers he mentored directly and indirectly. His timeless wisdom has become a staple in business schools, motivational programs, and self-help literature around the globe.

The Legacy of a Life Well Lived

Jim Rohn's journey from humble beginnings to personal transformation is a testament to the power of mentorship, self-discipline, and intentional growth. His legacy serves as a reminder that success is not just about financial wealth—it is about becoming the best version of yourself and helping others do the same.

As Rohn often said: "Success is nothing more than a few simple disciplines, practiced every day."

His message endures because it speaks to the universal desire for self-improvement and fulfillment. Jim Rohn's life exemplifies the idea that with the right mindset, the right habits, and the right guidance, anyone can create a life of meaning, impact, and success.

Diana Scharf's Success Story: Pioneer of the Vision Board and Goal-Setting Movement

"Goals are dreams with deadlines." — DIANA SCHARF,
AUTHOR AND SPEAKER

Diana Scharf became a renowned figure in the personal development world through her groundbreaking work on goal-setting strategies and the concept of vision boards. With a passion for helping others visualize and achieve their dreams, Scharf left an indelible mark on the self-help industry. Her journey to success is a story of innovation, focus, and a deep belief in the power of visualization.

A Background in Psychology and Motivation

Diana Scharf's early career was rooted in psychology and personal motivation. She initially worked in the corporate world, helping individuals and teams improve their productivity and focus. Her expertise in human behavior, combined with a curiosity about how people achieve personal success, laid the foundation for her life's work.

She became increasingly fascinated with the idea that thoughts and intentions shape outcomes. Through observation, research, and personal experience, Scharf realized that one of the most effective ways for people to achieve their dreams was through visualizing them clearly. This insight would become the cornerstone of her approach to goal-setting and personal development.

The Birth of the Vision Board Concept

In the 1970s, Diana Scharf introduced a simple yet revolutionary idea: the vision board—a tool to help people visualize their goals and dreams by creating a collage of inspiring images, words, and affirmations. The idea was rooted in the principle that when people see their goals represented visually, they are more likely to stay focused and motivated to achieve them.

The concept of a vision board quickly gained popularity, as it was easy to understand and apply. Athletes, entrepreneurs, and professionals began using vision boards to clarify their aspirations and map out their success. Scharf's method encouraged individuals to visualize their goals as already achieved, which fostered a mindset of abundance and possibility.

Impact on Personal Development and Business Success

Diana Scharf's innovative approach to goal-setting spread far beyond the personal development world. Vision boards became an essential tool not only for individuals but also for teams and organizations seeking to align their goals. Business leaders and entrepreneurs began using vision boards to articulate their visions for growth, innovation, and success.

Her work was further amplified when public figures and motivational speakers like Tony Robbins and Oprah Winfrey adopted and promoted the concept of visualization. Scharf's methods became part of larger conversations about the law of attraction, positive psychology, and personal empowerment.

Publications and Global Recognition

In addition to promoting the vision board concept, Diana Scharf authored books and conducted workshops on goal-setting, motivation, and self-improvement. Her publications emphasized the importance of clarity, intention, and persistence when pursuing dreams. Titles such as *"The Magic of Visualization"* and *"Creating the Life You Want"* became popular resources for anyone seeking to design their ideal future.

Scharf's work resonated deeply because it was accessible to people of all backgrounds. Whether someone wanted to achieve personal happiness, career success, or financial freedom, Scharf's philosophy was rooted in practical, achievable steps.

Leaving a Legacy of Transformation

Diana Scharf's legacy lies in empowering people to dream boldly and take concrete action toward their goals. She showed the world that success begins with a clear vision and focused intention. Through vision boards and her teachings on goal-setting, she gave individuals the tools to not only imagine their dreams but to turn them into reality.

Today, the influence of Diana Scharf is evident in countless personal development programs and goal-setting workshops. Her vision board method remains a cornerstone of modern self-help practices, proving that the power of visualization is as relevant today as it was when she first introduced it.

Scharf's message endures in the hearts and minds of those she inspired: "What you see is what you can become."

Her story serves as a reminder that every great accomplishment starts with a vision, and through dedication and focus, that vision can grow into something truly extraordinary.

Jana Kingsford's Success Story: The Queen of Big Dreams and Business Balance

"Balance is not something you find, it's something you create." — JANA KINGSFORD, MOTIVATIONAL SPEAKER AND AUTHOR

Jana Kingsford built her reputation as an inspiring entrepreneur, mentor, and lifestyle strategist by transforming her life's challenges into opportunities for growth. She is known for her empowering message of "Big Dreams, Small Steps," showing others how to balance ambitious goals with everyday life. Kingsford's story is one of resilience, creativity, and her relentless pursuit of balancing business success with family life.

From Overwhelm to Breakthrough

Jana's entrepreneurial journey began in the midst of personal struggle. As a young mother of three children, she faced the pressure of balancing motherhood with her desire to build a business. Like many aspiring entrepreneurs, she initially experienced burnout and frustration, feeling trapped between her family responsibilities and her business aspirations.

Her turning point came when she realized that success didn't require sacrificing family life—instead, it was about integrating both worlds harmoniously. This epiphany led to her core philosophy: "You can have it all, but not all at once." Jana's focus shifted to creating a business model that accommodated her lifestyle, not the other way around.

Building the Dream Life One Step at a Time

With her mantra of "Big Dreams, Small Steps," Jana began sharing her journey through blogs and videos. Her authenticity and relatability resonated with an audience of ambitious women struggling to juggle entrepreneurship and parenthood. Rather than selling overnight success, Jana emphasized the importance of small, consistent actions toward big goals.

She started hosting online programs and mentorships, focusing on mindset, business strategy, and productivity. Through her coaching, she provided practical advice on building an empire while staying present for her family. Her clients admired her for making business goals achievable and showing that "doing things imperfectly is better than not doing them at all."

The Rise of Her Personal Brand

Jana Kingsford's personal brand quickly gained momentum, and her message expanded to a global audience. She built a loyal following through social media by openly sharing the highs and lows of entrepreneurship. Her transparency about both business successes and challenges made her an authentic voice in the personal development and business space.

Jana launched courses, live events, and group coaching programs that focused on scaling businesses while maintaining balance. She emphasized the importance of leveraging time, energy, and priorities, encouraging women to take inspired action without sacrificing their well-being or relationships.

Empowering Women Entrepreneurs

Jana Kingsford has become a trusted mentor for women who want to pursue entrepreneurship without compromising their role as mothers or caretakers. Her signature programs, such as *Big Dreams Bootcamp*, are designed to help women create scalable, soul-aligned businesses. Jana's teaching philosophy centers on energy management, showing that productivity isn't just about time but about working from a place of passion and purpose.

She also advocates for building businesses online, leveraging digital platforms to create freedom-based careers. Her content empowers her audience to step into their full potential while embracing imperfections. Jana is known for saying, "Life doesn't need to be perfect to be beautiful."

117

Living the Dream on Her Own Terms

Today, Jana Kingsford continues to inspire women through coaching, online programs, and public speaking. She has built a lifestyle and business that reflect her core values—freedom, family, and impact. Jana's story exemplifies how entrepreneurship can be redefined to fit the life you desire, rather than following traditional molds of success.

Jana's journey from overwhelmed mother to successful business mentor is a testament to the power of mindset, perseverance, and intentional action. Her ability to inspire others to dream big while staying grounded makes her a sought-after speaker, coach, and influencer in the world of lifestyle entrepreneurship.

Through her work, Jana Kingsford continues to show that building a thriving business doesn't mean giving up what matters most—it means finding a way to do it all, your way.

———

Steven Pressfield's Success Story: The Champion of Creative Resistance and Master of Storytelling

"Start before you're ready. Good things happen when we trust the process and do the work." — STEVEN PRESSFIELD, BESTSELLING AUTHOR AND CHAMPION OF CREATIVE DISCIPLINE

"Overcoming writing blocks requires not just dedication, but a mastery of scheduling that aligns with your most productive periods, transforming potential into pages." — STEVEN PRESSFIELD, AUTHOR AND SCREENWRITER

Steven Pressfield's journey to success is a story of perseverance, creative struggle, and self-discovery. Known for his profound work on overcoming creative resistance and his bestselling historical novels, Pressfield's rise was not a straightforward path. His life exemplifies that success often comes to those who endure through rejection, failure, and relentless self-doubt. With works like *The War of Art* and *Gates of Fire*, Pressfield has become a voice for aspiring artists, entrepreneurs, and creators battling their own inner resistance.

From the Shadows of Struggle to the Light of Creation

Steven Pressfield didn't find success overnight. In fact, it took decades of failure before he published his first book. Born in Port of Spain, Trinidad, and raised in New York, Pressfield worked in various jobs—advertising, screenwriting, and manual labor—while chasing his dream of becoming a writer. He lived for years in near-poverty, grappling with personal failures and struggling to finish any significant creative work.

During his journey, Pressfield often faced rejection from publishers and Hollywood studios, leaving him in a constant battle with what he later coined as "Resistance"—the invisible force that holds back creative expression. This resistance wasn't just external but internal: self-doubt, procrastination, and fear of failure.

A Turning Point: Finding Purpose in the Struggle

After countless false starts and abandoned projects, Pressfield experienced a pivotal moment of clarity. He realized that his calling as a writer required him to embrace the struggle, to show up every day and do the work regardless of inspiration or recognition. This insight became the bedrock of his philosophy and eventually led to the creation of his most influential work, *The War of Art*.

Before publishing this seminal book, however, Pressfield found modest success in screenwriting, contributing to films like *King Kong Lives* and *Above the Law*. But even with these small wins, the journey remained difficult, and true recognition eluded him for years.

Breakthrough with *The Legend of Bagger Vance*

Pressfield's major breakthrough came with the publication of *The Legend of Bagger Vance* in 1995, a novel blending philosophy, spirituality, and golf. The book's narrative about inner growth and self-mastery struck a chord with readers and was later adapted into a film starring Will Smith and Matt Damon. This success gave Pressfield the momentum he needed to pursue more ambitious projects and reaffirmed his place as a storyteller with a unique perspective on life and creativity.

The War of Art: A Guide for Creators and Dreamers

In 2002, Pressfield released *The War of Art*, a life-changing book for creatives and entrepreneurs alike. Drawing from his personal struggles, the book tackles the challenges of creative resistance and provides readers with practical advice on how to overcome self-doubt, fear, and procrastination. It became a cult classic among artists, writers, and business leaders, resonating with those who face similar inner obstacles on their creative journeys. The book's message is simple yet profound: "The hardest part is starting. Do the work."

Master of Historical Fiction

Following his success with non-fiction, Pressfield continued writing, focusing on historical novels that reflected his deep interest in ancient warfare and human nature. Books like *Gates of Fire*, a novel about the Battle of Thermopylae, and *The Afghan Campaign*, which explores Alexander the Great's conquests, showcased Pressfield's ability to breathe life into history with rich storytelling and complex characters. His meticulous research and gripping narratives earned him a devoted readership and critical acclaim.

A Legacy of Inspiration and Impact

Steven Pressfield's work transcends genres and industries. Whether through his novels, screenplays, or motivational writings, he has left a profound mark on creators across disciplines. His core philosophy—showing up, embracing the struggle, and doing the work—has empowered countless individuals to pursue their passions against all odds.

Today, Pressfield continues to write and speak on creativity, sharing his experiences with those who need guidance through their own battles with resistance. His story is a testament to the idea that success is not about avoiding failure but about learning to persevere through it.

Through his books, Pressfield offers more than just storytelling; he provides a map to navigate the wilderness of creative ambition, inspiring others to keep pushing forward until they, too, find success.

Morten T. Hansen's Success Story: Leadership and Productivity Expert

"Do less, but obsess." — MORTEN T. HANSEN, MANAGEMENT PROFESSOR AND AUTHOR

Morten T. Hansen is a distinguished scholar, author, and management consultant who has reshaped how organizations approach leadership, collaboration, and productivity. As a former senior manager at the Boston Consulting Group and a professor at the University of California, Berkeley, Hansen combines academic rigor with real-world insight. His groundbreaking research, including concepts introduced in his book *Great at Work*, focuses on how individuals and teams can achieve more by doing less—but obsessing over what truly matters. Hansen's contributions to leadership studies have made him a sought-after speaker and consultant for organizations seeking to thrive in a competitive environment. His personal journey is one of continuous learning, strategic insight, and the relentless pursuit of excellence, inspiring countless professionals to rethink their approach to work and leadership.

Early Life and Academic Foundations

Morten T. Hansen, born and raised in Norway, began his journey with a passion for understanding human behavior, organizations, and the factors that drive exceptional performance. He pursued higher education in business and management, earning degrees from both the University of Oslo and the London School of Economics. His academic curiosity eventually led him to Stanford University, where he obtained his Ph.D. in Business, focusing on how organizations and teams can operate more efficiently through collaboration.

Early Career: A Scholar in Action

Hansen's career started in academia, where he took up research roles in leading institutions such as INSEAD and the Harvard Business School. His early work delved into organizational behavior, collaboration, and how companies could leverage internal synergy to unlock greater potential. While teaching and conducting research, Hansen developed a deep interest in discovering why some companies and individuals excel while others, even with similar resources, fall behind.

121

Writing *Collaboration: How Leaders Avoid the Traps, Create Unity, and Reap Big Results*

Hansen's research took a pivotal turn when he noticed that many organizations struggle with achieving productive teamwork. In 2009, he published *Collaboration: How Leaders Avoid the Traps, Create Unity, and Reap Big Results*. This influential book redefined the way businesses thought about teamwork, moving away from the assumption that collaboration is inherently good toward understanding when it works and when it doesn't. Hansen provided practical frameworks that identified how leaders could foster meaningful cooperation and avoid unnecessary complexity.

Expanding Thought Leadership: *Great at Work*

Hansen's reputation as a leading expert on performance was further solidified with the release of *Great at Work: How Top Performers Do Less, Work Better, and Achieve More*. This book, published in 2018, is the culmination of a five-year study involving thousands of employees across industries. Hansen discovered that top performers don't necessarily work longer hours; instead, they focus obsessively on a few key priorities and excel at those. His research identified practical strategies, such as disciplined focus and the "do less, then obsess" principle, which resonate with professionals seeking to achieve more without burnout.

Partnership with Jim Collins: Unlocking Success through Data

One of Hansen's defining collaborations was with renowned business author Jim Collins. Together, they co-authored *Great by Choice*, an exploration of how companies thrive in uncertainty and chaos. This book became a New York Times bestseller and offered compelling insights into why certain organizations outperform others, even in volatile environments. Their research introduced the concept of "10Xers"—leaders who achieve ten times more success than their peers through disciplined and consistent action.

Educator and Consultant for Global Leaders

Beyond writing, Hansen's work has had a significant impact in the classroom and the boardroom. As a professor at the University of California, Berkeley, Hansen teaches future leaders how to cultivate high performance and collaboration in their organizations. His consulting work spans multinational corporations, where he guides top executives on strategies to enhance teamwork and productivity.

Philosophy and Enduring Influence

Morten T. Hansen's philosophy centers on disciplined focus, purposeful collaboration, and making a meaningful impact. His research continues to inspire professionals at every level, encouraging them to rethink how they approach work and teamwork. Hansen's mantra of "doing less, but better" resonates in an age of information overload and constant demands, providing a much-needed framework for sustainable performance.

Legacy and Ongoing Impact

Hansen's books and research have become staples in the business community, influencing how companies strategize for success and adapt to change. His insights on collaboration, leadership, and personal effectiveness have empowered countless professionals to reimagine their approach to work. Whether through his books, teaching, or consulting, Morten T. Hansen continues to shape the future of business performance, helping leaders navigate the complexities of the modern workplace with clarity and focus.

Matt Goulart's Success Story: Building Brands in the Digital Age

"Social media is about the people! Not about your business. Provide for the people and the people will provide for you." — MATT GOULART, DIGITAL MARKETING EXPERT

Matt Goulart is a trailblazer in the world of digital marketing, known for his ability to merge technology with business strategy. As the founder of Ignite Digital, Goulart has built a reputation for helping businesses harness the power of the internet to achieve measurable success. With a passion for data-driven marketing and a commitment to staying ahead of industry trends, Goulart transformed his agency into one of the top digital marketing firms in North America. His journey from a tech-savvy entrepreneur to a thought leader in the digital space exemplifies how foresight, adaptability, and innovation can turn challenges into opportunities.

Early Life and Passion for Technology

Matt Goulart grew up fascinated by the intersection of technology and communication. From a young age, he showed an entrepreneurial spark, teaching himself coding and experimenting with web design. Goulart recognized early on that the internet was more than a place for entertainment—it was a space where businesses could grow, connect, and thrive. His passion for technology and marketing laid the foundation for his career in digital marketing.

Building the Foundation: Starting Ignite Digital

In 2008, Goulart founded Ignite Digital, a full-service digital marketing agency, with the goal of helping businesses succeed online. His mission was simple: to empower companies by leveraging the potential of digital platforms like Google, Facebook, and Instagram. In an era when many companies were still hesitant to embrace online marketing, Goulart saw an opportunity to fill that gap by offering data-driven strategies and expert insights.

Through Ignite Digital, Goulart built a reputation for delivering measurable results. His agency specialized in search engine optimization (SEO), pay-per-click (PPC) advertising, and content marketing—tools essential for businesses navigating the online marketplace. Goulart's unique ability to blend technical expertise with creative thinking quickly positioned him as a leader in the digital marketing space.

Overcoming Challenges and Expanding Influence

The road to success wasn't without obstacles. As digital marketing evolved rapidly, Goulart faced the challenge of staying ahead of industry trends and innovations. He invested heavily in research and development, continuously updating Ignite Digital's tools and practices to meet changing demands. This adaptability became a key differentiator for his company, helping it grow while competitors struggled to keep pace.

Goulart also prioritized client education, believing that businesses needed to understand digital marketing to appreciate its value. He offered workshops and consultations, teaching business owners how to build strong online presences and drive customer engagement. His commitment to transparency and education fostered trust and loyalty among clients.

Recognition and Influence in the Digital Marketing World

As Ignite Digital flourished, Goulart's expertise became widely recognized in the industry. He became a sought-after speaker at conferences, sharing insights on SEO, branding, and digital transformation. His thought leadership extended to online platforms, where he wrote articles and gave interviews on the latest trends in online marketing and entrepreneurship.

Goulart's influence grew beyond his agency. His innovative strategies and commitment to data-driven marketing earned him a reputation as one of the top minds in the digital space. He also became an advocate for the power of small businesses to thrive through effective digital marketing.

Legacy and Future Vision

Today, Matt Goulart's journey continues to inspire aspiring entrepreneurs and marketers. His success with Ignite Digital exemplifies the importance of foresight, adaptability, and innovation in an ever-changing industry. Goulart remains dedicated to helping businesses unlock their potential through digital marketing, leveraging emerging technologies to stay at the forefront of the industry.

His story is a testament to the transformative power of digital marketing when combined with a visionary mindset. Goulart's ability to see opportunity where others saw uncertainty has made him a leader in his field, and his legacy is one of empowering businesses to grow, evolve, and succeed in the digital age.

Sierra Bailey's Success Story: A Story of Passion and Transformation

"Writing is not about using big words to impress. It's about using simple words in an impressive way." — SIERRA BAILEY, ENTREPRENEUR AND WRITER

Sierra Bailey's journey from artist to business mentor is a story of passion, reinvention, and empowerment. Beginning her career as the founder of the jewelry brand Manic Trout, Bailey spent over a decade building a successful creative business. However, as she navigated the entrepreneurial world, she discovered her true calling—helping other small business owners thrive. Transitioning from jewelry designer to business coach, Bailey built a platform dedicated to equipping entrepreneurs with practical strategies for productivity, time management, and sustainable growth. Her journey showcases the power of embracing change, finding purpose, and turning personal experience into a tool for empowering others.

Early Life and the Artist's Path

Sierra Bailey began her career in the arts, working as a jewelry designer and creative entrepreneur. From a young age, Bailey had a passion for both artistry and problem-solving, which drove her to start her first business—a handcrafted jewelry line called Manic Trout. Over the course of 16 years, she built the brand from a small creative endeavor into a thriving business, with her pieces being featured in boutiques and media outlets nationwide.

The Shift to Entrepreneurship Coaching

As Bailey grew her creative business, she discovered a new passion—helping other entrepreneurs succeed. She noticed that many small business owners struggled with the operational aspects of running a business, such as marketing, time management, and scaling sustainably. Her experience in growing Manic Trout gave her valuable insights into these challenges, which she began sharing through blog posts, workshops, and consulting sessions.

Realizing there was a significant need for guidance among creative entrepreneurs, Bailey decided to pivot her career. She transitioned from being a full-time jewelry designer to becoming a business coach and mentor, specializing in helping small business owners structure their businesses for long-term success.

Building a New Brand and Community

In her new role as a mentor, Bailey launched Doers Shakers Makers, a platform that includes a podcast, courses, and a vibrant community for entrepreneurs. Her focus was to provide practical tools and advice to help small business owners become more productive, streamline operations, and stay motivated. She built a loyal following by offering actionable insights and relatable advice, inspiring entrepreneurs to thrive in competitive markets.

Success Through Authenticity and Connection

Bailey's success as a business mentor lies in her authenticity and deep connection with her audience. Rather than focusing solely on traditional business models, she advocates for finding joy in the work and creating businesses that align with personal values and goals. Her coaching sessions emphasize time management, goal-setting, and overcoming the fear of failure—common challenges faced by entrepreneurs.

Through public speaking, workshops, and her online presence, Bailey has become a sought-after voice in the world of entrepreneurship. Her journey is a testament to the power of reinvention and following one's passion, demonstrating that success is not just about profit but about building a meaningful life and career.

Legacy of Empowerment

Sierra Bailey's story reflects the importance of adaptability and personal growth. From jewelry designer to entrepreneur and business mentor, her journey illustrates that success is not linear but a continuous evolution. Today, she continues to empower small business owners by equipping them with the tools and confidence they need to turn their dreams into sustainable ventures, leaving a lasting impact on the creative and entrepreneurial communities.

———————

CHAPTER SIX

Storytelling in Marketing

In today's competitive business landscape, marketing messages are everywhere, making it increasingly difficult for companies to stand out. Storytelling offers a way to break through the noise and create meaningful connections with audiences. People respond to stories because they evoke emotion, inspire trust, and make brands more relatable. This chapter explores the strategic use of storytelling in marketing and how it transforms products, services, and companies into experiences customers want to engage with. Successful storytelling makes the audience the hero of the narrative, positioning the brand as the guide that helps them overcome challenges and achieve success.

Some of the most influential marketing campaigns weave compelling narratives about the founders, customers, or missions behind the business. For instance, Gary Vaynerchuk reminds us that "great marketing isn't about pushing products; it's about pulling people in." Similarly, Bernadette Jiwa emphasizes the significance of storytelling in creating an emotional connection, urging brands to share their unique journeys to resonate deeply with their audience. Storytelling is not limited to origin stories or testimonials; it can also take the form of real-time engagement, brand campaigns aligned with societal values, or playful narratives that capture attention in unique ways.

This chapter introduces key storytelling principles: authenticity, relevance, emotional appeal, and consistency. Authenticity ensures that your stories align with your company's values and mission, as highlighted by Neil Gaiman, who stresses the importance of crafting an authentic voice. Ann Handley echoes this sentiment by noting that good content creates meaningful connections, transforming followers into loyal advocates. Simon Sinek teaches us that "people don't follow you for what you do; they follow you for why you do it," reinforcing the idea that effective stories convey more than products—they embody purpose.

Different platforms allow for different types of storytelling. Jay Baer sees social media as a powerful tool for storytelling, emphasizing that "content marketing is fire, and social media is gasoline," indicating the synergy between storytelling and platform strategy. Jonah Sachs adds that video storytelling can ignite a deeper emotional response, creating a modern narrative experience that captivates audiences. This chapter will guide you in identifying the right formats—whether social media posts, blogs, videos, podcasts, or email newsletters—and aligning them with your brand's story to maximize impact.

We will also explore how storytelling integrates into your broader marketing strategy. Whether through high-level branding campaigns or customer-centric content, storytelling allows companies to engage authentically and consistently. Practical advice from experts like Neil Patel, who encourages businesses to use SEO to ensure stories are discoverable, highlights the technical side of effective storytelling.

At the heart of storytelling lies the goal of building meaningful connections with customers. David Ogilvy advises us to "open with the fire" when telling stories, ensuring that they grab attention from the start. The chapter also examines how well-told stories enhance customer loyalty by reinforcing shared values and emotions. As Jay Baer notes, engagement is crucial; every story should invite interaction and involvement from your audience.

By the end of this chapter, you will understand that storytelling is not just a creative endeavor but a strategic tool for cultivating loyalty and driving growth.

Successful storytelling engages customers emotionally, turning them into advocates who champion your brand and amplify your message. With guidance from experts like Neil Patel, Gary Vaynerchuk, and Ann Handley, you will learn to craft narratives that resonate deeply and inspire action. Through storytelling, you will transform your marketing efforts from a collection of promotional messages into a dynamic conversation that fosters community, trust, and sustainable success.

Gary Vaynerchuk's Success Story: How Gary Vee Hustled His Way to the Top

"Successful marketing is about identifying those unmet needs that people don't even know they have yet and finding innovative ways to meet them. When you truly understand your audience, you can create solutions that surprise and delight." — GARY VAYNERCHUK, CEO OF VAYNERMEDIA

"Adapt your techniques to each channel and its audience to ensure your message cuts through the noise and engages viewers." — GARY VAYNERCHUK, ENTREPRENEUR AND DIGITAL MARKETING EXPERT

"Turn your passion into profit: Let your website be more than a calling card; make it a cash register." — GARY VAYNERCHUK, ENTREPRENEUR AND SOCIAL MEDIA INFLUENCER

"Tumblr is the canvas where your audience doesn't just see your content; they interact with it, reshape it, and make it their own. Embrace this platform to discover just how dynamic and responsive your brand can be." — GARY VAYNERCHUK, ENTREPRENEUR AND SOCIAL MEDIA EXPERT

"Turn your social media into a revenue-generating machine. It's not just about being popular; it's about being profitable." — GARY VAYNERCHUK, ENTREPRENEUR AND SOCIAL MEDIA EXPERT

"Post-launch is when the real work begins. It's about amplifying your message and keeping the momentum alive, turning a successful launch into a sustained triumph." — GARY VAYNERCHUK, ENTREPRENEUR AND SOCIAL MEDIA INFLUENCER

"Social media is the modern marketplace, and mastering it requires turning every post, pin, and picture into an opportunity for engagement and conversion." — GARY VAYNERCHUK, ENTREPRENEUR AND SOCIAL MEDIA EXPERT

"Direct mail, enriched with modern insights, transforms from old-school to cutting-edge, offering a tactile dimension to our digital dialogues." — GARY VAYNERCHUK, ENTREPRENEUR AND SOCIAL MEDIA INFLUENCER

"Repurposing content is about seeing the many lives any single piece of writing can lead. It's economical, it's efficient, and it extends the reach of your original ideas to new audiences and formats." — GARY VAYNERCHUK, ENTREPRENEUR AND DIGITAL MARKETING EXPERT

Gary Vaynerchuk, often known simply as "Gary Vee," is a prime example of how hustle, foresight, and a relentless drive to innovate can turn an ordinary business into an empire. His story begins with humble beginnings but quickly escalates into a saga of success that spans multiple industries, including wine, media, and digital marketing.

Early Life and Family Business
Born in Belarus in 1975, Vaynerchuk immigrated to the United States with his family in 1978. Like many immigrant families, they struggled financially, but his father eventually saved enough money to open a liquor store in New Jersey, called Shopper's Discount Liquors. Gary worked at the store throughout his childhood and learned valuable lessons about hard work and entrepreneurship.

The Birth of Wine Library
In the late 1990s, after graduating from Mount Ida College in Massachusetts, Vaynerchuk saw the potential of the internet to transform business. He decided to take his family's liquor store online. Renaming the business Wine Library, he launched an e-commerce platform and began using digital marketing strategies to

grow its customer base. This was a bold move at a time when e-commerce was still in its infancy.

His biggest breakthrough came with Wine Library TV, a daily video blog (or vlog) in which Gary reviewed wines in a fun, accessible way. At a time when wine tasting was seen as an elite activity, Vaynerchuk's down-to-earth and entertaining style attracted a wide audience. He became known for his signature catchphrase "Crush It!" and his ability to make wine approachable for everyday people. Through Wine Library TV and other digital strategies, Vaynerchuk grew the family business from $3 million to $60 million in sales within just a few years.

Pivot to Media and Marketing

After transforming his family's business, Gary set his sights on a larger goal: helping others build their brands using the power of social media. In 2009, he co-founded VaynerMedia with his brother, AJ. The agency focused on providing social media and digital marketing strategies to Fortune 500 companies. With clients like PepsiCo, General Electric, and Johnson & Johnson, VaynerMedia quickly grew into a multi-million dollar business.

Gary was an early adopter of platforms like YouTube, Twitter, and Facebook, understanding the massive potential of social media long before most marketers did. His ability to stay ahead of trends, combined with his knack for storytelling, helped propel him into the spotlight.

Bestselling Author and Public Speaker

Gary Vaynerchuk's influence wasn't limited to business alone. He became a bestselling author, with books like *Crush It!* (2009), *The Thank You Economy* (2011), *Jab, Jab, Jab, Right Hook* (2013), and *#AskGaryVee* (2016). Each of these books emphasized the importance of hard work, perseverance, and leveraging the power of social media to build personal brands and businesses.

As a motivational speaker, Gary's energy and no-nonsense advice have made him a favorite at industry conferences. He's known for his direct and unfiltered speaking style, constantly encouraging people to stop making excuses and start taking action to build the life and business they want.

VaynerX and Expanding His Empire

In addition to VaynerMedia, Vaynerchuk launched VaynerX, a media and communications holding company, and Gallery Media Group, which focuses on contemporary digital publishing. He has also ventured into angel investing, backing successful companies like Facebook, Twitter, Tumblr, Venmo, and Uber early on.

In 2017, Vaynerchuk further expanded his brand by launching Empathy Wines, a direct-to-consumer wine business that leveraged his expertise in the wine industry and his powerful personal brand. In 2020, Empathy Wines was acquired by Constellation Brands, proving once again Gary's ability to create and scale businesses.

Crushing It: Gary's Success Formula

Gary Vee's success can be attributed to several key factors:

- **Hustle and Work Ethic**: From working in his family's store to building multiple companies, Gary is known for his relentless work ethic.

- **Early Adopter of Social Media**: Vaynerchuk recognized the potential of social media platforms before most marketers did, allowing him to build a massive audience.

- **Customer-Centric Focus**: Whether through content creation, marketing strategies, or running a business, Gary has always put customer experience and value first.

- **Personal Branding**: He has built a powerful personal brand that extends across multiple industries, becoming a go-to resource for entrepreneurs and businesses looking to grow.

Legacy and Influence

Today, Gary Vaynerchuk is one of the most influential figures in digital marketing, entrepreneurship, and social media. His no-excuses, motivational style continues to inspire millions to "crush it" and take control of their careers and lives.

Vaynerchuk's story is a testament to vision, perseverance, and the power of adapting to new technologies. From growing his family's liquor store to building a media empire, Gary Vee continues to be an innovator, constantly pushing the boundaries of what's possible in business and personal branding.

―――――――

Neil Gaiman's Success Story: Master Storyteller and Literary Visionary

"Building a brand is not just about exposure and presence; it's about crafting an identity that your audience can connect with deeply and consistently. Your brand is your promise to your reader." — NEIL GAIMAN, AUTHOR AND GRAPHIC NOVELIST

"Choosing your genre is like picking your battlefield. Know it well, and you'll find your stories not just surviving but thriving in the hearts and minds of your readers." — NEIL GAIMAN, ACCLAIMED AUTHOR

"Crafting your written voice is like fine-tuning a musical instrument; it's what turns noise into symphony." — NEIL GAIMAN, AUTHOR AND GRAPHIC NOVELIST

"Being an author isn't just about writing; it's about throwing your whole self behind your work and engaging with your readers on every level." — NEIL GAIMAN, AUTHOR

Neil Gaiman is a literary force who has redefined storytelling across genres, captivating audiences with his ability to weave fantasy, folklore, and reality into seamless narratives. From humble beginnings as a freelance journalist and comic book writer, Gaiman rose to become one of the most influential authors of our time. His works—spanning novels, graphic novels, children's books, and screenplays—transcend age and genre, appealing to readers of all kinds. Known for masterpieces such as *American Gods*, *The Sandman* series, and *Coraline*, Gaiman's talent lies in his unparalleled creativity, blending the familiar with the extraordinary. His journey from aspiring writer to internationally celebrated storyteller is a testament to the power of persistence, imagination, and daring to create worlds where dreams and nightmares coexist.

Early Life and Inspiration

Neil Gaiman was born on November 10, 1960, in Hampshire, England, and developed an early passion for books. His childhood was filled with stories from authors like C.S. Lewis, J.R.R. Tolkien, and Lewis Carroll, as well as comic books, which sparked his imagination. From a young age, Gaiman knew he wanted to become a writer, finding refuge and purpose in the world of storytelling. However, the path to fulfilling this dream was anything but conventional.

Breaking into Writing

Without formal training, Gaiman started his career as a journalist and freelance writer. This phase provided him with valuable insights into narrative construction while he conducted interviews and wrote reviews. However, his ultimate passion was writing fiction. With a deep love for fantasy and mythology, Gaiman sought a way to merge those elements into unique and compelling stories.

The Breakthrough with *The Sandman*

Gaiman's breakthrough came in 1988 when he collaborated with DC Comics to create *The Sandman*, a revolutionary comic book series about Dream, the lord of the dream world. The series blended mythology, history, and fantasy into an intricate narrative that captivated readers. *The Sandman* received critical acclaim and became one of the most influential comic book series of all time. It was also the first comic to win the World Fantasy Award, setting a new standard for the genre.

Transition to Novels

With the success of *The Sandman*, Gaiman transitioned into writing novels. In 1990, he co-wrote *Good Omens* with Terry Pratchett, a humorous take on the apocalypse that developed a loyal following. Gaiman continued to publish solo works, including *Neverwhere* (1996), *Stardust* (1999), and *American Gods* (2001), all of which became bestsellers. His stories often explore themes of identity, mythology, and the intersection of reality and fantasy, captivating audiences with their depth and originality.

Reaching New Audiences

Gaiman's storytelling versatility allowed him to write for all age groups. With *Coraline* (2002), a dark fantasy tale for children, he reached a younger audience. The book was met with widespread acclaim and was later adapted into an award-winning animated film. His ability to craft stories that resonate across generations has solidified his place as one of the most influential authors in modern literature.

Expanding Across Mediums

Gaiman's success is not limited to novels and comics. His work has been adapted into films, television series, radio dramas, and stage plays. Titles such as *American Gods* and *Good Omens* have been successfully translated to the screen, further expanding Gaiman's influence. His stories, regardless of medium, maintain a signature blend of fantasy, mythology, and profound insight.

Legacy and Philosophy

In addition to his storytelling prowess, Gaiman is a passionate advocate for libraries and literacy. He frequently shares advice with aspiring writers, encouraging them to embrace creativity and imperfection. His famous 2012 commencement speech, where he urged graduates to "make good art," has become a rallying cry for artists and creators around the world.

Continuing Influence

Neil Gaiman remains an enduring literary figure, with numerous awards including the Hugo, Nebula, and Bram Stoker awards to his name. His ability to craft narratives that inspire and challenge readers has made him a beloved author across generations. Through his books, adaptations, and public presence, Gaiman continues to inspire both readers and aspiring storytellers, showing that stories can shape the world in unexpected ways.

Jay Baer's Success Story: The Marketing Visionary Redefining Customer Experience

"Content is fire; social media is gasoline." — JAY BAER,
AUTHOR AND MARKETING EXPERT

"Integrating offline and online marketing isn't just about broadening reach; it's about creating a seamless dialogue between your book and its audience, ensuring every touchpoint reinforces and amplifies your message."
— JAY BAER, MARKETING CONSULTANT

"Effective offline engagement is about creating moments that are so impactful, they turn every handshake into a lasting impression and every live interaction into a loyal customer." — JAY BAER, MARKETING AND CUSTOMER SERVICE EXPERT

"Every piece of publicity should be seen not just as a chance to showcase, but a strategic opportunity to convert interest into tangible, profitable action." — JAY BAER, MARKETING AND CUSTOMER EXPERIENCE EXPERT

Jay Baer is a pioneering force in the world of marketing, known for transforming how businesses engage with their customers. With a focus on utility-driven marketing, Baer has built a career on the belief that the most effective marketing isn't about hype—it's about being genuinely helpful. As a bestselling author, dynamic keynote speaker, and founder of the renowned consulting firm Convince & Convert, Baer has guided countless businesses toward innovative customer engagement strategies. His practical insights into word-of-mouth marketing, social media, and customer experience have not only influenced global brands but also shaped the future of digital marketing. Baer's story is one of vision, adaptability, and a relentless commitment to helping businesses succeed by building trust and delivering real value.

Early Life and Entrepreneurial Spark
Jay Baer was born with a natural curiosity for marketing and communication, though his early career did not initially set him on the path of a marketing guru. Growing up in Arizona, Baer studied political science at the University of Arizona, which gave him insight into strategy, leadership, and influence. After dabbling in various roles, Baer discovered his passion for entrepreneurship, realizing that the future of marketing lay not in traditional strategies but in innovative, customer-first approaches. His journey to the top began with his belief that the best marketing isn't about promotion—it's about solving customer problems and building trust.

Early Ventures and Founding Mighty Interactive
In 1994, Baer saw the emerging potential of the internet and pivoted toward digital marketing. His first venture, Mighty Interactive, was a digital marketing agency that focused on helping companies build strong online presences in a rapidly

evolving digital landscape. During this period, Baer mastered the intricacies of content marketing, search engine optimization (SEO), and social media strategy. Mighty Interactive became a powerhouse in digital marketing, serving clients from diverse industries and setting the foundation for Baer's future in the customer experience space.

Convince & Convert: A Marketing Consultancy Empire

In 2008, Baer founded Convince & Convert, the consulting firm that propelled him into the upper echelon of marketing thought leaders. Convince & Convert focuses on customer experience (CX) strategies, helping companies bridge the gap between marketing promises and customer satisfaction. The firm also works with leading global brands, including Nike, Hilton, and Oracle. Baer's consultancy quickly became renowned for offering practical advice on building trust and loyalty through exceptional customer service and engagement.

Baer developed a unique approach: "helpful marketing." He urged companies to move beyond advertising to focus on delivering real value to customers, believing that being useful is the most effective way to earn loyalty. His motto, "What would happen if your marketing was so good that people would pay for it?" became a guiding principle for the industry.

Thought Leadership and Bestselling Books

Baer's success was not confined to consulting. He made his mark as a thought leader through keynote speaking and writing bestselling books. His first major success came with *Youtility: Why Smart Marketing is About Help, Not Hype*, which became a New York Times and Amazon bestseller. The book introduced his concept of marketing as a service, emphasizing that businesses must focus on providing useful, relevant content rather than flashy promotions.

Following the success of *Youtility*, Baer authored several other influential books, including *Talk Triggers*—a groundbreaking exploration of word-of-mouth marketing—and *Hug Your Haters*, which emphasized the importance of turning customer complaints into opportunities for brand loyalty. These books cemented Baer's status as a leader in the customer experience revolution.

The Power of Public Speaking and Social Influence

Baer's dynamic speaking style and knack for storytelling made him one of the most sought-after keynote speakers in the marketing industry. He regularly speaks at conferences, helping companies and marketers understand the changing dynamics of customer expectations in the digital age. His thought-provoking and humorous delivery makes his insights memorable and actionable, leading him to keynote major events such as Content Marketing World and Social Media Marketing World.

Baer also leveraged his social media influence, establishing himself as an authority on platforms like LinkedIn and Twitter. His podcasts, including *Social Pros*, have become go-to resources for marketers seeking practical advice from industry experts.

Key Partnerships and Industry Recognition

Baer's ability to anticipate marketing trends and guide companies toward innovative strategies earned him numerous accolades. He has been recognized as one of the world's top influencers in marketing and customer experience by Forbes and has built partnerships with major global companies seeking to enhance their customer engagement efforts. Baer's work has had a profound influence on how businesses view marketing—not just as a way to sell products, but as an integral part of delivering exceptional experiences.

Philosophy and Legacy

At the heart of Jay Baer's success is his unwavering belief that marketing must be built on trust, transparency, and utility. He transformed the marketing landscape by proving that businesses thrive not by shouting louder but by serving their customers better. Baer continues to inspire entrepreneurs, marketers, and companies to align their strategies with the principles of helpfulness, relevance, and empathy.

His lasting legacy lies in shifting the focus from transactional marketing to relational marketing. Through Convince & Convert, his books, and public speaking, Baer has taught countless professionals that meaningful customer engagement is the key to long-term success. His work serves as a beacon for those navigating the complexities of the digital marketplace, proving that when businesses prioritize their customers' needs, both the company and its audience thrive.

Ann Handley's Success Story: The Trailblazer Who Transformed Digital Marketing and Storytelling

"Tools and resources are the keys to unlocking your business's full potential."
— ANN HANDLEY, MARKETING EXPERT

"Email marketing is about weaving a personal narrative that reaches the inbox like a letter from an old friend, turning each message into a moment of connection and each newsletter into a chapter of your ongoing story."
— ANN HANDLEY, DIGITAL MARKETING PIONEER

"Effective content is not about overwhelming your audience but resonating with them. Define your themes clearly, and they'll echo across your brand's story."
— ANN HANDLEY, DIGITAL MARKETING

"Visual content is the emotional bridge between your message and your audience. Master it, and you master engagement." — ANN HANDLEY, DIGITAL MARKETING PIONEER AND WRITER

"Pinterest is more than just a collection of images; it's a powerful tool for visual storytelling that can draw readers into your narrative and build lasting engagement." — ANN HANDLEY, DIGITAL MARKETING PIONEER AND AUTHOR

"Effective copywriting is both an art and a science, employing persuasive language to weave compelling narratives that drive action."
— ANN HANDLEY, DIGITAL MARKETING EXPERT AND AUTHOR

"Establishing online authority is about crafting content that doesn't just speak to your audience but speaks for them, turning every post and article into a cornerstone of your industry's conversation." — ANN HANDLEY, DIGITAL MARKETING PIONEER

"Writing for PR is not just about filling space with words; it's about crafting messages that act as conduits for connection, turning every sentence into a strategy and every word into a weapon." — ANN HANDLEY, DIGITAL MARKETING PIONEER

"Good content isn't about good storytelling. It's about telling a true story well." — ANN HANDLEY, DIGITAL MARKETING PIONEER AND WRITER

"Content is not just king; it's the wizard, the shopkeeper, and the knight at the round table. Good content tells a story that resonates, educates, and motivates readers to come back for more." — ANN HANDLEY, DIGITAL MARKETING PIONEER AND WRITER

Ann Handley, a pioneer in content marketing and digital storytelling, is celebrated as one of the most influential voices in modern marketing. As an author, entrepreneur, and speaker, Handley has reshaped how businesses connect with audiences through authentic, engaging content. Her journey is a testament to the power of creativity, consistency, and a deep understanding of audience needs.

Early Life and the Love for Writing

Ann Handley grew up with a love for writing and storytelling, fueled by her natural curiosity and ability to capture the essence of everyday experiences. From a young age, she recognized the power of words to connect with people and share ideas. Her passion for writing would later become the cornerstone of her career in content marketing.

After completing her education, Handley began her career as a journalist, working for publications such as The Boston Globe. The experience of writing for newspapers gave her a deep understanding of audience engagement and the importance of delivering value through compelling stories.

The Shift to Digital Media: Co-Founding ClickZ

In the late 1990s, as the internet was rapidly changing the media landscape, Handley recognized the potential of digital platforms to connect businesses with their customers. Seizing the opportunity, she co-founded ClickZ, one of the world's first online publications dedicated to digital marketing.

ClickZ quickly gained traction as a go-to resource for marketers navigating the new world of online marketing. Handley's focus on delivering practical, relevant insights helped the publication grow, attracting a loyal readership. Her ability to blend storytelling with technical expertise set ClickZ apart from other publications, making it a trusted source for marketing professionals.

In 2000, ClickZ was acquired by a media company, marking a significant milestone in Handley's career. The experience of building and scaling a digital media company taught her valuable lessons about content strategy, audience engagement, and the evolving dynamics of online marketing.

Content Marketing: A New Era of Storytelling

Following the sale of ClickZ, Handley focused on helping businesses embrace content as a powerful tool for building relationships and driving growth. She joined MarketingProfs, an educational platform providing marketing training and resources, where she became the Chief Content Officer—one of the first people in the industry to hold such a title.

At MarketingProfs, Handley spearheaded efforts to transform how businesses approach content marketing. She emphasized the importance of creating valuable, audience-centric content that resonates with customers and builds trust. Her belief that marketing should be meaningful, not just promotional, became the foundation of her philosophy.

Authoring 'Content Rules' and 'Everybody Writes'

In 2010, Handley co-authored "Content Rules" with C.C. Chapman, a book that became one of the first definitive guides to content marketing. The book introduced the idea that businesses of all sizes could use content to attract, engage, and retain customers—a revolutionary concept at the time. "Content Rules" quickly became a bestseller, establishing Handley as a thought leader in the content marketing space.

Building on the success of *Content Rules*, Handley published "Everybody Writes: Your Go-To Guide to Creating Ridiculously Good Content" in 2014. This book focused on the art and science of writing for the digital age, offering practical tips and advice for marketers, entrepreneurs, and content creators. *Everybody Writes* became a bestseller and is widely regarded as a must-read for anyone creating content.

In 2022, Handley released an updated version of Everybody Writes, reinforcing her belief that great content starts with clear, thoughtful writing and must adapt to changing trends in digital communication.

A Visionary Speaker and Educator

Handley's ability to simplify complex marketing concepts and deliver them with humor and authenticity has made her a sought-after speaker at conferences around the world. She has keynoted events such as Content Marketing World and INBOUND, inspiring audiences to embrace creativity and tell better stories.

Through her workshops and speaking engagements, Handley encourages businesses to focus on storytelling, authenticity, and building meaningful connections with customers. She emphasizes that marketing is about helping, not hyping, and that every piece of content should add value to the audience's experience.

Building a Community and Influencing the Industry

Beyond writing and speaking, Handley has cultivated a vibrant online community, engaging with her audience through social media, newsletters, and blog posts. Her newsletter, "Total Annarchy," delivers insights, tips, and personal reflections, embodying her unique voice and keeping her followers inspired.

Handley's influence extends far beyond individual businesses—she has become a mentor to aspiring marketers and content creators, shaping the direction of the industry. Her focus on community building, collaboration, and continuous learning reflects her belief that great marketing is rooted in genuine relationships.

Lessons from Ann Handley's Success

1. **Writing is a Superpower:** Handley believes that writing is the foundation of all great content and marketing, and she encourages everyone to improve their writing skills.

2. **Be Authentic:** Handley's content stands out because of its authenticity—she emphasizes the importance of connecting with audiences through real, relatable stories.

3. **Create Value, Not Noise:** Her philosophy is centered on delivering meaningful content that adds value to the audience, rather than overwhelming them with promotions.

4. **Adapt to Change:** Handley's ability to stay ahead of industry trends has kept her at the forefront of the digital marketing landscape.

5. **Community is Key:** She has built strong connections with her audience and believes that relationships are the heart of great marketing.

Conclusion: A Legacy of Meaningful Marketing

Ann Handley's journey from journalist to content marketing pioneer is a powerful example of how creativity, authenticity, and dedication to helping others can drive lasting success. Through her work at MarketingProfs, her bestselling books, and her engaging keynote speeches, Handley has inspired businesses to embrace the power of storytelling and create content that truly matters.

As a writer, speaker, and community builder, Handley continues to shape the future of marketing, encouraging marketers to think differently, write boldly, and connect meaningfully with their audiences. Her legacy is not just about marketing—it's about building trust, inspiring change, and using words to make the world a better place.

———————

Neil Patel's Success Story: From Teenage Hustler to Digital marketing Mogul

"A business plan should be more than a set of figures and forecasts—it should tell a compelling story. Make it engaging and insightful, so it not only informs but excites your readers about your vision and potential."
— NEIL PATEL, MARKETING EXPERT AND ENTREPRENEUR

"Traffic is the lifeblood of any website. It's not just about attracting eyes, it's about captivating hearts and engaging minds. Make your site a destination, not just a detour." — NEIL PATEL, CO-FOUNDER OF CRAZY EGG, HELLO BAR, AND KISSMETRICS

"Create content that pleases your audience's intellect and tickles their curiosity. If they enjoy it, they'll come back for more." — NEIL PATEL, A LEADING ONLINE MARKETING EXPERT

"Mastering online ads means turning every banner and classified into a digital handshake, extending a personal invitation to engage and connect with your brand." — NEIL PATEL, Digital Marketing Expert

"Enhancing your online visibility isn't just about being seen; it's about being memorable, crafting a digital presence so vibrant it turns first-time viewers into lifelong followers." — NEIL PATEL, DIGITAL MARKETING EXPERT

"Great marketing starts with clear goals. If you don't know where you're going, every campaign is a shot in the dark." — NEIL PATEL, DIGITAL MARKETING EXPERT

Neil Patel is one of the most influential voices in digital marketing and SEO, known for helping companies grow their online presence and drive massive traffic to their websites. His journey from a teen entrepreneur to the co-founder of successful businesses and a global thought leader is a story of hustle, resilience, and mastery of the ever-evolving world of online marketing.

Early Beginnings: Hustling from the Start
Neil Patel's entrepreneurial spirit showed early. Born in London and raised in California, Patel grew up in a middle-class family that instilled a strong work ethic. During high school, Neil started selling CD burners and later moved on to car parts to make extra cash. His entrepreneurial instincts kicked in when he realized he could make more money if he had his own website. This curiosity would eventually lead him to discover the power of SEO (Search Engine Optimization).

At just 15 years old, Patel built his first website, only to realize that traffic didn't magically appear. He paid a marketing firm to help him, but the results were disappointing. Determined not to rely on others, he decided to learn SEO himself—and this marked the beginning of his journey into the world of digital marketing.

First Business Ventures

By the time he was in college, Patel was already working as a freelance consultant, offering SEO and digital marketing services to small businesses. His first significant success came when he co-founded Advice Monkey, a job board similar to Monster.com. Though the project didn't become the blockbuster he'd hoped for, it taught Patel valuable lessons about growth strategies, user experience, and the importance of traffic.

His early struggles and experience in driving organic traffic became the bedrock of his career. Patel soon realized that many companies were eager to pay for marketing expertise, but they lacked the know-how to build and scale their online presence. This unmet need set the stage for his next business ventures.

Co-Founding Successful Marketing Companies

In his early 20s, Patel co-founded Crazy Egg, a heat mapping tool that helps businesses understand how users interact with their websites. Crazy Egg gave companies insights into user behavior, such as where visitors click, scroll, and engage the most. This innovation made it easier for companies to optimize their websites for conversions.

Crazy Egg's success was followed by Patel co-founding KISSmetrics, a web analytics platform designed to track customer behavior over time. These tools gave businesses the power to analyze their sales funnels and improve customer journeys, solidifying Patel's reputation as an innovator in the marketing world.

Building a Personal Brand and Becoming a Thought Leader

As Patel's ventures grew, so did his desire to give back and share his knowledge. He started blogging about SEO, content marketing, and growth hacking. His blog, NeilPatel.com, quickly became a go-to resource for marketers and entrepreneurs, offering free, in-depth guides on how to grow websites and businesses through SEO and digital strategies.

What made Patel stand out was his generosity with knowledge. While many marketing experts gated their insights behind expensive courses or memberships, Patel shared his expertise for free. This approach not only earned him trust and credibility but also helped build his personal brand into one of the most recognizable in the industry.

Entrepreneurial Success and Industry Influence

Over the years, Patel has consulted for Fortune 500 companies like Amazon, Microsoft, NBC, and General Motors, helping them grow their online traffic. He has also invested in and advised numerous startups. Patel's knack for staying ahead of trends has made him a sought-after speaker at industry conferences worldwide, and he continues to influence the way businesses approach SEO and digital marketing.

In 2017, Patel co-founded Ubersuggest, an SEO tool designed to help businesses optimize their websites and content strategies. Ubersuggest has become one of the most widely used SEO tools globally, cementing Patel's position as a leader in the digital marketing space.

Awards and Recognition

Patel's success hasn't gone unnoticed. He has been recognized as a Top 100 Entrepreneur Under 30 by President Obama and was named a Top 100 Entrepreneur Under 35 by the United Nations. His work has been featured in major media outlets, including Forbes, Inc., Entrepreneur, and The Wall Street Journal.

Adapting to Change and Giving Back

What sets Patel apart is his adaptability in the face of a fast-changing industry. He is constantly refining his strategies and tools to keep pace with Google algorithm updates and new digital trends. Patel's ability to reinvent himself and his businesses has kept him relevant in an industry known for its rapid evolution.

In addition to his entrepreneurial ventures, Patel continues to educate and mentor aspiring entrepreneurs. Through his YouTube channel, podcast, and blog, he reaches millions of followers, offering practical advice on everything from SEO to scaling businesses.

Legacy and Impact

Today, Neil Patel stands as one of the most influential figures in digital marketing. His journey from teenage entrepreneur to global thought leader is a testament to the power of persistence, passion, and continuous learning. Patel has not only built successful businesses but has also created a lasting impact by democratizing marketing knowledge, empowering people to grow their businesses through digital tools.

Conclusion

Neil Patel's story is one of ambition, resilience, and generosity. From his early ventures to the founding of tools like Crazy Egg and Ubersuggest, Patel has proven time and time again that consistent learning and sharing knowledge are key to long-term success. His legacy goes beyond entrepreneurship—Patel has become a mentor and guide to millions of marketers and entrepreneurs worldwide, leaving a lasting mark on the digital marketing industry.

Bernadette Jiwa's Success Story: Crafting Success Through the Art of Storytelling

"Storytelling in branding isn't just about weaving tales; it's about crafting narratives that resonate deeply, giving life and substance to both publisher and product." — BERNADETTE JIWA, BRAND STORYTELLING EXPERT AND AUTHOR

Bernadette Jiwa has redefined what it means to build brands and connect with customers by focusing on storytelling at the heart of business success. Growing up in Australia, she developed a keen awareness of how narratives shape people's decisions and emotions. Jiwa's career has been dedicated to helping businesses leverage that power, teaching entrepreneurs and corporations alike how to build authentic connections with their audiences. Through her books, consulting, and blog, *The Story of Telling*, Jiwa has become a trusted voice in marketing, guiding organizations to shift from transactional relationships to meaningful engagement. Her innovative insights continue to influence how brands evolve and stand out in an increasingly noisy marketplace.

Early Life and Passion for Stories

Bernadette Jiwa grew up in Australia, where her fascination with human connections and storytelling began at an early age. As a curious child, she was captivated by how stories shaped people's emotions, actions, and decisions. Her background in communications and marketing laid the groundwork for her later work in helping brands use storytelling to create meaningful customer experiences.

A New Approach to Marketing

Jiwa's career began in various marketing roles, but she quickly realized that traditional advertising methods were often impersonal and ineffective. She believed the key to building lasting relationships between brands and customers wasn't in flashy campaigns but in meaningful storytelling. Driven by this insight, Jiwa ventured into entrepreneurship, determined to shift the narrative around how businesses connect with their audiences.

Building a Platform and Gaining Recognition

Bernadette launched her blog, *The Story of Telling*, where she shared insights on the power of narrative in business. Her unique perspective on storytelling as a tool for brand building resonated with readers, quickly gaining traction. She distilled her approach into several best-selling books, including *Make Your Idea Matter*, *Difference*, and *The Fortune Cookie Principle*. These books emphasized the idea that every product, service, or business can stand out by articulating a compelling story—one that makes a meaningful difference in the lives of customers.

A Thought Leader in Branding and Innovation

Jiwa's influence grew as she became a sought-after speaker, consultant, and advisor to entrepreneurs and corporations around the world. Her work has helped organizations rethink how they present themselves, focusing not just on what they sell but on how they make their customers feel. Jiwa's success lies in her ability to articulate complex ideas about business innovation in simple, actionable terms, inspiring both small startups and established brands to harness the power of storytelling.

Recognition and Legacy

Named by SmartCompany as one of Australia's Top Business Thinkers, Jiwa continues to make an impact with her writing and consulting work. Her philosophy is that businesses thrive not by shouting the loudest but by creating authentic connections with their customers through story-driven experiences. Today, she is considered one of the most influential voices in marketing, brand storytelling, and customer engagement.

Jiwa's journey from marketer to global thought leader exemplifies the importance of understanding human connection in business. Her success story proves that storytelling is not just a tool for marketing—it's the foundation of impactful, sustainable business practices.

————

Jonah Sachs' Success Story: Pioneering Empowerment Marketing through Storytelling

"Your brand is a story unfolding across all customer touch points."
— JONAH SACHS, AUTHOR AND ENTREPRENEUR

Jonah Sachs is a trailblazer in the world of marketing, best known for revolutionizing the way brands communicate with their audiences. As the co-founder of Free Range Studios and the author of *Winning the Story Wars*, Sachs recognized early on that compelling storytelling could shape public perception and foster deeper brand engagement. He pioneered a new form of marketing centered on empowerment and authenticity, rather than fear-based manipulation. Through viral campaigns like *The Meatrix* and *The Story of Stuff*, Sachs proved that brands could inspire action and create lasting social change by telling stories that connect with people's values and aspirations. His work has redefined marketing, encouraging businesses to harness the emotional power of storytelling to spark movements and drive impact.

Early Life and Creative Beginnings
Jonah Sachs was drawn to creativity and storytelling from a young age. Growing up in the suburbs of Philadelphia, he immersed himself in literature, mythology, and art, fascinated by how stories shape culture and influence behavior. His passion for storytelling stayed with him throughout his studies at Wesleyan University, where he majored in anthropology, focusing on how narratives impact human society.

The Birth of Free Range Studios and a New Marketing Philosophy
In the early 2000s, Sachs co-founded Free Range Studios, a creative agency with a mission to harness the power of storytelling for good. His approach was

150

unconventional—he believed that the traditional marketing model of pushing products and services onto consumers was outdated. Instead, Sachs sought to create "empowerment marketing," where brands offer meaningful stories that engage, inspire, and resonate with audiences on a deeper level.

One of Free Range Studios' early projects was "The Meatrix," a viral animated series designed to raise awareness about factory farming. Released in 2003, it combined humor, creativity, and advocacy, generating millions of views worldwide. The overwhelming success of "The Meatrix" established Sachs as a pioneer of viral content and showed the potential of storytelling to drive social change and influence public opinion.

Empowerment Marketing and the Success of Viral Campaigns
Building on the success of "The Meatrix," Sachs and his team at Free Range Studios developed campaigns that focused on telling stories with a purpose. He believed that people connect with brands that align with their values and aspirations. Sachs encouraged companies to adopt narratives that empowered their audiences rather than manipulate them, creating partnerships built on trust.

His work has had a significant impact, helping clients ranging from nonprofits to Fortune 500 companies reshape their brand messaging. By shifting the focus from products to people's values and beliefs, Sachs redefined the rules of marketing in the digital age.

Authoring "Winning the Story Wars" and Beyond
In 2012, Sachs published his influential book *Winning the Story Wars*, which crystallized his philosophy of storytelling and empowerment marketing. In the book, he argues that in a world of information overload, only the brands that tell honest, meaningful, and engaging stories will stand out. The book has become a must-read for marketers, entrepreneurs, and creatives seeking to understand the power of narratives in shaping cultural movements.

Through his consulting work, speaking engagements, and writing, Sachs continues to champion the idea that storytelling is the most effective tool for fostering meaningful change and building lasting connections. His approach resonates with businesses and organizations that aspire to do more than sell products—they aim to inspire and make a difference.

Legacy and Lasting Influence

Jonah Sachs has left an indelible mark on modern marketing, proving that stories can change not just individual behavior but entire cultural conversations. His work has redefined what it means to engage with audiences in the 21st century, moving beyond mere transactions to create experiences that resonate on a personal level. Sachs remains committed to empowering businesses and individuals to use storytelling as a force for good, inspiring a new generation of marketers to create campaigns that matter.

———

CHAPTER SEVEN

Building an Audience Online

In the digital age, building an audience online is both an art and a science. Businesses thrive by engaging with the right people in the right places, turning casual visitors into loyal followers. Creating a thriving audience is about more than just accumulating numbers—it's about fostering a community of individuals who believe in your brand, engage with your content, and become your most valuable advocates. This chapter explores how to strategically cultivate and grow your online audience through the use of content, social media, and digital marketing tools.

Mari Smith reminds us that "building a community is about more than just gathering an audience. It's about creating an environment where every interaction adds value, and every member feels like they belong." Whether you're starting with a blog, social media presence, or website, the goal is to build meaningful relationships, turning viewers into loyal advocates. Jeff Bezos emphasizes the importance of treating every online touchpoint as an opportunity for connection, stating, "Your brand is what other people say about you. It's your job to make sure they have a great story to tell."

Creating an audience requires understanding where your ideal followers gather and what they care about. Rand Fishkin teaches that "optimized content wins," highlighting the importance of knowing how to make your content discoverable. This means you must not only create engaging content but also foster conversation, respond to comments, and engage your audience consistently. Platforms like LinkedIn can become powerful tools for audience building if used thoughtfully and authentically, as Darren Rowse notes about the importance of finding the right platforms for your message.

Consistency is key in building an online following. Tim Ferriss emphasizes that "consistency breeds familiarity, and familiarity breeds trust." This chapter explores strategies for maintaining a consistent voice and presence across platforms, ensuring your audience stays connected with your brand. Sheryl Sandberg advises businesses to "focus on building a community, not just a following," underscoring the importance of aligning content with your audience's needs and values.

Technical know-how plays a crucial role in audience growth. Joe Pulizzi highlights the necessity of integrating content marketing into your overall strategy, as "the right content, delivered at the right time, can create powerful connections." Understanding how to make your content discoverable ensures it reaches the right people, and effective use of digital tools is essential for meeting your audience where they are.

Beyond the technical strategies, this chapter discusses the importance of testing and adapting. As Sheryl Sandberg points out, "Social media's power lies in its ability to evolve with your audience's changing tastes." Continuous evaluation and adjustment based on real-time feedback and analytics are vital for success.

Building an audience online is not just about numbers but about cultivating meaningful connections. Mari Smith explains that "your database isn't just a collection of names; it's a doorway to new relationships." Whether it's through newsletters, social media, or blogs, the focus is on creating interactions that build trust and foster loyalty.

This chapter will guide you in creating a sustainable strategy for building and nurturing an online audience. You'll learn how to leverage blogs, social media platforms, email lists, and SEO to grow your following strategically. With insights from Mari Smith, Rand Fishkin, and Sheryl Sandberg, you'll understand how to align your messaging, stay consistent, and continuously engage your audience. By building a strong community around your brand, you turn followers into loyal supporters who not only purchase your products but also share your message, helping your business thrive in the long term.

Mari Smith's Success Story: The Queen of Facebook Marketing

"Content is king, but engagement is queen, and the lady rules the house!"
— MARI SMITH, RENOWNED SOCIAL MEDIA
THOUGHT LEADER AND SPEAKER

"Knowing your audience is the key to success. If you can speak to their hearts, they'll follow you anywhere." — MARI SMITH, SOCIAL MEDIA EXPERT
AND FACEBOOK MARKETING PRO

Mari Smith, widely known as the "Queen of Facebook," has built a remarkable career as one of the foremost social media strategists in the world. With a background rooted in both interpersonal communication and digital marketing, Mari was quick to recognize the transformative power of online platforms like Facebook. Her early adoption and mastery of social media tools allowed her to develop a personal brand synonymous with relationship-driven marketing. Through her consulting, books, and keynote talks, Mari has empowered countless entrepreneurs and companies to harness the potential of social media for business growth. With her signature blend of warmth, expertise, and actionable insights, Mari continues to shape the ever-evolving landscape of digital marketing, inspiring businesses to connect meaningfully with their audiences.

Humble Beginnings and Early Passion for Networking
Born in Canada and raised in rural Scotland, Mari Smith's journey to becoming a globally recognized social media expert began with humble roots. Her initial career in the service industry sparked her fascination with human behavior and

the power of communication. In the late 1990s, as the internet began reshaping the way people connected, Smith discovered the potential of online communities and became deeply engaged in digital networking.

Discovering Social Media's Power

In the early 2000s, Mari relocated to San Diego, where she immersed herself in digital marketing and personal branding. When Facebook opened its platform to the public in 2006, Smith saw its potential not just as a social tool but as a game-changing marketing channel. Her early adoption of Facebook and intuitive understanding of how it could drive business growth set her apart from others. Mari dedicated herself to mastering Facebook's ever-evolving features and algorithms, building a personal brand around her expertise in social media engagement and strategy.

Becoming the "Queen of Facebook"

Smith's breakthrough came as businesses started seeking guidance on using Facebook to connect with their audiences effectively. Known for her warmth and engaging speaking style, Mari quickly gained popularity as a social media strategist. She began conducting workshops and consulting for companies of all sizes, helping them navigate the emerging social media landscape. By 2009, she was recognized as one of the world's leading experts on Facebook marketing, earning the unofficial title of "Queen of Facebook."

Global Recognition and Influence

Mari's career skyrocketed as she authored books, including *The New Relationship Marketing*, and became a sought-after keynote speaker at global conferences. Her ability to translate complex digital strategies into actionable insights made her a trusted advisor to both entrepreneurs and Fortune 500 companies. Smith's consulting firm, Mari Smith International, continues to shape the social media strategies of top brands around the world.

Impact and Legacy

Smith's influence extends beyond marketing strategies. She emphasizes building genuine relationships and creating meaningful engagement online, inspiring businesses to shift from transactional marketing to relationship-driven connections. Mari has also used her platform to promote personal development and encourage individuals to align their online presence with their core values.

Today, Mari Smith is not only recognized as a social media pioneer but also as a thought leader whose practical advice and strategies empower businesses to thrive in the digital era. Her story illustrates the power of vision, adaptability, and a genuine passion for helping others succeed in the fast-changing world of social media.

======

Rand Fishkin's Success Story: From SEO Underdog to Marketing Visionary

"Clear, actionable objectives are the backbone of any successful business. Without them, you're just throwing darts in the dark. Define your goals with precision, track them relentlessly, and adjust as needed to stay on course." — RAND FISHKIN, FOUNDER OF MOZ AND SPARKTORO

"SEO isn't just about being found by search engines. It's about being found by the right people—your future readers. It's about connecting those seeking to discover with the stories you've told." — RAND FISHKIN, CO-FOUNDER OF MOZ AND INBOUND.ORG

"SEO is about making your site understandable to search engines and your content discoverable by the right audience. It's not just science, it's an art form that requires creativity, insight, and persistence." — RAND FISHKIN, CO-FOUNDER OF MOZ AND SPARKTORO

Rand Fishkin, co-founder of Moz and SparkToro, is a fascinating figure in the world of digital marketing. Known for his transparency, resilience, and innovative approach to search engine optimization (SEO), Fishkin built his reputation by navigating personal and professional challenges. His journey from a struggling entrepreneur to one of the most recognized experts in SEO is a compelling story of persistence, creativity, and reinvention.

Early Life and the Creation of Moz
Rand Fishkin was born on July 10, 1979, in Seattle, Washington. He grew up surrounded by books and computers, fostering a love for learning and technology.

In the early 2000s, Fishkin dropped out of the University of Washington and began working with his mother, Gillian Muessig, at her small web design business.

However, by 2003, the business was facing financial difficulties. Clients increasingly asked for help improving their visibility on search engines—something Fishkin knew little about. Driven by necessity, Fishkin threw himself into learning SEO (search engine optimization). He began documenting everything he learned on a personal blog, hoping it would attract clients to their struggling business.

Moz: From SEO Blog to SaaS Giant

Fishkin's blog, initially called SEOmoz, quickly gained traction. SEO was still a nascent field, and few people shared information openly. Fishkin's transparent approach—publishing everything from SEO tactics to personal struggles—resonated with marketers and entrepreneurs. Over time, the blog evolved into a thriving online community.

By 2007, SEOmoz pivoted from consulting to becoming a software-as-a-service (SaaS) company, developing tools to help businesses improve their search engine rankings. The company's suite of tools offered features like keyword research, backlink analysis, and rank tracking, which became indispensable for marketers.

Moz's success didn't happen overnight. In fact, Fishkin and his team went through periods of failure, near-bankruptcy, and personal burnout. Yet, Fishkin's passion for transparent marketing and building community-driven products helped Moz become a leader in the SEO space.

The Whiteboard Friday Phenomenon

One of Fishkin's most popular contributions to the SEO community is Whiteboard Friday—a video series where Fishkin explained complex SEO topics in a simple, engaging format. His down-to-earth personality, iconic yellow sneakers, and signature mustache made him an approachable figure in a technical field often dominated by jargon.

Whiteboard Friday not only attracted a loyal audience but also established Moz as an authority in digital marketing. Fishkin's ability to break down complex ideas into digestible content helped countless businesses and marketers improve their SEO efforts.

Challenges and Departure from Moz

Despite Moz's success, Fishkin's journey wasn't without setbacks. In his memoir, "Lost and Founder," Fishkin candidly discusses the challenges he faced as an entrepreneur—struggling with anxiety, imposter syndrome, and the pressures of scaling a startup. His honesty about these challenges endeared him to many in the entrepreneurial community.

In 2014, Fishkin stepped down as CEO of Moz, citing burnout and the need for fresh leadership. Although he remained involved with the company in other roles, tensions grew as Moz's focus shifted toward paid advertising tools rather than the SEO products Fishkin had championed. In 2018, Fishkin made the difficult decision to leave Moz and embark on a new entrepreneurial journey.

SparkToro: Reinventing Audience Intelligence

After leaving Moz, Fishkin co-founded SparkToro with Casey Henry in 2018. SparkToro is an audience intelligence platform that helps businesses identify where their target customers are spending time online—an alternative to traditional SEO and paid advertising strategies. Fishkin's goal with SparkToro was to help marketers better understand their audiences without relying solely on Google and Facebook's advertising ecosystems.

SparkToro reflects Fishkin's evolution as a marketer. While SEO was once the primary focus, Fishkin realized that understanding audience behavior—beyond search engines—was becoming increasingly important for effective marketing. SparkToro's success demonstrates that Fishkin's innovative thinking and community-focused approach remain as relevant as ever.

Transparency, Vulnerability, and Thought Leadership

Throughout his career, Fishkin has been known for his unapologetic honesty. In his memoir, *Lost and Founder*, Fishkin provides a rare, behind-the-scenes look at the challenges of entrepreneurship. Unlike many business books that glorify success, Fishkin's memoir is filled with stories of mistakes, missed opportunities, and lessons learned the hard way. His willingness to share failures as openly as successes set him apart from other leaders in the tech world.

Fishkin also champions mental health and work-life balance, challenging the traditional startup culture that glorifies hustle and burnout. His story encourages entrepreneurs to define success on their own terms and prioritize well-being over relentless growth.

Key Lessons from Rand Fishkin's Success

1. **Transparency Builds Trust:** Fishkin's open sharing of his experiences, both good and bad, helped him build a loyal community.

2. **Adapt and Evolve:** Fishkin transitioned from SEO to audience intelligence, proving the importance of staying ahead of industry trends.

3. **Prioritize Mental Health:** His candid discussions about burnout and anxiety encourage entrepreneurs to take care of their well-being.

4. **Community Matters:** Fishkin's success was rooted in creating value for others and building strong connections within the marketing community.

5. **It's Okay to Fail:** Fishkin's memoir teaches that failure is part of the journey, and the lessons learned along the way are invaluable.

Conclusion: A Legacy of Innovation and Authenticity

Rand Fishkin's journey from a struggling entrepreneur to a pioneering voice in digital marketing is a testament to the power of authenticity, innovation, and resilience. Whether through Moz, Whiteboard Fridays, SparkToro, or his memoir, Fishkin's contributions have shaped the way marketers think about SEO, audience engagement, and entrepreneurship.

His story reminds us that success isn't just about achieving financial goals—it's about staying true to your values, learning from failures, and building meaningful connections along the way. Fishkin's legacy continues to inspire marketers and entrepreneurs to embrace transparency, prioritize mental health, and explore new frontiers with curiosity and creativity.

―――――――

Sheryl Sandberg's Success Story: Empowering Women and Transforming Leadership

"Test relentlessly and adapt swiftly. The power of social media lies in its ability to evolve with the audience's ever-changing tastes and preferences."
— SHERYL SANDBERG, COO OF FACEBOOK

"Unlocking the full potential of social media ads means more than just posting; it's about crafting targeted messages that engage and convert, turning followers into fans and customers." — SHERYL SANDBERG, TECHNOLOGY EXECUTIVE AND AUTHOR

"Crafting a unified brand story across multiple platforms is key to forging a deep, lasting connection with your audience, turning casual encounters into a consistent narrative that pulls them closer." — SHERYL SANDBERG, TECHNOLOGY EXECUTIVE AND AUTHOR

"Operational excellence isn't about doing more work in less time, but about enhancing the quality of your work and the efficiency of your processes to elevate the entire organization." — SHERYL SANDBERG, COO OF FACEBOOK

"Risk management is the fine art of navigating uncertainties, protecting your assets while positioning your business for future growth." — SHERYL SANDBERG, TECHNOLOGY EXECUTIVE AND AUTHOR

"Protecting your creative rights isn't just about safeguarding today's work; it's about securing your legacy for tomorrow." — SHERYL SANDBERG, COO OF FACEBOOK

Sheryl Sandberg, one of the most influential women in technology and business, is best known for her tenure as the Chief Operating Officer (COO) of Facebook and for her groundbreaking book, "Lean In." Sandberg's journey is a remarkable story of ambition, resilience, and advocacy for gender equality in the workplace. Her success is rooted not only in her sharp business acumen but also in her ability to lead through personal challenges and inspire others to redefine their potential.

Early Life and Education: Building a Foundation of Excellence

Sheryl Kara Sandberg was born on August 28, 1969, in Washington, D.C., and raised in Miami, Florida. From an early age, Sandberg demonstrated academic excellence and a passion for leadership. She excelled in school and became class president in high school, setting the stage for her future career in leadership.

In 1991, Sandberg earned a bachelor's degree in Economics from Harvard University, where she graduated summa cum laude and was mentored by renowned economist Lawrence Summers. Impressed by her talent, Summers took Sandberg under his wing, and she served as his research assistant while he was Chief Economist at the World Bank.

Sandberg later pursued her MBA at Harvard Business School, where she earned top honors. Her time at Harvard nurtured her analytical thinking and problem-solving skills, preparing her for a career at the intersection of business and policy.

Early Career: From Government to Tech

After earning her MBA, Sandberg followed Lawrence Summers to Washington, D.C., when he became U.S. Treasury Secretary under President Bill Clinton. Sandberg worked as Chief of Staff at the U.S. Treasury Department, where she gained valuable experience managing complex government operations.

Following the end of the Clinton administration, Sandberg moved to Silicon Valley, drawn by the opportunities in the rapidly evolving tech industry. She joined Google in 2001, where she played a pivotal role in building the company's online advertising platform, AdWords, which became one of the company's biggest revenue generators. During her time at Google, Sandberg led global operations for Google's ad products and was instrumental in growing the company's advertising business into a multi-billion-dollar operation.

Joining Facebook: Transforming a Social Network into a Business Powerhouse

In 2008, Sandberg made the career-defining decision to join Facebook as Chief Operating Officer. At the time, Facebook was a young social network with millions of users but limited revenue. Mark Zuckerberg, Facebook's CEO, recognized Sandberg's ability to bring structure and strategy to fast-growing organizations, and she became one of his closest collaborators.

Sandberg's arrival at Facebook marked a turning point for the company. She developed Facebook's advertising strategy, transforming the platform into one of the most profitable digital advertising companies in the world. Under her leadership, Facebook's advertising revenue grew exponentially, and the company successfully navigated its IPO in 2012, becoming one of the most valuable tech companies in history.

Sandberg's expertise in scaling businesses and managing operations was instrumental in Facebook's evolution from a social network into a global technology giant. She was credited with building Facebook's business model, diversifying its revenue streams, and helping the company expand internationally.

Lean In: Advocating for Gender Equality and Empowering Women
In 2013, Sandberg published "Lean In: Women, Work, and the Will to Lead," a book that would cement her status as a thought leader and advocate for gender equality. The book encourages women to embrace leadership roles and push past societal barriers that often hold them back in the workplace.

"Lean In" became a global bestseller, sparking conversations about gender inequality in corporate environments and inspiring the formation of Lean In Circles, small peer groups that support women in their personal and professional growth. Sandberg's call for women to "lean in" to their careers and negotiate for leadership roles resonated with millions, igniting a movement toward more inclusive workplaces.

Despite receiving both praise and criticism, Sandberg's bold advocacy for gender equity changed the conversation around workplace diversity, unconscious bias, and leadership. Her work continues to inspire women to pursue leadership opportunities while advocating for organizational policies that support work-life balance.

Personal Challenges and Resilience
In 2015, Sandberg faced a devastating personal tragedy when her husband, Dave Goldberg, passed away unexpectedly. Goldberg, who was the CEO of SurveyMonkey, had been Sandberg's closest partner and supporter. His death left her to navigate life as a single mother while managing the demands of leading one of the world's most influential companies.

In the aftermath of her husband's passing, Sandberg wrote "Option B: Facing Adversity, Building Resilience, and Finding Joy" with psychologist Adam Grant. The book explores grief, resilience, and the power of community support in overcoming life's challenges. Sandberg's vulnerability and openness in sharing her personal journey resonated with many, offering hope to those facing similar losses.

Her experience with grief also deepened her commitment to supporting employees through personal challenges, advocating for better workplace policies such as bereavement leave and family support.

Impact and Leadership Style
Sandberg's leadership style is marked by transparency, empathy, and results-driven execution. She is known for her ability to build high-performing teams and scale businesses efficiently. At Facebook, she fostered a culture of collaboration and was instrumental in mentoring future leaders within the organization.

In addition to her work at Facebook, Sandberg has served on the boards of Walt Disney Company and Women for Women International and has supported numerous philanthropic causes related to education, gender equality, and public health.

Stepping Down from Facebook and New Chapters
After 14 years at Facebook, Sandberg announced in 2022 that she would be stepping down as COO to focus on philanthropy and personal projects. While her tenure at Facebook was marked by incredible growth, it also came with challenges, including scrutiny over Facebook's handling of user privacy, misinformation, and political content.

Despite these controversies, Sandberg's contributions to Facebook remain undeniable. She played a crucial role in transforming the platform into one of the most influential companies in the world and pioneered innovative strategies in digital advertising and corporate leadership.

Lessons from Sheryl Sandberg's Success

1. **Embrace Leadership Roles:** Sandberg's career demonstrates the importance of taking initiative and seizing leadership opportunities.

2. **Balance Ambition with Empathy:** Sandberg's leadership blends strategic execution with empathy, creating a culture of collaboration.

3. **Support Women in Leadership:** Through "Lean In," Sandberg has shown the power of mentorship and advocacy in promoting workplace diversity.

4. **Adapt Through Adversity:** Sandberg's ability to navigate personal loss and professional challenges illustrates the importance of resilience.

5. **Champion Work-Life Balance:** Her advocacy for better workplace policies highlights the need to support employees holistically.

Conclusion: A Legacy of Empowerment and Innovation

Sheryl Sandberg's journey from government service to tech pioneer is a powerful example of visionary leadership and advocacy for social change. As the COO of Facebook, she played a pivotal role in scaling the platform into a global giant, all while championing gender equality and workplace inclusion through her books and public speaking.

Sandberg's impact extends far beyond the business world. Her work continues to inspire women to pursue leadership roles, challenge societal norms, and build supportive communities. Through her personal and professional journey, Sandberg has shown that success is not just about climbing the corporate ladder— it's about using influence to empower others and lead with purpose and resilience.

———

Tim Ferriss' Success Story: The Master of Lifestyle Design and Productivity

"Expanding your reach beyond the book is about creating an ecosystem around your ideas, transforming every chapter into a doorway that opens up new opportunities for engagement and influence."
— TIM FERRISS, ENTREPRENEUR AND AUTHOR

"Snapchat offers a window into your book's soul. Use its visual storytelling power to captivate and convert your audience in real-time."
— TIM FERRISS, AUTHOR AND ENTREPRENEUR

"Batching and scheduling content is about being proactive, not reactive. It allows you to be present in the moment while ensuring your future is taken care of." — TIM FERRISS, AUTHOR AND ENTREPRENEUR

"Building a reputation as an expert doesn't happen by accident; it's a deliberate act of crafting your narrative and leveraging publicity to ensure that when your industry speaks, it's your voice they use as the benchmark."
— TIM FERRISS, AUTHOR AND ENTREPRENEUR

"Podcasting is the new personal touchpoint—a tool so intimate that it gives each listener the feeling of an in-depth, personal conversation that, at its best, can move mountains and minds." — TIM FERRISS, AUTHOR AND PODCASTER

Tim Ferriss, an entrepreneur, author, podcaster, and self-experimenter, rose to fame by questioning conventional norms and inspiring millions to rethink how they live and work. Best known for his book *The 4-Hour Workweek*, Ferriss introduced the world to the concept of lifestyle design, promoting efficiency, time freedom, and personal fulfillment. His journey is one of relentless curiosity, experimentation, and a deep commitment to self-improvement.

Ferriss attended Princeton University, where he studied East Asian Studies. His time at Princeton sparked an interest in unconventional paths to success, and he began to realize that real-world experience and practical knowledge were often more valuable than traditional education.

Building a Business and Burning Out
After graduating from Princeton, Ferriss started BrainQUICKEN, a sports nutrition supplements company, in the early 2000s. While the business grew steadily, Ferriss found himself working 14-hour days and drowning in emails, phone calls, and meetings. He soon realized that despite the financial success, the constant stress was unsustainable, prompting him to rethink how he approached work and life.

In search of a better way to manage his time, Ferriss began experimenting with productivity hacks, outsourcing tasks, and automating parts of his business. His goal was to free himself from the day-to-day operations and explore the world— a dream he had long put on hold.

166

The 4-Hour Workweek: A Game-Changer

During his travels, Ferriss refined his ideas about lifestyle design—the concept of deliberately creating a life aligned with personal values rather than societal expectations. In 2007, he published "The 4-Hour Workweek: Escape 9-5, Live Anywhere, and Join the New Rich."

The book became a global phenomenon, landing on multiple bestseller lists, including The New York Times and Wall Street Journal. It introduced revolutionary ideas such as:

1. **Pareto Principle (80/20 Rule):** Focus on the 20% of activities that produce 80% of the results.

2. **Outsourcing:** Delegate repetitive tasks to virtual assistants and external services.

3. **Mini-Retirements:** Take extended breaks throughout life rather than waiting for traditional retirement.

4. **Automation:** Use tools and systems to automate business operations.

The book resonated with entrepreneurs, freelancers, and corporate professionals looking to escape the rat race and design more meaningful lives. It redefined what it meant to be successful and sparked a global movement of digital nomads and remote workers.

Becoming a Thought Leader and Podcaster

Following the success of *The 4-Hour Workweek*, Ferriss wrote additional books focusing on health, fitness, and performance optimization. His subsequent works—*The 4-Hour Body*, *The 4-Hour Chef*, and *Tools of Titans*—became bestsellers as well, further establishing Ferriss as a leading voice in the self-improvement and productivity space.

In 2014, Ferriss launched The Tim Ferriss Show, a podcast where he interviews high achievers across disciplines, from athletes and artists to CEOs and scientists. His guests include luminaries like Elon Musk, Arnold Schwarzenegger, and Brené Brown. The show became a massive success, surpassing 900 million downloads and earning numerous awards.

Ferriss's podcast focuses on deconstructing success, exploring the habits, tools, and routines of top performers. His ability to ask insightful questions and extract actionable insights made the podcast an essential resource for those seeking self-improvement and peak performance.

A Life of Experimentation and Public Transparency

Ferriss is known for treating his life as a series of experiments. Whether it's learning a new language in record time, exploring psychedelics for mental health, or practicing fasting and meditation, Ferriss shares his successes and failures openly with his audience. This willingness to push boundaries and document his journey transparently has earned him a dedicated following.

His "Fear-Setting" exercise, which involves visualizing the worst-case scenarios of a decision, has become a popular tool for managing fear and anxiety. Ferriss's approach encourages individuals to confront their fears head-on and take calculated risks in pursuit of their dreams.

Mental Health and Personal Challenges

Despite his public success, Ferriss has been candid about mental health struggles. In several interviews, he has spoken openly about battling depression and anxiety, as well as exploring therapy, meditation, and psychedelic treatments to manage his mental well-being. His transparency has helped destigmatize mental health issues in the entrepreneurial community and foster conversations about the importance of mental resilience.

In 2020, Ferriss announced that he was scaling back his public commitments to focus on personal growth and relationships, reinforcing his belief that success isn't just about achievements but also about well-being and balance.

Investing and Philanthropy

Ferriss has also been a successful early-stage investor, backing companies like Uber, Shopify, Twitter, and Duolingo. His keen eye for emerging trends and willingness to bet on innovative ideas helped him achieve substantial financial success beyond his books and podcasts.

In recent years, Ferriss has become involved in philanthropy, focusing on causes related to mental health research, education, and psychedelic-assisted therapy. He has donated millions to organizations working in these fields, using his platform to advocate for innovative mental health treatments.

Lessons from Tim Ferriss's Success

1. **Question the Norms:** Ferriss challenges conventional thinking, encouraging people to design lives aligned with their values.

2. **Embrace Experimentation:** Treat life as a series of tests to learn what works and what doesn't.

3. **Optimize for Freedom:** Success isn't about working more—it's about creating time and space for what matters most.

4. **Leverage Outsourcing and Automation:** Free up time by delegating tasks and automating processes.

5. **Prioritize Mental Health:** Success is incomplete without mental and emotional well-being.

Conclusion: A Legacy of Lifestyle Design and Self-Optimization

Tim Ferriss's journey from burnt-out entrepreneur to lifestyle design pioneer is a powerful example of rethinking success. His books, podcast, and public experiments have inspired millions to take control of their lives, pursue meaningful goals, and prioritize well-being.

Ferriss's legacy lies not just in his achievements but in the movement he sparked—a generation of individuals who seek freedom, fulfillment, and personal growth beyond the constraints of traditional career paths. Through his continuous exploration of what it means to live a good life, Ferriss reminds us that success is not just about how much you achieve, but how intentionally you live.

Jeff Bezos' Success Story: From Garage Startup to Global Giant

"Planning for the long-term isn't about predicting the future, but about preparing to adapt to whatever the future holds, ensuring sustainability and resilience in an ever-changing world." — JEFF BEZOS, FOUNDER AND FORMER CEO OF AMAZON

"Your brand is what people say about you when you're not in the room." — JEFF BEZOS, FOUNDER OF AMAZON

"Data is the great revealer. Properly interpreted, it cuts through assumptions and exposes the truth about what really drives sales and engagement." — JEFF BEZOS, FOUNDER OF AMAZON

"Email is not just a method of communication; it's a vital tool for building your brand's identity and ensuring consistent engagement." — JEFF BEZOS, ENTREPRENEUR AND FOUNDER OF AMAZON

"Mastering Amazon and Shopify isn't just about selling; it's about strategically positioning your products so they don't just exist in the marketplace—they dominate it." — JEFF BEZOS, FOUNDER OF AMAZON

"Digital advertising demands that we not only adapt to change but anticipate it, ensuring we're always a step ahead in the game." — JEFF BEZOS, ENTREPRENEUR AND FOUNDER OF AMAZON

"Writing a business plan forces you into disciplined thinking if you do an intellectually honest job. An idea may sound great in your mind, but when you put down the details and numbers, it may fall apart." — JEFF BEZOS, FOUNDER OF AMAZON

"Understanding trademark law isn't just about protecting what's yours; it's about staking a claim in the marketplace that no one can challenge." — JEFF BEZOS, FOUNDER OF AMAZON

"Claiming ownership of your creative work is the first step towards turning your art into an asset. Secure your rights, and you secure your future." — JEFF BEZOS, FOUNDER OF AMAZON

"Distribution is about making sure your product meets your customers where they are, in the way they want to be met." — JEFF BEZOS, FOUNDER OF AMAZON

Jeff Bezos is one of the most iconic entrepreneurs of our time, known for revolutionizing e-commerce, founding Amazon, and transforming the way the world shops. His journey to becoming the world's richest person (at various times) is a story of vision, innovation, and relentless determination. Here's how Bezos started and rose to success.

Early Life and Career

Born on January 12, 1964, in Albuquerque, New Mexico, Jeff Bezos displayed a knack for innovation and entrepreneurship from a young age. As a child, he spent his summers on his grandfather's ranch in Texas, tinkering with mechanical projects and learning the value of hard work. Bezos was also an excellent student, excelling in academics, particularly in science and technology.

He graduated summa cum laude from Princeton University in 1986 with degrees in electrical engineering and computer science. After Princeton, Bezos worked in various roles on Wall Street, including at firms like Bankers Trust and D. E. Shaw & Co., where he became the youngest vice president at the firm. Although he had a promising career in finance, Bezos had bigger dreams.

The Big Idea: The Birth of Amazon

In 1994, Bezos came across a startling statistic: the internet was growing at 2,300% per year. Sensing a massive opportunity, he decided to leave his lucrative position at D. E. Shaw and take a bold leap into the unknown. He moved to Seattle and began working on an idea that would change the world: an online bookstore.

Bezos founded Amazon (initially called "Cadabra") in the garage of his rented home in Bellevue, Washington. His idea was simple but revolutionary: to create an online marketplace where customers could buy books more conveniently and at lower prices than traditional bookstores offered. He started with books because they were easier to ship and had broad appeal, but Bezos had much bigger ambitions right from the start.

Amazon's Early Growth

On July 16, 1995, Bezos launched Amazon.com, selling its first book and offering a catalog of over one million titles. Word spread quickly about this new, convenient way to buy books online. Within its first month, Amazon was shipping books to all 50 U.S. states and over 45 countries.

Even though Bezos had created a new business model, he was well aware of the need for patience and long-term thinking. He reinvested Amazon's early profits back into the business, focusing on building infrastructure, customer satisfaction, and innovation. By 1997, just two years after its launch, Amazon went public, raising $54 million.

From Books to Everything: Expanding Amazon

Although Amazon started as an online bookstore, Bezos always envisioned something much larger: a place where people could buy anything and everything online. In the early 2000s, Amazon expanded beyond books to sell music, electronics, toys, clothing, and more, turning it into the "everything store" it is today.

Under Bezos' leadership, Amazon pioneered key innovations such as personalized product recommendations, user reviews, and 1-click ordering. These features helped differentiate Amazon from its competitors and revolutionized the e-commerce experience for consumers.

Relentless Focus on Customer Experience

One of the key drivers behind Amazon's success was Bezos' unwavering focus on customer satisfaction. He believed that building trust and loyalty with customers was the key to long-term success, even if it meant sacrificing short-term profits. Amazon consistently prioritized convenience and affordability, introducing Amazon Prime in 2005, a subscription service that offered fast, free shipping—eventually adding streaming video and music services as well.

Bezos also encouraged a culture of experimentation at Amazon, where failures were seen as part of the process of discovering new and better ways to serve customers. While some innovations, like the Fire Phone, flopped, others—like Kindle and Amazon Web Services (AWS)—became wildly successful.

Disrupting Multiple Industries

Beyond e-commerce, Bezos transformed numerous industries, from cloud computing with AWS to entertainment with Amazon Studios. AWS became a major profit driver for Amazon, providing cloud services to businesses around the world. Meanwhile, Amazon Studios helped the company enter the world of original content, producing award-winning films and TV shows.

In 2017, Bezos further shook up the retail world by acquiring Whole Foods, expanding Amazon's presence in brick-and-mortar stores while integrating the grocery chain with its online ecosystem.

Space Exploration: Blue Origin

But Bezos' ambitions weren't confined to Earth. In 2000, he founded Blue Origin, a space exploration company with the mission of making space travel more accessible and affordable. Much like Elon Musk's SpaceX, Bezos' goal is to make humanity a multi-planetary species, believing that space is crucial to the future of civilization.

Blue Origin has made significant advancements in rocket technology, working toward a future where humans can live and work in space.

Wealth and Influence

As Amazon grew, so did Bezos' personal wealth. In 2020, he briefly became the first person in history to amass a net worth over $200 billion. However, despite his wealth, Bezos remained hands-on with Amazon until 2021, when he stepped down as CEO to focus on other ventures like Blue Origin.

His impact on business and culture is undeniable. Bezos transformed how people shop, how businesses handle cloud computing, and how industries adapt to the digital age.

Bezos' Legacy: Visionary Leader and Risk-Taker

Jeff Bezos' success can be attributed to his visionary thinking, customer obsession, willingness to take risks, and relentless drive to innovate. From selling books in his garage to running one of the largest companies in the world, Bezos never shied away from challenging the status quo and pushing boundaries.

His legacy is more than just building Amazon—he's reshaped entire industries and fundamentally altered how consumers engage with technology, commerce, and entertainment.

In the words of Bezos himself: *"If you do build a great experience, customers tell each other about that. Word of mouth is very powerful."*

Darren Rowse's Success Story: From Hobby Blogger to Digital Entrepreneur

"Monetizing your digital space isn't just about earning revenue; it's about enhancing your content with relevant, thoughtful ad placements that add value for your audience while enriching your bottom line."
— DARREN ROWSE, PROFESSIONAL BLOGGER
AND FOUNDER OF PROBLOGGER

Darren Rowse is a trailblazer in the world of professional blogging, known for transforming a personal passion into a thriving entrepreneurial venture. As the founder of ProBlogger and Digital Photography School, Rowse built two influential platforms that empower aspiring bloggers and photographers worldwide. Through a blend of transparency, community building, and practical advice, Rowse has helped countless individuals turn their online hobbies into sustainable careers. His story exemplifies how consistency, strategic thinking, and a passion for sharing knowledge can lead to long-lasting success in the ever-evolving digital landscape.

Early Beginnings: A Passion for Writing and Photography
Darren Rowse's journey to becoming a highly influential figure in the blogging world started as a personal experiment. Born and raised in Melbourne, Australia, Rowse was passionate about writing and photography. In 2002, he launched his first blog as a way to share his thoughts and experiences online. What began as a hobby quickly became a learning experience as Rowse explored the potential of blogging as a platform for personal expression and community building.

Finding His Niche: ProBlogger and Digital Photography School

Rowse's early blogs were diverse, but as he gained experience, he saw the potential of niche blogging. In 2004, he launched ProBlogger, a blog dedicated to helping others make a living from blogging. Around the same time, he founded Digital Photography School, providing tips and tutorials to aspiring photographers. Both sites quickly gained traction, and Rowse's success cemented him as an expert in monetizing blogs and building online communities.

Growing Through Transparency and Teaching

What set Rowse apart from other early bloggers was his transparency. He openly shared his journey, including successes and failures, making his insights relatable to his audience. His step-by-step guides, practical advice, and focus on building genuine connections resonated with readers looking to follow in his footsteps. Rowse wasn't just creating content—he was teaching others how to succeed in the growing digital landscape.

Monetization and Community Building

Rowse explored multiple streams of income, including affiliate marketing, sponsorships, eBooks, and online courses. His approach to monetization was always community-focused, ensuring that his content provided value first. This philosophy allowed ProBlogger and Digital Photography School to grow into trusted resources for bloggers and photographers worldwide.

Expanding His Influence: ProBlogger Events and Podcasts

Rowse extended his reach beyond blogging by launching the ProBlogger podcast, where he shared insights on entrepreneurship, marketing, and digital content strategies. Additionally, he organized ProBlogger events, bringing bloggers and influencers together to learn, network, and grow their businesses. These events fostered a sense of community and expanded Rowse's influence within the industry.

Legacy and Impact

Today, Darren Rowse is regarded as a pioneer of professional blogging. His ability to blend authenticity with strategic content creation has inspired countless bloggers to pursue their passions and build sustainable online businesses. ProBlogger and Digital Photography School remain active and influential, continuing to empower creators around the globe. Rowse's story exemplifies how passion, persistence, and a willingness to share knowledge can transform a personal hobby into a thriving entrepreneurial journey.

Joe Pulizzi's Success Story: The Visionary Who Revolutionized Marketing through Content

"Offering free content is like casting a wide net with bait so irresistible, it not only catches but also nurtures the fish, guiding them seamlessly from casual browsers to loyal customers." — JOE PULIZZI, CONTENT MARKETING EXPERT

"An engaging online media room acts as your brand's digital front door, not just welcoming visitors but captivating them, turning every entry into an opportunity for discovery and connection." — JOE PULIZZI, FOUNDER OF CONTENT MARKETING INSTITUTE

Joe Pulizzi is widely recognized as one of the founding figures of the content marketing movement, transforming the way businesses connect with their audiences. As the founder of the Content Marketing Institute (CMI) and the visionary behind Content Marketing World, Pulizzi's groundbreaking work redefined marketing by emphasizing storytelling, trust, and value-driven content. At a time when companies were focused on traditional advertising and sales tactics, Pulizzi introduced the idea that businesses should think and act like publishers—offering content that educates and engages their audiences. His innovative approach not only gave rise to a global industry but also empowered countless businesses to succeed by building meaningful relationships with their customers. Through his books, podcasts, and speaking engagements, Pulizzi continues to inspire marketers and entrepreneurs to embrace the power of storytelling, making him one of the most influential thought leaders in modern marketing.

Early Life and Career Beginnings
Joe Pulizzi's journey to becoming a leading figure in content marketing began in Cleveland, Ohio. With a background in communications and marketing, Pulizzi

initially worked in traditional media and corporate marketing roles. However, he quickly realized that most businesses were approaching marketing the wrong way—focusing too much on selling and not enough on building trust with their audience through valuable content.

The Birth of Content Marketing Institute

Pulizzi's dissatisfaction with conventional marketing led him to take a leap of faith. In 2007, he founded the Content Marketing Institute (CMI), a pioneering organization designed to help businesses create compelling content that attracts and retains customers. At a time when content marketing was a relatively unknown concept, Pulizzi's vision centered on the belief that businesses could succeed by acting more like publishers—offering content that informs, entertains, and educates.

CMI's rise was initially challenging. Pulizzi worked tirelessly to build credibility, grow a community, and establish content marketing as a strategic discipline. Through CMI's blog, podcasts, and events, Pulizzi became the go-to authority on content marketing.

Content Marketing World: Building a Global Movement

In 2011, Pulizzi launched Content Marketing World, an annual conference that brought marketers from around the globe together to learn, collaborate, and share insights. The event quickly became the largest gathering of content marketers, drawing industry leaders, innovators, and marketing professionals seeking to deepen their expertise.

CMI's success was further bolstered by the release of "Epic Content Marketing" in 2013, a book that became a must-read for marketing professionals. In the book, Pulizzi outlined how businesses could achieve sustainable success by focusing on storytelling, audience-building, and long-term strategy.

Selling CMI and Expanding His Legacy

In 2016, after years of building CMI into a powerhouse, Pulizzi sold the company to UBM (now part of Informa), solidifying its place as a leading global resource for content marketers. However, Pulizzi's entrepreneurial journey didn't end there. Following the sale, he embarked on new ventures, including writing more books, launching the Content Inc. podcast, and founding the Orange Effect

Foundation, which helps children with speech disorders receive the therapy they need.

The Power of Content and Community

Throughout his career, Pulizzi has emphasized that the heart of successful content marketing lies in focusing on the needs of the audience. He encourages businesses to build relationships, foster trust, and create valuable experiences through storytelling. His insights have fundamentally changed how companies view marketing, making content a strategic priority rather than a side project.

Conclusion: A Visionary and Mentor

Joe Pulizzi's journey from a frustrated marketer to the founder of a global content marketing movement is a testament to the power of vision, persistence, and community-building. His influence has shaped an entire industry, helping thousands of businesses and marketers succeed through the art of storytelling. With his continued work in education and philanthropy, Pulizzi remains a passionate advocate for the transformative potential of content marketing, leaving behind a legacy that continues to inspire marketers around the world.

CHAPTER EIGHT

Mastering Social Media Platforms

Mastering social media platforms is no longer an optional strategy in today's business environment—it's a necessity. Social media offers businesses unparalleled opportunities to connect, engage, and build relationships with their audience. This chapter dives deep into how to leverage the most popular platforms to promote your brand, build credibility, and drive conversions. Each platform is unique, requiring a tailored approach to maximize engagement and ensure your message resonates with your audience.

Jack Dorsey reminds us, "Twitter is a dance floor for ideas," highlighting the platform's fast-paced nature and the value of real-time interaction. Simply being present is not enough; businesses must learn to navigate each platform's specific nuances. Mark Zuckerberg emphasizes that "the best marketing doesn't feel like marketing," underscoring the importance of authenticity in connecting with your audience. This chapter covers key strategies for major platforms such as

Instagram, Facebook, Twitter, LinkedIn, Pinterest, and emerging platforms like TikTok.

On Instagram, the visual content is paramount. Malcolm Gladwell notes that "the power of storytelling is in the details," and Instagram enables businesses to express their identity and connect with followers on a personal level. Biz Stone adds that "the best way to make a difference is to take a chance," encouraging brands to embrace creativity in their visual storytelling efforts. Ann Handley encourages businesses to use Pinterest as "a powerful tool for visual storytelling that draws readers into your narrative," emphasizing the platform's potential for engagement.

Building a brand voice across social media platforms requires consistency and authenticity. Jonathan Lister advises, "Speak to your audience in their language about what's in their heart," emphasizing the importance of empathy in social media messaging. This chapter explores how businesses can craft a distinct, authentic voice that remains consistent across platforms while adapting to each platform's unique style. W. Edwards Deming, the renowned statistician, famously said, "Without data, you're just another person with an opinion." Monitoring metrics ensures you understand what works and what doesn't, allowing you to refine your strategy continuously.

The importance of social media advertising is also discussed in this chapter. Harper Reed illustrates that "mastering online ads means creating genuine connections," highlighting how advertising on platforms like Facebook and Instagram can foster direct relationships with your audience. Mark Zuckerberg notes that effective communication can transform promotional messages into meaningful conversations, emphasizing the need for brands to engage thoughtfully.

Effective social media strategies don't just aim to gather followers but cultivate engaged communities. Malcolm Gladwell explains, "Building a community is not just about gathering an audience—it's about creating an environment where every interaction adds value." Engaged followers are more likely to become brand advocates, sharing your content and amplifying your message organically.

Mastering social media platforms means more than posting content—it requires thoughtful strategy, continuous learning, and adaptation. This chapter provides a comprehensive guide to using each platform effectively, from crafting the perfect Instagram post to leveraging LinkedIn for professional growth. With insights from Jack Dorsey, Jonathan Lister, and Biz Stone, you'll learn how to build meaningful relationships, stay ahead of trends, and drive real business results. Whether you're just starting or looking to refine your strategy, this chapter equips you with the tools needed to thrive on social media and grow your brand with purpose and impact.

====

Jack Dorsey's Success Story: From Coder to Social Media Visionary

"Twitter is a dance floor for ideas. Engage correctly, and your message will echo far beyond your initial reach." — JACK DORSEY, CO-FOUNDER OF TWITTER AND TECHNOLOGY ENTREPRENEUR

Jack Dorsey is a name synonymous with innovation in both the tech and financial sectors. As the co-founder of Twitter, the platform that revolutionized real-time communication, and Square, the fintech company that redefined mobile payments, Dorsey's career reflects a deep understanding of how technology can reshape industries. Known for his unconventional leadership style and relentless focus on simplicity, Jack has not only built tools that foster conversation and financial empowerment but also navigated challenges with resilience. His story is one of persistence, adaptability, and visionary thinking—qualities that continue to inspire entrepreneurs and innovators worldwide.

Early Beginnings: The Love for Coding and Communication
Jack Dorsey's journey to becoming a tech giant began in his childhood. Born and raised in St. Louis, Missouri, Jack showed an early fascination with maps, communication networks, and technology. As a teenager, he developed programming skills and built open-source software to help dispatch taxis and couriers—laying the groundwork for his future endeavors in streamlining communication.

181

The Birth of Twitter: Capturing the Power of Short Communication

After moving to California and working in various tech companies, Jack found himself captivated by the idea of real-time communication. Alongside co-founders Biz Stone, Evan Williams, and Noah Glass, Jack developed a microblogging platform in 2006 that would allow people to share thoughts in short, instant messages. This idea evolved into Twitter, with Jack sending the very first tweet: *"just setting up my twttr."*

Though initially met with skepticism, Twitter gained popularity as a revolutionary platform where breaking news, activism, and global conversations unfolded in real time. Jack's vision to create a public messaging space reshaped how the world communicates, from celebrity culture to political movements.

Challenges and a Comeback: From CEO to Entrepreneurial Growth

Jack's road to success was not without its challenges. After internal conflicts, he stepped down as Twitter's CEO in 2008 but stayed involved with the company. During his time away, Jack founded Square (now known as Block, Inc.), a fintech company enabling mobile payments, particularly aimed at small businesses and independent merchants. The seamless integration of technology with finance made Square a leader in the payment industry.

In 2015, Jack returned as Twitter's CEO to rejuvenate the platform, navigating challenges like user growth and content moderation. Under his leadership, Twitter launched innovative features while maintaining its status as the digital hub for real-time conversation.

Impact on Technology and Society

Jack Dorsey's ventures have redefined industries beyond communication. Twitter became a critical platform for journalism, activism, and politics, while Square democratized financial services for small business owners. Jack's dual success reflects his ability to identify gaps in communication and finance, creating accessible solutions to bridge them.

Personal Philosophy: Minimalism and Focus

Jack is known for his unconventional lifestyle, advocating for minimalism, fasting, and meditation to maintain focus. His distinctive approach to business and life reflects a desire for simplicity and efficiency, influencing his leadership style and product innovation. Jack's relentless curiosity and commitment to shaping meaningful technologies continue to define his career.

Legacy and Influence

Today, Jack Dorsey's influence extends across technology, finance, and entrepreneurship. As both a founder of Twitter and Square, he has shown the importance of perseverance, vision, and adaptability. His ability to balance innovation with societal needs has positioned him as one of the most influential figures in tech, leaving a lasting legacy of communication and financial empowerment in the digital age.

Jonathan Lister's Success Story: Mastering the Art of Customer Engagement and Sales

"Speak to your audience in their language about what's in their heart."
— JONATHAN LISTER, LINKEDIN'S VICE PRESIDENT
OF SALES SOLUTIONS

Jonathan Lister stands as a prime example of how strategic leadership and customer engagement can drive business success in the modern age. With a career rooted in the art of relationship-driven sales, Lister has built a reputation as a visionary leader who understands the evolving dynamics between companies and their customers. Best known for his transformative work at LinkedIn, Lister has shaped how businesses approach sales and engagement, emphasizing authenticity, long-term connections, and adaptive strategies. His journey from business operations to becoming a thought leader in sales solutions demonstrates the power of aligning technology, empathy, and leadership to create meaningful business impact.

Early Life and Professional Beginnings

Jonathan Lister's journey began with a passion for connecting people and crafting meaningful interactions. With a background in business administration, Lister quickly discovered that his strengths lay in the intricate dance of sales, leadership, and customer engagement. Early in his career, he gained valuable experience in marketing and operations at top-tier organizations, where he developed a keen understanding of what makes customers tick and how businesses can authentically connect with them.

Climbing the Corporate Ladder

Lister's breakthrough came when he joined LinkedIn, the professional networking giant. As Vice President of Sales Solutions, he played a pivotal role in transforming the platform's offerings, helping businesses leverage LinkedIn for growth through strategic relationships and targeted marketing. He demonstrated that sales were no longer just transactional but relationship-driven, paving the way for future success in the business landscape. His ability to blend sales strategies with authentic engagement positioned him as a key leader in the organization.

LinkedIn Success and Influence

Under Lister's leadership, LinkedIn's Sales Solutions division expanded rapidly. He introduced innovative ways for companies to use the platform, not just for recruitment but as a tool to connect with audiences meaningfully. His emphasis on speaking to the customer's heart—not just their mind—resonated across industries. This approach positioned LinkedIn as an indispensable tool for business professionals, and Lister emerged as a thought leader on sales engagement.

Beyond LinkedIn: Thought Leadership and Impact

Lister's insights on customer engagement have shaped modern sales practices. He advocates for adaptive strategies that evolve with the changing needs of customers and markets. His work emphasizes the importance of building lasting relationships over quick wins, showing companies how to craft meaningful dialogues that result in sustainable growth. Through speaking engagements, interviews, and mentorship, he continues to share his wisdom with aspiring leaders.

Legacy and Continuing Influence

Jonathan Lister's career exemplifies the power of authentic connection in business. His contributions have redefined sales strategies, shifting the focus from transactions to relationships. Today, Lister's influence extends beyond LinkedIn, as companies worldwide adopt his customer-first mindset. His journey serves as an inspiration for those looking to blend technology, engagement, and leadership to create meaningful business impact.

W. Edwards Deming's Success Story: The Architect of Modern Quality Management

"Without data, you're just another person with an opinion."
— W. Edwards Deming, Statistician and
Quality Control Expert

W. Edwards Deming, a pioneer in the world of quality management, is widely credited with transforming modern business practices through his innovative approach to continuous improvement and statistical process control. Born in 1900, Deming's passion for data-driven processes and collaboration led him from academic pursuits to becoming a driving force behind the post-World War II economic revival of Japan. His groundbreaking philosophy emphasized long-term success over short-term gains, empowering organizations to focus on quality, employee engagement, and customer satisfaction. Though initially recognized overseas, Deming's teachings eventually reshaped industries worldwide, influencing methodologies like Total Quality Management, Lean, and Six Sigma, leaving a lasting legacy in the pursuit of business excellence.

Early Life and Education

W. Edwards Deming was born on October 14, 1900, in Sioux City, Iowa, and grew up on a farm in Wyoming. Raised with a strong work ethic and a curiosity about problem-solving, Deming pursued higher education, earning degrees in electrical engineering and mathematics. He completed his PhD in mathematical physics from Yale University in 1928, setting the foundation for his career in academia, research, and consulting.

Career Beginnings and Transformation

Deming initially worked as a statistician at the U.S. Department of Agriculture and later with the U.S. Census Bureau. His expertise in statistical methods led him to explore ways data could be used to improve processes. During this period,

Deming became influenced by Walter A. Shewhart's pioneering work on statistical process control, which inspired him to connect mathematics and manufacturing to boost quality and efficiency.

The Turning Point: Post-War Japan

Deming's defining career breakthrough came after World War II, when he was invited to help rebuild Japan's devastated economy. In 1950, the Union of Japanese Scientists and Engineers (JUSE) brought Deming to Japan, where he introduced statistical quality control methods and a philosophy of continuous improvement. His ideas emphasized collaboration between management and workers, focusing on long-term growth rather than short-term gains. Japanese executives embraced Deming's teachings, incorporating them into manufacturing, and within a few decades, Japanese products became renowned for quality worldwide.

Key Contributions and the Deming Philosophy

Deming's philosophy, often summarized as the "System of Profound Knowledge," emphasized four interconnected areas: appreciation for a system, understanding variation, theory of knowledge, and psychology. His focus on "continuous improvement" (Kaizen) and statistical quality control revolutionized industries not only in Japan but also globally. His 14 Points for Management became a blueprint for achieving sustainable business success through leadership, teamwork, and customer satisfaction.

One of Deming's most influential ideas was that "quality drives profitability." He believed that better products and services create loyal customers, which in turn reduce costs associated with rework, defects, and customer complaints. Deming also emphasized the importance of empowering employees at all levels to take ownership of their work, fostering an environment of trust and learning.

Recognition and Lasting Legacy

Though he was relatively unknown in his home country for much of his career, Deming's impact became recognized in the 1980s, when American companies, particularly in manufacturing, faced competition from superior Japanese products. His ideas on quality management and operational excellence were finally embraced by U.S. businesses, and Deming became a sought-after speaker and consultant. His teachings laid the foundation for what would later become known as Total Quality Management (TQM) and Lean Manufacturing.

Deming's legacy continues to shape industries around the world. His work influenced the Six Sigma methodology and remains embedded in today's quality management systems. Major corporations, such as Toyota, General Electric, and Ford, have applied Deming's principles to achieve long-term success.

Conclusion

W. Edwards Deming's journey from an academic to a transformative figure in business showcases the power of innovation, continuous learning, and collaboration. His dedication to improving processes and products through data-driven methods reshaped global manufacturing, giving rise to movements like Lean and Six Sigma that remain relevant today. More than just a statistician or consultant, Deming was a pioneer of modern quality management, inspiring generations of businesses to prioritize quality, empower employees, and strive for excellence. His life's work exemplifies how persistence, a commitment to knowledge, and visionary thinking can create profound and lasting change.

Mark Zuckerberg's Success Story: From Dorm Room Dream to Global Tech Leader

"Social media is the new frontier for copyright law; navigating it requires a clear understanding of both its power and its pitfalls. Creators must be vigilant to protect their work while engaging with this dynamic platform."
— MARK ZUCKERBERG, CEO OF FACEBOOK

"Social media is the new frontier for copyright law; navigating it requires a clear understanding of both its power and its pitfalls. Creators must be vigilant to protect their work while engaging with this dynamic platform."
— MARK ZUCKERBERG, CEO OF FACEBOOK

"Technology and social media have brought power back to the people."
— MARK ZUCKERBERG, CEO OF FACEBOOK

Mark Zuckerberg's rise from a curious young coder to the founder of one of the most influential companies in the world is a testament to the power of vision and ambition. Known for co-creating Facebook (now Meta) from his dorm room at Harvard University, Zuckerberg transformed a college networking site into a global platform that redefined how people connect and interact. His journey is one of bold ideas, rapid growth, and overcoming challenges in the fast-paced world of technology. As both a tech innovator and a philanthropist, Zuckerberg has left an indelible mark on the digital age, cementing his legacy as a leader who changed the landscape of social media and global communication forever.

Early Life and Passion for Programming
Born in 1984 in White Plains, New York, Mark Zuckerberg exhibited an early talent for computers and programming. Encouraged by his supportive parents, he began coding at a young age, developing computer games and software. His father, a dentist, hired a tutor to nurture Mark's skills further. While still in high school, Mark built a messaging program called "ZuckNet" to enable communication between his father's home office and family members—a precursor to the interconnected world he would help create.

Harvard Beginnings and the Birth of Facebook
In 2002, Zuckerberg enrolled at Harvard University, where he quickly became known for his exceptional programming skills. During his sophomore year, he developed "Facemash," a controversial app that allowed students to rank their peers' photos. Although the project was shut down by the university, it sparked the idea for a larger platform—one that would connect people within Harvard and beyond.

In February 2004, Zuckerberg, along with co-founders Eduardo Saverin, Andrew McCollum, Dustin Moskovitz, and Chris Hughes, launched **Facebook** from his dorm room. Originally limited to Harvard students, the platform rapidly expanded to other universities, capturing the imaginations of students with its promise of social connectivity.

Expansion and Explosive Growth
By 2005, Facebook received its first major investment of $12.7 million from Accel Partners, fueling its growth. Zuckerberg and his team opened the platform to the public, expanding beyond academia. Facebook's intuitive design and

seamless user experience set it apart, allowing it to surpass competitors like MySpace.

The company's innovative approach to social networking, combined with Zuckerberg's vision for global connectivity, attracted millions of users. By 2012, Facebook had reached a landmark 1 billion users. The platform became more than just a social network; it evolved into a major force in advertising, digital communication, and global culture.

Leadership and Business Success

Zuckerberg's relentless focus on innovation helped Facebook navigate challenges, including controversies surrounding privacy and misinformation. Under his leadership, Facebook acquired major companies like Instagram, WhatsApp, and Oculus VR, solidifying its dominance in the tech industry. Zuckerberg's emphasis on long-term vision, strategic growth, and bold decision-making earned him recognition as one of the most influential entrepreneurs of the 21st century.

Philanthropy and Legacy

In addition to his business achievements, Zuckerberg has committed significant resources to philanthropy. Along with his wife, Priscilla Chan, he established the Chan Zuckerberg Initiative in 2015, pledging to donate the majority of their wealth to charitable causes focused on education, healthcare, and scientific research.

Conclusion

Mark Zuckerberg's journey from a college student with a big idea to the CEO of Meta (formerly Facebook) is a story of vision, resilience, and unrelenting ambition. His impact on the digital world has reshaped the way people connect and communicate globally, making him a pivotal figure in the evolution of social media. Through both his technological innovations and philanthropic efforts, Zuckerberg continues to influence the future of communication, business, and society.

Malcolm Gladwell's Success Story: The Master Storyteller Who Redefined How We Think

"Understanding your audience is the cornerstone of successful writing. It's about engaging with their desires and fears to craft stories that resonate deeply and endure over time." — MALCOLM GLADWELL, AUTHOR AND JOURNALIST

"Embracing your local roots in your marketing efforts doesn't just build a fan base—it plants the seeds of enduring support that grow and thrive along with your literary career." — MALCOLM GLADWELL, AUTHOR AND JOURNALIST

"Establishing yourself as a market expert is less about claiming expertise and more about demonstrating it in ways that engage, educate, and resonate with your audience." — MALCOLM GLADWELL, AUTHOR AND JOURNALIST

"Building a legacy with your book involves more than just a launch; it's about creating a continuous dialogue with your readers and keeping the book alive in their minds and hearts for years." — MALCOLM GLADWELL, JOURNALIST AND BESTSELLING AUTHOR

Malcolm Gladwell is a bestselling author, journalist, and public speaker who has captivated audiences with his unique ability to blend storytelling with deep insights into human behavior, psychology, and social phenomena. From humble beginnings in rural Canada to becoming one of the most influential thinkers of the 21st century, Gladwell's journey is a testament to the power of curiosity, persistence, and unconventional thinking.

Early Life and Education

Born on September 3, 1963, in Fareham, England, to a Jamaican psychotherapist mother and a British mathematics professor father, Gladwell moved to Canada as a child. His parents' professions profoundly shaped his intellectual curiosity and lifelong fascination with people and systems. Raised in Ontario, he was an avid reader and an insightful observer from a young age.

Gladwell attended Trinity College at the University of Toronto, where he studied history. Though initially unsure about his future career, he became increasingly drawn to journalism as a way to explore big ideas and make sense of the world. After graduating in 1984, he set out on a path that would eventually make him one of the most celebrated non-fiction writers of his generation.

Early Career in Journalism
Gladwell's first job in journalism was with The American Spectator in Indiana. Later, he moved to Washington, D.C., where he began covering business and science for the Washington Post. It was during this period that Gladwell honed his ability to identify patterns and connect seemingly unrelated ideas—a skill that would become his signature style.

Despite facing rejection for certain articles early in his career, Gladwell persisted. He thrived on curiosity-driven reporting and unconventional angles, gaining a reputation for his ability to ask questions that others didn't think to ask. His writing was insightful, engaging, and grounded in narrative storytelling—a rare combination in journalism.

The Breakthrough with *The New Yorker*
Gladwell's big break came in 1996 when he joined The New Yorker as a staff writer. His knack for exploring complex topics through captivating stories made him a standout voice. Two of his early New Yorker essays—"The Tipping Point" and "The Coolhunt"—explored how ideas spread and how trends catch on. These articles would lay the foundation for his first bestselling book.

***The Tipping Point* and Instant Fame**
In 2000, Gladwell published his first book, "The Tipping Point: How Little Things Can Make a Big Difference." The book examined how small, seemingly insignificant events can trigger widespread social changes—like how fads start or crime rates suddenly drop. It became an instant bestseller, resonating with readers who appreciated its blend of data, psychology, and storytelling.

"The Tipping Point" established Gladwell as a thought leader, earning him a spot on bestseller lists and making him a sought-after public speaker. The success of the book marked the beginning of a new genre of narrative non-fiction, inspiring other writers to explore big ideas through storytelling.

Building on Success with *Blink* and *Outliers*

Gladwell followed up with "Blink: The Power of Thinking Without Thinking" in 2005, a book that explored the science behind snap judgments and intuition. Once again, Gladwell's ability to weave research and real-world examples made the book a bestseller. Readers appreciated his ability to explain how people make decisions in the blink of an eye, offering insights into the hidden processes of the human mind.

In 2008, Gladwell published "Outliers: The Story of Success," which explored the factors that contribute to extraordinary success. Gladwell challenged the idea that success is solely the result of talent, introducing concepts like the 10,000-Hour Rule, which argues that mastery in any field requires at least 10,000 hours of practice. "Outliers" became one of Gladwell's most popular books and cemented his reputation as a cultural thinker who could shift public perception on topics as varied as education, sports, and economics.

Expanding Influence with *David and Goliath* and *Talking to Strangers*

Gladwell continued to explore unexpected themes with books like "David and Goliath" (2013), which reexamines the idea of strength and weakness by showing how underdogs can triumph in seemingly impossible situations.

In 2019, he published "Talking to Strangers: What We Should Know about the People We Don't Know," which delves into the miscommunication and misunderstandings that occur when people encounter those different from themselves. The book explored case studies involving law enforcement, international diplomacy, and criminal trials, challenging readers to think differently about trust and perception.

Podcasting and New Ventures

In 2016, Gladwell expanded into podcasting, launching "Revisionist History," a show that reexamines overlooked or misunderstood events and ideas. The podcast quickly became a hit, showcasing Gladwell's ability to spin a compelling narrative across a variety of topics—from sports scandals to moral philosophy.

In 2018, Gladwell co-founded Pushkin Industries, a media company focused on producing high-quality podcasts. Pushkin's success reflects Gladwell's ability to stay relevant in an ever-changing media landscape, using new platforms to continue engaging with his audience.

Thought Leadership and Public Speaking

Gladwell has become one of the most influential public intellectuals of the modern era. His work has redefined how people think about success, behavior, and society. As a sought-after speaker, he has delivered keynote addresses at conferences, universities, and corporate events, where he shares his insights on topics ranging from innovation to diversity.

Awards and Recognition

Gladwell's influence and achievements have earned him numerous awards and accolades. Time magazine named him one of the 100 Most Influential People in the World in 2005. His books have sold millions of copies worldwide, and his ideas have become part of popular culture—sparking discussions in business, education, psychology, and beyond.

Conclusion: A Legacy of Curiosity and Storytelling

Malcolm Gladwell's journey from curious journalist to bestselling author and podcast creator is a story of embracing the unexpected, challenging assumptions, and finding meaning in the ordinary. His ability to translate complex concepts into engaging narratives has made him a favorite among readers and listeners alike.

Gladwell's legacy is one of intellectual curiosity, inspiring others to think differently, question the status quo, and embrace the power of storytelling. With each new book and podcast episode, he continues to push boundaries, proving that the key to success lies not just in knowledge—but in how we tell the story of the world around us.

===

Biz Stone's Success Story: Innovator, Entrepreneur, and Co-Founder of Twitter

"Timing, perseverance, and ten years of trying will eventually make you look like an overnight success." — BIZ STONE, CO-FOUNDER OF TWITTER

Biz Stone is a visionary entrepreneur whose work has reshaped the landscape of digital communication. Best known as a co-founder of Twitter, Stone has built his career on the intersection of technology, creativity, and social impact. From his early days working on one of the first blogging platforms to launching game-changing startups, Stone has always focused on connecting people and empowering them to share ideas. His story is one of resilience and innovation, demonstrating how unconventional thinking and a passion for storytelling can lead to extraordinary success. Stone's journey serves as an inspiration to entrepreneurs, encouraging them to build ventures that not only thrive but also leave a positive mark on the world.

Early Life and the Spark of Creativity

Biz Stone, born Christopher Isaac Stone on March 10, 1974, in Boston, Massachusetts, had a humble beginning. With limited financial means growing up, Stone developed an innate ability to find creative solutions to challenges. His early life was shaped by a passion for art and design, interests that would later play a role in his tech ventures. Stone attended Northeastern University and the University of Massachusetts but left before completing his degree, following his belief that real-world experience was more valuable than traditional education.

Early Career and the Birth of Blogging

Stone's first taste of the digital world began when he co-founded Xanga, one of the earliest blogging platforms. This venture introduced him to the growing power of social networking and online communities. Stone then joined Google, where he worked on Blogger, an acquisition that gave him a front-row seat to the evolution of user-generated content. During his time at Google, Stone honed his skills in product development and gained valuable insight into how digital platforms could facilitate human connection.

Founding Twitter: A New Era of Communication

In 2006, Biz Stone joined forces with Jack Dorsey, Evan Williams, and Noah Glass to create what would become Twitter, a platform that revolutionized real-time communication. Initially developed as a side project at Odeo, Twitter was built on the simple concept of sharing thoughts in 140-character messages. Stone's focus on user experience and community-building helped shape Twitter's core identity as a fast, accessible platform for sharing ideas, breaking news, and connecting people globally.

Though the early days of Twitter were challenging—with slow adoption and technical issues—Stone's belief in the product never wavered. The turning point came during major world events, such as the 2009 Iranian elections, when Twitter became a vital tool for activists and journalists. Stone's emphasis on openness and simplicity allowed Twitter to become more than just a social network—it became a platform for freedom of expression and global conversations.

Expanding His Influence: Beyond Twitter

After leaving Twitter in 2011, Stone continued to explore new ways to combine technology, design, and storytelling. He co-founded Jelly, a Q&A-based search engine that leveraged crowdsourcing to answer user questions. While Jelly was eventually acquired by Pinterest, it reflected Stone's enduring passion for innovative solutions that empower users.

In addition to his entrepreneurial ventures, Stone became a thought leader and philanthropist, supporting causes related to education, animal welfare, and public health. He also published books, including *Things a Little Bird Told Me*, in which he shared lessons from his journey in entrepreneurship and leadership.

Legacy and Impact

Biz Stone's impact extends far beyond Twitter. His work has fundamentally shaped the way people communicate and engage with information in the digital age. Known for his belief that technology should serve humanity, Stone remains a prominent advocate for creativity, empathy, and social good in business. Through his ventures and public speaking, he encourages entrepreneurs to build with purpose, reminding them that success isn't just about profits—it's about making the world a better place.

Stone's journey from a young dreamer to a co-founder of one of the most influential social media platforms illustrates the power of resilience, innovation, and a belief in the transformative potential of ideas. His story continues to inspire a new generation of entrepreneurs to think boldly and act compassionately.

Harper Reed's Success Story: Innovating at the Intersection of Technology

"Building your author brand on Amazon is about turning your profile into a beacon for your audience, where every element—from your bio to your book list—tells a compelling story that invites readers into your world." — HARPER REED, BRAND STRATEGIST

Harper Reed has built a career at the crossroads of technology, creativity, and social impact. A visionary technologist and entrepreneur, Reed's journey spans multiple domains, from revolutionizing e-commerce to transforming digital campaigning. Known for his unconventional approach, Reed has become a pioneer in blending community-driven innovation with cutting-edge technology. Whether leading product development at Threadless or building the groundbreaking digital infrastructure for Obama's 2012 re-election campaign, Reed's ability to connect technology with meaningful solutions continues to shape the tech landscape. His story is a remarkable example of how embracing curiosity and unconventional thinking can drive both business success and societal impact.

Early Life and Passion for Technology

Harper Reed was born with an inherent curiosity about technology, growing up in a household that encouraged creative exploration. From an early age, he was drawn to computers, spending hours experimenting with coding and software. Reed's interest in technology deepened during his years at Cornell College, where he pursued philosophy and computer science. His unconventional path of blending humanities and tech would later become a cornerstone of his approach to problem-solving and entrepreneurship.

Pioneering Innovation at Threadless

Reed's first major success came as the CTO of Threadless, a pioneering online T-shirt company that revolutionized e-commerce by crowdsourcing designs from its community. Reed spearheaded Threadless's technology platform, building systems that allowed customers to interact directly with the brand. Under his leadership, Threadless grew into a global community-driven business, earning recognition for its innovation in retail and digital interaction. Reed's success at

Threadless cemented his reputation as a tech-savvy leader who could seamlessly combine technology with creativity to drive growth.

Transforming Digital Campaigning with Obama for America

In 2012, Reed was recruited as the Chief Technology Officer for Obama for America, leading the technology team behind President Barack Obama's re-election campaign. Reed's team built one of the most sophisticated digital infrastructures ever used in a political campaign, leveraging data analytics, mobile apps, and social media to engage voters. His work helped revolutionize how technology was used in modern campaigning, setting new standards for political technology.

Entrepreneurial Ventures and Startup Success

After his work on the campaign, Reed channeled his passion for innovation into entrepreneurial ventures. He founded Modest; a mobile commerce startup designed to enhance the shopping experience. Modest was later acquired by PayPal, further solidifying Reed's reputation as a talented entrepreneur who could build scalable, impactful solutions.

Impact and Legacy in Technology and Civic Engagement

Harper Reed's career is marked by a blend of entrepreneurship, technological innovation, and social impact. Beyond his ventures, he continues to champion the use of technology to solve meaningful problems, working on projects in civic tech and open-source initiatives. Reed also shares his expertise through speaking engagements, where he advocates for diversity in tech and encourages entrepreneurs to embrace unconventional thinking.

Lessons from Harper Reed's Success

- **Innovation through Community**: At Threadless, Reed demonstrated the power of crowdsourcing and community-driven innovation.

- **Leveraging Data for Impact**: His work on Obama's re-election campaign showcased how technology and data can transform engagement and outreach.

- **Entrepreneurial Agility**: Reed's journey reflects the importance of being adaptable and taking risks, whether in startups or corporate environments.

From pioneering e-commerce innovations to transforming digital campaigning, Harper Reed's story is a testament to the power of combining creativity, technology, and social responsibility. His career continues to inspire those who seek to leverage technology not just for profit but for meaningful change.

———————

CHAPTER NINE

Email Marketing and
Website Success

In an era where digital communication is paramount, email marketing and a well-optimized website are vital components for any successful business strategy. These tools not only enhance customer engagement but also drive conversions and build long-lasting relationships. This chapter explores how to harness the power of email marketing alongside effective website strategies to create a seamless experience for your audience.

Bruce Schneier, a prominent security expert, highlights the importance of trust in digital communication, stating, "The future of privacy is about managing trust." Building trust through email marketing involves delivering value, ensuring privacy, and engaging your audience consistently. Marissa Mayer, former CEO of Yahoo, emphasizes that "people are more likely to engage with content that feels personal," underscoring the need for targeted messaging that resonates with individual preferences.

Joanna Penn, a successful author and entrepreneur, stresses the significance of integrating email marketing with content strategy. She notes, "Your email list is your most valuable asset," illustrating how nurturing this asset can lead to sustained growth. This chapter will guide you in creating compelling email campaigns that not only capture attention but also drive traffic to your website.

Sundar Pichai, CEO of Google, emphasizes the importance of user experience, stating, "A good user experience can mean the difference between success and failure." Your website must be intuitive, mobile-friendly, and visually appealing to keep visitors engaged. Scot Belsky, co-founder of Behance, adds that "creative work is driven by collaboration and community," highlighting the role of design in fostering an interactive online environment.

Analyzing performance is crucial for both email marketing and website success. Avinash Kaushik, a digital marketing expert, points out that "what gets measured gets improved." This chapter will cover essential analytics tools and metrics that help you assess the effectiveness of your email campaigns and website performance. Understanding these insights allows for data-driven decisions that enhance user experience and engagement.

Finally, Don Schultz, a pioneer in integrated marketing communications, reminds us that "the customer is at the center of everything." Successful email marketing and website strategies prioritize the customer journey, ensuring that every interaction adds value and fosters loyalty.

By the end of this chapter, you will be equipped with actionable strategies to leverage email marketing and optimize your website effectively. You'll learn how to create engaging content, build trust with your audience, and analyze performance metrics to drive continuous improvement. With the right tools and insights from industry leaders like Bruce Schneier, Marissa Mayer, and Joanna Penn, you'll transform your email and web presence into powerful assets that contribute to your overall business success.

Bruce Schneier's Success Story: The Security Guru Who Made Cryptography Cool

"Security is not a product, but a process. It's more than a feature, it's a necessity. Protecting your data is akin to protecting your reputation in the digital age." — BRUCE SCHNEIER, CYBERSECURITY EXPERT AND AUTHOR

Bruce Schneier is a renowned security technologist, author, and public speaker, often called the "security guru" for his contributions to cryptography, cybersecurity, and privacy. His career spans decades of innovation, advocacy, and thought leadership in the field of information security. Here's how Schneier built his reputation and became one of the most influential voices in cybersecurity.

Early Life and Education

Born in 1963, Schneier grew up with a keen interest in math and technology. He studied physics at the University of Rochester before shifting his focus to computer science. Later, he earned a Master's degree in Computer Science from American University in Washington, D.C. His passion for cryptography, combined with his analytical thinking, set him on a path to become one of the most respected experts in security.

The Birth of a Security Guru

Schneier's rise to prominence began with the publication of "Applied Cryptography" in 1994. The book became a foundational text in the field, making the once-obscure science of encryption accessible to a broader audience of engineers, developers, and policymakers. It provided not only technical explanations but also working code, giving people the tools to build secure systems.

"Applied Cryptography" quickly became a must-read for anyone working in the information security field, and Schneier's name became synonymous with practical, effective cryptographic solutions.

Founding Counterpane and Advancing Security Practices

In 1999, Schneier founded Counterpane Internet Security, one of the first companies to offer Managed Security Services (MSS). Counterpane helped organizations monitor their networks for threats and vulnerabilities—long before cybersecurity became the household term it is today. Schneier's approach revolutionized how companies thought about security, focusing on monitoring, prevention, and continuous improvement.

Counterpane was later acquired by BT (British Telecom), solidifying Schneier's reputation as a leading entrepreneur and visionary in the cybersecurity space.

Author, Advocate, and Thought Leader
Schneier's career extends far beyond business ventures. He has written over a dozen books, covering topics from encryption and network security to the intersection of technology and society. Some of his most notable works include:

- "Secrets and Lies: Digital Security in a Networked World" (2000) – Explores the realities of security threats in the age of interconnected systems.

- "Liars and Outliers" (2012) – Examines trust in human systems and the role of security.

- "Click Here to Kill Everybody: Security and Survival in a Hyper-Connected World" (2018) – Discusses the vulnerabilities of the Internet of Things (IoT) and the risks posed by an increasingly connected world.

Schneier also maintains an influential blog where he shares his insights on privacy, technology policy, and emerging threats in cybersecurity. His straightforward, no-nonsense approach to these issues has made him a go-to expert for journalists, academics, and policymakers.

Advocacy for Privacy and Ethical Technology
As technology continued to evolve, Schneier became increasingly concerned with issues of privacy and government surveillance. Following the revelations by Edward Snowden about mass surveillance programs in 2013, Schneier emerged as a key voice advocating for user privacy and responsible encryption. He has testified before Congress and advised government agencies on technology policy, urging for a balance between national security and individual freedoms.

Schneier has also criticized practices like backdoors in encryption systems, arguing that weakening encryption for the sake of government access undermines security for everyone.

Teaching and Ongoing Influence

Schneier is currently a lecturer and fellow at the Harvard Kennedy School, where he teaches about technology and public policy. His work focuses on the intersection of cybersecurity, privacy, and democracy, exploring how technological decisions impact society at large. His teaching helps bridge the gap between technical knowledge and policy-making, ensuring that future leaders understand the implications of technological decisions.

Legacy and Impact

Bruce Schneier's career is a testament to foresight, dedication, and clarity in a complex field. He transformed cryptography from an arcane science into a practical tool, helped businesses rethink how they approach cybersecurity, and continues to advocate for responsible technology use. Through his books, business ventures, and public speaking, Schneier has left an indelible mark on the way we think about digital security and privacy in the modern world.

Conclusion

Bruce Schneier's journey from cryptography enthusiast to global thought leader demonstrates the power of vision and expertise in solving real-world problems. Whether it's through his books, blogs, or teaching, Schneier has empowered individuals, companies, and governments to navigate the challenging landscape of digital security with insight and integrity.

———

Marissa Mayer's Success Story: Pioneering Success in Silicon Valley

"Creating the right site map and structure is like building a strong foundation for a skyscraper. It ensures that your site not only stands tall but is also seen from miles away." — MARISSA MAYER, FORMER CEO OF YAHOO

Marissa Mayer stands as one of the most influential figures in modern technology, known for her pioneering leadership and visionary contributions to the digital world. From her early days as the first female engineer at Google to her transformative tenure as CEO of Yahoo, Mayer's career exemplifies innovation, resilience, and an unyielding passion for design and user experience. Her ability to thrive in the male-dominated tech industry, coupled with her data-driven approach to product development, cemented her reputation as a trailblazer. Mayer's journey from shaping Google's most iconic products to spearheading Yahoo's evolution demonstrates the power of strategic leadership and creative problem-solving in an ever-changing landscape.

Early Life and Education
Born in Wausau, Wisconsin, in 1975, Marissa Mayer exhibited a love for mathematics and science from a young age. A high achiever in school, she initially aimed to become a doctor but later shifted her focus to computer science. Mayer attended Stanford University, where she earned both a Bachelor's degree in symbolic systems and a Master's degree in computer science, with a specialization in artificial intelligence. Her passion for technology and problem-solving set the foundation for her future career in Silicon Valley.

Rise to Prominence at Google
Mayer's big break came in 1999 when she became Google's 20th employee and first female engineer. At Google, Mayer played a pivotal role in shaping the company's most iconic products, such as Google Search, Gmail, and Google Maps. She also spearheaded the minimalist design of Google's search homepage, which became one of the brand's most recognizable features. Mayer's focus on simplicity, usability, and innovation earned her a reputation as one of the tech industry's leading product designers.

Over the course of 13 years, Mayer climbed the ranks at Google, eventually serving as Vice President of Search Products and User Experience. Her work was instrumental in growing Google's core search business into the behemoth it is today. Mayer's dedication to data-driven design and user-centric innovation became hallmarks of her leadership style.

Taking the Helm at Yahoo

In 2012, Mayer made headlines when she became the CEO of Yahoo, making her one of the most prominent female leaders in tech. Her mission was to revitalize the struggling company by fostering a culture of innovation and investing in mobile technologies. Under her leadership, Yahoo acquired Tumblr and several other tech startups to strengthen its mobile and social media presence.

Mayer also restructured Yahoo's product offerings, focusing on core services such as email, news, and finance. Though her tenure at Yahoo had mixed results, she was credited with modernizing the company's infrastructure and culture, positioning it for a lucrative sale to Verizon in 2017 for nearly $4.5 billion.

Life Beyond Yahoo and Entrepreneurial Ventures

After stepping down from Yahoo, Mayer co-founded Lumi Labs (later renamed Sunshine), a tech startup focusing on artificial intelligence to enhance everyday tasks like scheduling and organization. This venture demonstrated her ongoing commitment to innovation and problem-solving.

Legacy and Impact

Marissa Mayer's career reflects her ability to thrive in fast-moving, high-stakes environments. As a trailblazer for women in tech, she broke barriers, showing that leadership and innovation are not confined by gender. Mayer's influence can be seen not only in the products she shaped at Google but also in her leadership at Yahoo during a pivotal time in its history.

Her legacy serves as an inspiration for aspiring tech entrepreneurs, emphasizing the importance of perseverance, creativity, and the willingness to take risks—even in the face of uncertainty.

Joanna Penn's Success Story: From Burnout to Bestselling Author and Creative Entrepreneur

"Creating an author platform is vital for a new author's success, and creating a brand is the basis for the platform. You need to know what you are creating before you start!" — JOANNA PENN, AUTHOR AND PUBLISHING EXPERT

Joanna Penn is a powerhouse in the world of self-publishing, a bestselling author, and the voice behind the influential The Creative Penn podcast and blog. Her journey is one of reinvention, passion, and perseverance, as she transformed herself from a stressed corporate professional into a thriving creative entrepreneur. Here's how she made her mark and became a trusted mentor for writers and entrepreneurs around the globe.

Breaking Free from Corporate Burnout

Joanna Penn began her career in the corporate world, working as a consultant for large companies in the UK, New Zealand, and Australia. While her career was financially rewarding, it left her emotionally drained and creatively unfulfilled. Long hours, relentless travel, and work that didn't align with her passions led her to burnout.

It was during this period that she realized she needed a major life change. Penn knew she had a creative itch—she'd always loved writing—but had never thought of it as a possible career path. Determined to find a more fulfilling way of life, she decided to write a book. This would become the first step in a journey that would completely change her trajectory.

The Early Steps into Publishing

In 2007, Penn wrote her first non-fiction book, "How to Enjoy Your Job . . . Or Find a New One." But what she thought would be a straightforward process quickly became an eye-opener. At the time, traditional publishing seemed like the only way to publish a book, but the industry gatekeepers proved difficult to navigate. Unfazed, Penn turned to self-publishing—a move that would ultimately shape her future career.

Realizing how many other authors were facing similar challenges, she launched The Creative Penn blog in 2008 to share her experiences and insights about the self-publishing journey. The blog quickly gained traction as she demystified the process of publishing and empowered writers to take control of their careers.

Building The Creative Penn Brand

Over the next few years, Penn expanded her platform to become a trusted resource for aspiring and established authors alike. The Creative Penn blog and podcast became go-to sources for tips on writing, self-publishing, book marketing, and entrepreneurship. Penn's candid style, combined with her in-depth knowledge, resonated with authors looking for practical advice and inspiration.

Through her blog, Penn built a community of creatives who embraced the idea that authorship could be a viable business. She tackled topics beyond writing, discussing issues like mindset, productivity, and multiple streams of income, helping writers think like entrepreneurs.

Becoming a Bestselling Author

Penn didn't stop with non-fiction. As she immersed herself in the world of publishing, she discovered a love for writing fiction. Under the pen name J.F. Penn, she began publishing thrillers and supernatural suspense novels. Books like "Stone of Fire" and "Desecration" showcased her ability to blend storytelling with historical and religious themes.

Her novels found a dedicated readership, proving that self-published fiction could thrive outside the confines of traditional publishing. Penn's success as a fiction author not only fueled her creative drive but also gave her firsthand insights into the challenges and rewards of being a full-time writer.

Multiple Streams of Income and Entrepreneurial Success

Joanna Penn is a firm believer in creating multiple income streams—a principle she has followed throughout her career. Beyond book royalties, she has built her business through courses, public speaking, affiliate marketing, coaching, and consulting. Her books on writing and publishing, such as "How to Market a Book" and "Successful Self-Publishing," are widely regarded as must-reads for indie authors.

Penn emphasizes the importance of creative independence and long-term thinking. She encourages writers to think beyond a single book, advising them to focus on building a sustainable creative career.

Navigating the Changing Landscape of Publishing

Penn has also become an advocate for embracing technology in the writing world. She discusses emerging trends like AI-assisted writing, audiobooks, and direct-to-reader platforms, helping authors stay ahead in a constantly evolving industry. Her openness to change and willingness to experiment with new ideas set her apart as a thought leader in self-publishing.

Even during challenging times—like the 2020 pandemic—Penn's message to creatives remained consistent: adapt, evolve, and keep creating.

Legacy and Ongoing Influence

Today, Joanna Penn is one of the most respected figures in the self-publishing industry. Through The Creative Penn, her books, courses, and podcast, she has empowered thousands of writers to take charge of their creative journeys. Her practical advice, positivity, and forward-thinking approach continue to inspire a new generation of authors to embrace independent publishing as a path to success.

Conclusion: A Creative Life Well Lived

Joanna Penn's story is a testament to the power of reinvention, creativity, and resilience. From corporate burnout to entrepreneurial success, she has built a career that aligns with her passions and values. Her journey exemplifies how anyone can create a life of purpose and freedom by pursuing what they love—and by sharing their knowledge to uplift others along the way.

———

Sundar Pichai's Success Story: From Humble Beginnings to Leading Google and Alphabet

"AI will transform every industry, but its greatest impact will be helping us manage our most valuable resource: time." — SUNDAR PICHAI, CEO OF GOOGLE

"By harnessing AI and AR, we're not just advertising books; we're creating immersive experiences that captivate and engage readers like never before." — SUNDAR PICHAI, CEO OF ALPHABET INC. AND GOOGLE

"Long-term growth requires more than initial success; it demands persistent innovation and strategic planning to adapt and thrive in an evolving market." — SUNDAR PICHAI, CEO OF ALPHABET INC. AND GOOGLE

"In the digital age, vigilance in protecting your trademark is not optional—it's critical. Treat your online brand presence as you would your most valuable asset, because in many ways, it is." — SUNDAR PICHAI, CEO OF GOOGLE

"Digital piracy isn't just a nuisance; it's a direct challenge to intellectual property rights and a threat to creators everywhere. We must adapt and enforce with vigilance to protect our works in the digital age."
— SUNDAR PICHAI, CEO OF GOOGLE

Sundar Pichai's journey from India to the helm of Google and Alphabet is a remarkable story of determination, hard work, and visionary leadership. Known for his humble demeanor and strategic insight, Pichai's rise to success demonstrates how curiosity, adaptability, and empathy can shape a leader's path and drive innovation at a global scale.

Early Life and Education: A Childhood Rooted in Learning
Sundar Pichai was born on June 10, 1972, in Madurai, Tamil Nadu, India, and grew up in Chennai. Raised in a middle-class family, Pichai lived in a modest two-room apartment with his parents and younger brother. His father worked as an electrical engineer at a British conglomerate, and his mother was a stenographer. Despite their limited resources, Pichai's parents valued education and curiosity, encouraging him to explore science and technology from a young age.

Pichai displayed exceptional memory and problem-solving skills early on, impressing his teachers with his ability to recall phone numbers and facts effortlessly. His interest in technology began when his family acquired a rotary phone—a device that fascinated him and sparked his lifelong passion for communication and innovation.

He earned a degree in Metallurgical Engineering from the Indian Institute of Technology (IIT) Kharagpur, one of the most prestigious engineering institutions in India. Recognizing his potential, Pichai's professors encouraged him to pursue higher studies abroad.

Pursuing Higher Education and Discovering Silicon Valley
After graduating from IIT, Pichai earned a scholarship to Stanford University, where he pursued a master's degree in Material Sciences and Engineering. Adjusting to life in the U.S. was challenging—Pichai arrived with limited financial resources and relied on the support of his family back in India. Despite

the obstacles, Pichai excelled academically and quickly immersed himself in the culture of Silicon Valley.

After completing his master's, Pichai pursued an MBA from the Wharton School of the University of Pennsylvania, where he was named a Siebel Scholar and Palmer Scholar for his academic achievements. His combination of technical expertise and business acumen positioned him perfectly for the emerging tech boom in the early 2000s.

Joining Google: The Early Years

Pichai joined Google in 2004 as Vice President of Product Management, initially working on the Google Toolbar—a browser extension that allowed users to access Google search from Internet Explorer and other browsers. At the time, Google was focused on expanding its search capabilities, and the toolbar played a critical role in driving early traffic and adoption.

Pichai's ability to simplify complex problems, collaborate effectively, and lead teams soon became evident. His success with the Google Toolbar earned him a key role in developing Google Chrome, the company's web browser. Pichai's team launched Google Chrome in 2008, despite skepticism about entering a market dominated by Internet Explorer and Firefox.

Chrome's success was phenomenal—within a few years, it became the world's most popular browser, known for its speed, simplicity, and user experience. Pichai's leadership in Chrome's development showcased his strategic foresight and ability to anticipate user needs, helping Google solidify its dominance on the web.

Climbing the Ranks: From Products to Platforms

Following the success of Chrome, Pichai took on increasingly larger responsibilities at Google. He led the development of critical products such as Google Drive, Gmail, and Google Maps, which became integral to Google's ecosystem.

Pichai's reputation as a collaborative and thoughtful leader continued to grow. In 2013, he took over management of Android, the world's largest mobile operating system, following the departure of its founder, Andy Rubin. Under Pichai's guidance, Android's adoption surged, and it became the foundation of Google's mobile strategy, powering billions of smartphones globally.

Pichai's focus on user-centric innovation and his ability to manage large teams across multiple products positioned him as one of Google's top executives. His leadership style, characterized by humility, empathy, and consensus-building, earned him the trust of both his colleagues and the company's founders, Larry Page and Sergey Brin.

Becoming CEO: Leading Google and Alphabet

In 2015, Google underwent a major restructuring, creating a parent company called Alphabet to oversee its various businesses, including Google, Waymo, DeepMind, and Verily. As part of this transition, Pichai was named CEO of Google, giving him responsibility for Google's core products and services, including search, ads, and cloud computing.

Pichai's leadership proved instrumental in expanding Google's reach while maintaining its culture of innovation. He focused on AI-driven advancements and led the development of Google Assistant, Google Photos, and improvements to Google Search powered by machine learning. His steady leadership during times of rapid change helped Google thrive in an increasingly competitive landscape.

In 2019, Pichai's role expanded further when Larry Page and Sergey Brin stepped down from their day-to-day roles, making Pichai the CEO of Alphabet as well. Now overseeing one of the world's largest and most influential technology companies, Pichai continues to drive Google's evolution into areas like artificial intelligence, cloud computing, and sustainability.

Navigating Challenges and Controversies

Pichai's tenure as CEO has not been without challenges. Google has faced scrutiny over privacy concerns, antitrust investigations, and employee protests related to workplace policies. Pichai has worked to address these issues through greater transparency and organizational reforms, emphasizing ethical practices in AI development and diversity and inclusion initiatives.

Despite external pressures, Pichai remains focused on long-term innovation and responsible leadership. His calm, methodical approach has helped guide Alphabet through turbulent periods, earning him respect as a steady and thoughtful leader in the tech industry.

Leadership Philosophy: Humility, Innovation, and Empathy

Pichai's leadership style is often described as humble and approachable. Unlike many high-profile CEOs, Pichai avoids the spotlight, preferring to empower his teams and focus on collaborative problem-solving. He believes in listening to different perspectives and building consensus, fostering an environment where innovation can thrive.

Pichai is also known for emphasizing the importance of education and lifelong learning. In interviews, he often speaks about the transformative power of technology and education, and he has advocated for policies that promote digital literacy and access to technology globally.

Key Lessons from Sundar Pichai's Success

1. **Stay Curious and Adaptable:** Pichai's ability to pivot from engineering to product management exemplifies the importance of adaptability.

2. **Lead with Empathy:** Pichai's humble leadership style fosters collaboration and trust among his teams.

3. **Focus on User Needs:** His success with Chrome and Android demonstrates the value of understanding and anticipating user behavior.

4. **Manage through Change:** Pichai's steady leadership during Google's restructuring and challenges showcases the importance of resilience.

5. **Empower Others:** Pichai's preference for empowering his teams reflects the belief that great leaders create opportunities for others to succeed.

Conclusion: A Visionary Leader for the Future

Sundar Pichai's journey from Chennai to Silicon Valley is a powerful example of how education, perseverance, and humility can unlock extraordinary opportunities. Through his work at Google and Alphabet, Pichai has helped shape the future of technology, driving AI-powered innovation and digital transformation across industries.

As he continues to lead one of the world's most influential companies, Pichai's legacy will be defined not just by technological breakthroughs but also by his commitment to responsible leadership and global impact. His story serves as an inspiration for aspiring leaders worldwide, proving that success is not just about ambition—it's about leading with purpose, empathy, and a passion for making the world better.

Scott Belsky's Success Story: Building Creative Empires from Scratch

"Mastering Amazon is not just about selling books; it's about understanding a vast ecosystem and using it to strategically position your work where eyes are most likely to land." — SCOTT BELSKY, AUTHOR AND ENTREPRENEUR

"Time management is not just about finding more hours in the day; it's about creating a workflow that allows you to be more creative, effective, and less stressed." — SCOTT BELSKY, ENTREPRENEUR AND AUTHOR

Scott Belsky is a visionary entrepreneur, author, and creative advocate known for revolutionizing the way artists and innovators share their work. As the co-founder of Behance, the largest online platform for creative portfolios, Belsky bridged the gap between inspiration and organization for millions of creatives worldwide. His work extends beyond entrepreneurship; Belsky has become a thought leader, authoring influential books like *"Making Ideas Happen"* and *"The Messy Middle,"* which offer insight into the complexities of turning ideas into reality. From leading product development at Adobe to investing in top startups like Pinterest and Uber, Belsky's career exemplifies the power of persistence, creativity, and strategic thinking. His journey is an inspiring blueprint for those who aspire to blend creativity with business acumen and make a lasting impact on the world.

Early Life and Education

Scott Belsky's journey to becoming a leading figure in the creative world began with a fascination for both business and design. Raised in Massachusetts, Belsky had a natural curiosity about entrepreneurship and innovation. He earned a degree from Cornell University and later pursued an MBA at Harvard Business School, where he began to explore the intersection of creativity and business strategy. Belsky's education laid the foundation for his future career, equipping him with the skills and insights needed to build a bridge between creatives and structured business processes.

The Birth of Behance

While working as a consultant, Belsky realized that many creative professionals struggled with organization and project management, often sacrificing productivity for inspiration. Seeing a gap in the market, he co-founded Behance in 2006, a platform that would become the largest online creative network in the world. His goal was simple but profound: to help creatives showcase their portfolios and find new opportunities while bringing more efficiency to their workflows.

Behance's success didn't come easily. Belsky and his team operated out of a small New York City apartment, bootstrapping the business and working tirelessly to gain traction. Despite the challenges, Belsky's belief in the platform's potential never wavered. His persistence paid off, as Behance began to attract attention from creatives and brands alike, becoming an indispensable hub for the global design community.

Acquisition by Adobe and New Ventures

In 2012, Adobe acquired Behance for $150 million, solidifying the platform's role as the go-to resource for creative professionals. Belsky stayed on as Adobe's Chief Product Officer, where he played a pivotal role in transforming the company's product strategy. He led the development of Adobe's Creative Cloud, a subscription-based service that revolutionized how creatives accessed tools and software.

After spending several years at Adobe, Belsky transitioned to new ventures. He co-founded and became an investor in several companies, including Pinterest, Uber, and Warby Parker. Through his involvement in these startups, Belsky gained a reputation as a forward-thinking advisor who could guide businesses toward sustainable success.

Author, Speaker, and Advocate for Creativity

Beyond entrepreneurship, Belsky became a bestselling author, penning books like "Making Ideas Happen" and "The Messy Middle," which offer practical advice on turning creative ideas into reality. His writing reflects his deep understanding of the creative process, particularly the challenges faced in navigating uncertainty and overcoming obstacles along the way.

Belsky is also a sought-after speaker and thought leader, regularly sharing insights on how creativity and business can coexist. He emphasizes the importance of perseverance, adaptability, and discipline—traits that he believes are essential for any creative professional aiming for long-term success.

Legacy and Impact

Scott Belsky's journey from entrepreneur to industry leader illustrates the power of vision, persistence, and a commitment to empowering creatives. His work with Behance revolutionized how artists, designers, and innovators connect with opportunities, leaving an indelible mark on the creative industry. Through his roles at Adobe, his investments, and his books, Belsky continues to inspire creatives to push boundaries and turn their ideas into meaningful ventures.

Belsky's story is a testament to the fact that success often lies at the crossroads of creativity and business acumen. His ability to blend these two worlds has not only changed the lives of countless creatives but also reshaped the way businesses approach innovation and design.

Avinash Kaushik's Success Story: Pioneering the World of Digital Analytics

"Effective monitoring in digital marketing doesn't just measure success—it anticipates it, transforming data into a strategic compass that guides every decision towards triumph." — AVINASH KAUSHIK, DIGITAL MARKETING EVANGELIST

Avinash Kaushik, a trailblazer in the realm of digital analytics, has redefined how businesses approach data-driven strategies. From his roots in India to becoming one of the most influential voices in the global marketing community, Kaushik's journey is one of passion, persistence, and innovation. His ability to transform complex data into actionable insights has empowered organizations to make smarter decisions and prioritize meaningful customer interactions. As an author, speaker, and Google's Digital Marketing Evangelist, Kaushik's influence extends far beyond corporate walls, inspiring countless marketers to embrace analytics as a powerful tool for growth and transformation. His story is a testament to how curiosity and a passion for learning can shape industries and spark lasting change.

Early Life and Career Beginnings

Avinash Kaushik, born in India, developed an early fascination with problem-solving and data. After completing his engineering degree, Kaushik moved to the United States to pursue further education, earning an MBA. His curiosity about technology and business soon led him to the world of digital marketing and analytics—a field where data-driven insights were just starting to gain relevance.

Breaking into Digital Analytics

Kaushik's big break came when he joined Intuit, where he took on the challenge of transforming the company's web analytics strategy. His innovative approach to measuring online performance emphasized actionable insights over raw data, marking him as a forward thinker in the industry. During this time, Kaushik became an advocate for simplicity in analytics—transforming complex data into meaningful business outcomes.

Google and Thought Leadership

Kaushik's unique perspective on analytics didn't go unnoticed. In 2008, he was hired by Google, where he became the Digital Marketing Evangelist. In this role, he developed strategies to educate businesses on how to use analytics effectively, helping organizations understand the power of data to drive growth and improve customer experiences. His work with Google elevated Kaushik into a global thought leader, making him a sought-after speaker at conferences and events.

Writing and Influencing the Industry

Kaushik's influence extends beyond his corporate roles. He authored two best-selling books, *Web Analytics: An Hour a Day* and *Web Analytics 2.0*, both of which became essential reading for marketers and data professionals. His books demystified web analytics, providing readers with a roadmap to use data creatively and effectively in business. Additionally, his popular blog, *Occam's Razor*, became a go-to resource for those looking to stay ahead in the evolving world of digital analytics.

Impact on the Digital Marketing Community

Avinash Kaushik's emphasis on focusing on key performance indicators (KPIs) rather than vanity metrics reshaped the way businesses think about success online. He advocates for "care over clicks," encouraging companies to prioritize customer experience and meaningful interactions over simple traffic numbers. Kaushik's teachings have empowered countless businesses to make smarter decisions by leveraging data, fundamentally changing the landscape of digital marketing.

Legacy and Ongoing Influence

Today, Avinash Kaushik continues to inspire through his public speaking, consulting, and thought leadership. His work has bridged the gap between technology, marketing, and business, making data accessible and actionable for organizations of all sizes. Kaushik's story demonstrates that success in a digital world comes not from just collecting data but from using it to tell stories, solve problems, and create meaningful change. His journey serves as a reminder that with passion, curiosity, and innovation, anyone can leave a lasting impact in the world of business analytics.

Don Schultz's Success Story: The Father of Integrated Marketing Communications

"Social media creates communities, not markets." — DON SCHULTZ, MARKETING PIONEER AND PROFESSOR

Don Schultz revolutionized the world of marketing with his groundbreaking concept of Integrated Marketing Communications (IMC). A visionary thinker, Schultz reshaped how businesses approach customer engagement by promoting the idea that all communication efforts—whether advertising, sales, or public relations—should align seamlessly to deliver a unified message. With an extensive career in both academia and consulting, Schultz's influence has extended across industries and continents. His work emphasized the importance of a customer-centric strategy, proving that consistent, cohesive communication is key to building lasting relationships in a fragmented media landscape. His legacy endures in the practices of modern marketers, many of whom still rely on his pioneering principles to navigate the complexities of today's multichannel world.

Early Life and Education

Don Schultz, known as the father of Integrated Marketing Communications (IMC), had an enduring passion for communication, strategy, and business. Born and raised in the Midwest, Schultz pursued his undergraduate degree at the University of Oklahoma, where he developed a foundational understanding of advertising. His early experiences in advertising sparked his interest in how different messages influence consumer behavior. He later completed a master's degree in marketing and earned a Ph.D. in mass communications, paving the way for a groundbreaking career in academia and consulting.

Career Beginnings and the Birth of IMC

Schultz's career began in traditional advertising agencies, where he spent several years working with major brands and businesses. However, it was during his time in the corporate world that Schultz identified a significant gap in the marketing landscape. Companies were using multiple channels to promote their products— advertising, sales promotions, public relations—but the messages were often inconsistent and fragmented. Schultz saw the need for a more cohesive approach that aligned all communication efforts toward a unified strategy.

In the late 1980s, Schultz joined the faculty at Northwestern University's Medill School of Journalism, where he would lay the foundation for what would become his life's work: Integrated Marketing Communications. His approach emphasized the importance of coordinating various marketing tools and channels—such as advertising, direct marketing, public relations, and sales efforts—into a seamless communication strategy centered around the customer.

Pioneering the IMC Movement

In 1993, Schultz co-authored *Integrated Marketing Communications: Pulling it Together & Making it Work*, which quickly became the definitive textbook for students and marketers alike. The book introduced IMC as a groundbreaking framework that placed the customer at the center of all communication strategies, marking a departure from the traditional, product-focused marketing methods. His insights revolutionized how brands approached marketing, shifting the focus toward building long-term customer relationships through consistent messaging.

IMC became a fundamental concept embraced by both academia and the corporate world. Schultz's work inspired marketers to break down silos within their organizations, aligning advertising, sales, and PR efforts to deliver a unified brand experience. His influence extended globally, with universities adopting his teachings and multinational corporations integrating his principles into their campaigns.

Legacy and Continued Impact

Throughout his career, Schultz authored more than 13 books and countless research papers, further refining the principles of IMC. He also consulted for leading companies, including Coca-Cola, McDonald's, and Procter & Gamble, helping them implement IMC strategies that drove growth and customer loyalty. His ability to blend academic theory with practical business insights made him a sought-after speaker at conferences worldwide.

Even after his retirement from teaching, Schultz remained an active voice in the marketing community, contributing thought leadership on emerging trends in digital media and data-driven marketing. His work has left a lasting legacy, shaping how marketers approach communication in an increasingly complex, multichannel world.

Lessons from Don Schultz's Success

- **Customer-Centric Strategy:** Schultz emphasized the importance of focusing on the customer experience across all communication channels.

- **Unified Communication:** He demonstrated how aligning messages across departments could amplify a brand's impact and foster stronger customer relationships.

- **Adaptability:** Schultz's work evolved with changing technology, proving the enduring relevance of IMC in the digital age.

- **Educational Influence:** His commitment to teaching and mentoring has empowered countless students and professionals to think more strategically about marketing.

Conclusion: A Visionary in Marketing Strategy

Don Schultz's legacy as the pioneer of Integrated Marketing Communications is a testament to his visionary thinking and passion for strategic marketing. His contributions transformed how businesses communicate, helping organizations foster meaningful connections with customers through consistent, cohesive messaging. Schultz's work continues to influence marketers, educators, and business leaders, proving that a customer-focused, integrated approach to communication is essential in today's competitive landscape.

CHAPTER TEN

Business Expansion and Innovation

In a rapidly evolving market, business expansion and innovation are essential for sustained growth. Successful entrepreneurs understand that expansion is not just about increasing size but about strategically identifying opportunities to deliver greater value, reach new markets, and innovate beyond existing products and services. This chapter explores how to plan for business growth while fostering a culture of innovation that keeps a company relevant and adaptable in an ever-changing world.

Satya Nadella, CEO of Microsoft, emphasizes that "technology is the linchpin of modern business strategy, not merely supporting operations but propelling them into new frontiers." Expanding a business requires strategic foresight—knowing not only where to grow but also how to maintain alignment with the company's values and vision. Whether it's expanding to new locations or scaling operations digitally, this chapter emphasizes the importance of deliberate, value-driven growth.

However, expansion without innovation can lead to stagnation. Elon Musk exemplifies this principle by continually pushing the boundaries of technology and innovation with companies like Tesla and SpaceX, demonstrating that successful leaders embrace change and leverage innovation to unlock growth potential. Business expansion often involves risk, and managing this risk effectively is critical. Howard Schultz, former CEO of Starbucks, advises that "risk is the price you pay for opportunity," highlighting the importance of evaluating expansion opportunities wisely.

This chapter provides tools to assess expansion options—whether through entering new markets, creating joint ventures, or acquiring other businesses. With clear planning and calculated risk management, companies can grow with confidence while protecting their core operations. Charles Duhigg, author of *The Power of Habit*, underscores the significance of refining internal processes to maintain efficiency, reminding us that "organizations grow through the habits they cultivate."

Entering new markets—whether regional or global—demands adaptability and local insight. Sam Walton, founder of Walmart, noted, "The secret to success is to be yourself. You can't change the world if you don't know who you are." Understanding cultural differences, legal requirements, and market trends is essential for smooth transitions and sustainable operations.

At the heart of any successful expansion is a mindset of continuous learning and reinvention. Jack Ma, co-founder of Alibaba, highlights the importance of flexibility, stating, "In the face of change, you have to be willing to adapt and grow." Innovation means being willing to change course when necessary, allowing businesses to evolve in response to market dynamics.

Collaboration plays a key role in business expansion. Howard Schultz emphasizes that "great things in business are never done by one person; they're done by a team of people." Partnering with the right individuals, companies, or organizations can open doors to new markets, generate fresh ideas, and create mutually beneficial opportunities that drive innovation.

In this chapter, you'll discover strategies for evaluating expansion opportunities, managing growth, and fostering innovation at every level of your business.

Drawing insights from leaders like Satya Nadella, Jack Ma, and Elon Musk, this chapter equips you with the tools to scale your business thoughtfully and sustainably. Whether you're considering entering new markets or developing groundbreaking solutions, mastering expansion and innovation will position your business for continued success in today's dynamic marketplace.

Satya Nadella's Success Story: The Visionary Leader Behind Microsoft's Renaissance

"Embracing change within your business structure isn't just about survival; it's about seizing opportunities to innovate and lead in your industry."
— SATYA NADELLA, CEO OF MICROSOFT

"Registering a trademark is like planting a flag in your market space—it declares your presence and protects your territory." — SATYA NADELLA, CEO OF MICROSOFT

"Technology is the linchpin of modern business strategy, not merely supporting operations but propelling them into new frontiers of efficiency and innovation." — SATYA NADELLA, CEO of Microsoft

"Collaboration is the secret ingredient that amplifies success. When we combine our strengths, we don't just add value—we multiply it."
— SATYA NADELLA, CEO OF MICROSOFT

Satya Nadella's journey from a curious young engineer in India to the transformational CEO of Microsoft is a story of innovation, resilience, and empathetic leadership. Born with a passion for technology and a hunger for learning, Nadella's career path took him across continents and industries, shaping him into a leader ready to guide one of the world's largest tech companies through a challenging era. With a strategic focus on cloud computing, AI, and cultural transformation, Nadella revitalized Microsoft, positioning it as a leader in the modern tech landscape. His leadership reflects a balance of technical expertise and emotional intelligence, creating a powerful legacy of growth and impact.

Early Life and Education

Satya Nadella was born on August 19, 1967, in Hyderabad, India, into a middle-class family with strong academic roots. His father, a civil servant, and his mother, a Sanskrit professor, instilled in him the values of curiosity and continuous learning. From an early age, Nadella was fascinated with technology, a passion that would become the foundation for his future career. After earning a Bachelor's degree in Electrical Engineering from the Manipal Institute of Technology, he pursued higher education abroad. He completed his Master's in Computer Science at the University of Wisconsin-Milwaukee and later earned an MBA from the University of Chicago Booth School of Business.

Joining Microsoft: The Early Years

Nadella joined Microsoft in 1992, at a time when the tech giant was dominating the software industry. He started in engineering roles, working on Windows NT, a foundational operating system. His early contributions helped him gain a reputation as a problem-solver with deep technical expertise and an aptitude for leadership. Over the years, he steadily rose through the ranks by taking on key roles, including Vice President of Microsoft Business Solutions and leadership in Microsoft's Server & Tools division.

Transforming Microsoft's Cloud Strategy

One of Nadella's most notable achievements before becoming CEO was his work in cloud computing. As the leader of Microsoft's Cloud and Enterprise Group, Nadella spearheaded the company's transition to the cloud by driving the development and growth of Azure, Microsoft's cloud platform. Under his leadership, Azure grew to become a powerful competitor to Amazon Web Services (AWS), positioning Microsoft as a leader in cloud technology. This shift marked a pivotal moment, transforming Microsoft's business model from primarily software-based to cloud-first, ensuring its relevance in a rapidly changing tech landscape.

Becoming Microsoft's CEO

In 2014, Nadella succeeded Steve Ballmer as Microsoft's CEO. At the time, the company was facing challenges, with stagnant growth and an uncertain future in mobile and cloud computing. Nadella brought a fresh vision that emphasized collaboration, innovation, and openness. He shifted the company's focus from

"Windows-first" to "cloud-first and mobile-first," embracing partnerships with competitors like Linux, Salesforce, and even Google. His leadership style, marked by empathy and inclusiveness, also fostered a new cultural transformation within Microsoft, moving it toward a growth mindset and more agile ways of working.

Key Successes and Innovations

Under Nadella's leadership, Microsoft's stock value soared, and the company once again became one of the most valuable in the world. He oversaw the successful acquisition of LinkedIn, expanded Azure's capabilities, and enhanced Microsoft's portfolio with products like Microsoft Teams and Office 365. His approach to innovation has been future-focused, driving investments in artificial intelligence, mixed reality, and quantum computing.

Nadella also emphasized corporate responsibility, advocating for sustainability and accessibility. His leadership during the COVID-19 pandemic was widely praised, as Microsoft's remote working tools like Teams became essential in supporting businesses, schools, and organizations worldwide.

Personal Philosophy and Legacy

Nadella's personal philosophy is rooted in continuous learning and empathy. His book, *"Hit Refresh,"* reflects his belief in the power of renewal—both personal and professional. He credits much of his personal growth to his family, particularly his son, Zain, who had special needs. Nadella often speaks about the impact Zain's challenges had on his leadership style, teaching him patience, empathy, and resilience.

The Impact of Satya Nadella

Satya Nadella's tenure at Microsoft is widely regarded as one of the most successful corporate turnarounds in modern history. His leadership not only revitalized the company but also redefined what it means to lead with empathy and vision. Through bold decision-making, strategic innovation, and a relentless focus on culture, Nadella ensured Microsoft's continued success in a rapidly evolving tech landscape, leaving an indelible mark on both the company and the industry at large.

———————

Jack Ma's Success Story: From Rejection to Global Success

"Looking ahead, the frontiers of entrepreneurship will be driven by a blend of artificial intelligence, sustainability, and hyper-connectivity, challenging today's entrepreneurs to think globally and act ethically."
— JACK MA, FOUNDER OF ALIBABA GROUP

"Going global with your book is not just about selling in new markets; it's about understanding and connecting with readers across cultures. It's a powerful way to expand your impact and influence on a worldwide stage."
— JACK MA, FOUNDER OF ALIBABA GROUP

"Artificial Intelligence is revolutionizing trademark management by automating complex processes, enhancing accuracy, and providing predictive insights that allow for proactive brand protection strategies." — JACK MA, FOUNDER OF ALIBABA GROUP

Jack Ma's journey is one of the most inspiring entrepreneurial success stories of the modern era. From humble beginnings in Hangzhou, China, to building a multi-billion-dollar global tech empire, Ma's rise to fame and fortune was anything but smooth. Rejected by schools, denied jobs, and underestimated by his peers, he demonstrated remarkable resilience and vision. Ma's creation of Alibaba, a company that revolutionized e-commerce, not only transformed the digital landscape in China but also impacted global trade. Known for his charismatic leadership and optimistic philosophy, Ma's story exemplifies how determination, creativity, and the power to embrace failure can lead to extraordinary success. His legacy goes beyond business, influencing leadership, innovation, and philanthropy worldwide.

Humble Beginnings

Jack Ma was born in 1964 in Hangzhou, China, at a time when opportunities were scarce. Coming from modest roots, he encountered rejection repeatedly, whether in school admissions or job applications, even being turned down for a position at KFC. However, his early struggles cultivated in him a relentless drive to prove himself and make a difference.

Discovering the Internet

During a trip to the United States in 1995, Ma was introduced to the internet for the first time. Fascinated by its potential, he noticed that China lacked any significant online presence. Sensing an opportunity, he launched his first internet venture, a website called "China Pages," to promote Chinese companies globally. Though the project faced challenges, it ignited Ma's passion for entrepreneurship and the power of digital commerce.

Founding Alibaba

In 1999, with just $60,000 pooled from friends, Ma founded Alibaba from his apartment in Hangzhou. The platform aimed to connect small Chinese manufacturers with international buyers, providing a digital marketplace that could empower businesses. Although he lacked technical skills, Ma's vision and leadership united a group of talented individuals to bring Alibaba to life. The company endured early financial struggles and skepticism from competitors, but Ma's belief in the potential of e-commerce kept the team focused.

Overcoming Challenges and Scaling Globally

The early days of Alibaba were challenging, with fierce competition and doubts about profitability. However, Ma remained determined, focusing on long-term growth over short-term profits. His ability to rally his team and sustain their motivation played a pivotal role in navigating these hurdles. The company achieved a breakthrough when it secured major rounds of investment from SoftBank and Yahoo, enabling it to scale operations.

Leadership Philosophy and Public Persona

Jack Ma's leadership style was unconventional, emphasizing perseverance, optimism, and adaptability. He believed in empowering his employees with a strong sense of mission and purpose, fostering a unique culture within Alibaba. Ma became known for his charisma, humor, and inspirational public speeches, often sharing personal stories of failure and resilience.

IPO and Global Influence

In 2014, Alibaba's initial public offering (IPO) on the New York Stock Exchange became the largest in history, raising $25 billion and cementing Ma's place on the global business stage. Under his guidance, Alibaba expanded into new sectors such as fintech with Alipay, logistics with Cainiao, and cloud computing through Alibaba Cloud, transforming it into a global tech conglomerate.

Retirement and Legacy

In 2019, Ma stepped down as chairman of Alibaba to focus on philanthropy, particularly in education and environmental sustainability. His journey from a struggling teacher to a globally recognized entrepreneur has inspired millions, proving that perseverance, vision, and the willingness to embrace change can turn even the most unlikely dreams into reality. Today, Jack Ma's story remains a testament to the power of resilience, innovation, and the belief that "never give up" can unlock incredible possibilities.

———————

Howard Schultz's Success Story: Brewing Success Through Vision and Resilience

"Effective branding is a journey, not a destination. It's about charting a course that is uniquely yours and navigating it with the precision of a seasoned captain, ready to adjust sails as the market winds change."
— HOWARD SCHULTZ, Former CEO of Starbucks

"Building a brand that crosses international borders isn't just about visibility, it's about strategic adaptation. You must tailor your trademarks to resonate globally while respecting local nuances." — HOWARD SCHULTZ, FORMER CEO OF STARBUCKS

"True leadership is rooted in ethical practices that foster trust and respect. It's about leading by example and maintaining integrity in every decision and action." — HOWARD SCHULTZ, FORMER CEO AND CHAIRMAN OF STARBUCKS

"Expanding nationally requires understanding that what works in one state may not work in another. Adaptability and local insight are keys to successful multi-state expansion." — HOWARD SCHULTZ, FORMER CEO OF STARBUCKS

Howard Schultz's journey from humble beginnings in a Brooklyn housing project to building one of the most iconic brands in the world is a story of vision, persistence, and purpose. Inspired by his father's struggles in low-wage jobs, Schultz developed a deep commitment to building a business that prioritized both people and profits. His discovery of Starbucks and his bold vision to transform it from a coffee bean supplier into a global café experience revolutionized how the world consumes coffee. Through a focus on quality, community, and employee well-being, Schultz not only grew Starbucks into a global powerhouse but also redefined business leadership by integrating social responsibility. His life's work reflects a deep belief that businesses can do well by doing good, leaving a lasting legacy that transcends the coffee cup.

Humble Beginnings and Early Influences

Howard Schultz grew up in a Brooklyn housing project, where financial hardship shaped his desire to achieve more for himself and his family. Watching his father struggle through various low-paying jobs without health benefits deeply influenced Schultz's commitment to create a company that would treat employees with dignity and respect. Driven by ambition, Schultz became the first in his family to attend college, earning a degree from Northern Michigan University. His early career began in sales at Xerox, but his true passion ignited when he discovered a small coffee company named Starbucks in 1981.

The Starbucks Vision Takes Root

Schultz joined Starbucks as Director of Retail Operations and Marketing in 1982. While on a business trip to Milan, Italy, he became captivated by the Italian coffee culture—where cafés were not just places to drink coffee but hubs of community connection. Schultz envisioned recreating this atmosphere back in the United States, transforming Starbucks from a mere coffee bean supplier into a social experience centered around espresso beverages.

Challenges, Setbacks, and Determined Growth

Initially, Schultz's vision met resistance from the original Starbucks founders, who were hesitant to shift the company's focus. Undeterred, Schultz left Starbucks in 1985 and launched his own coffeehouse, Il Giornale, successfully replicating the Italian-style café experience. In 1987, Schultz acquired Starbucks, merging it with Il Giornale, and began expanding the brand nationwide. However, growth didn't come easily. Schultz faced skepticism from investors and battled operational challenges as he sought to differentiate Starbucks from other coffee chains.

A Global Coffee Empire Emerges

Schultz's leadership and relentless pursuit of excellence turned Starbucks into a global phenomenon. By focusing on product quality, customer experience, and employee well-being—offering benefits like stock options and health care even to part-time workers—he fostered loyalty both among customers and staff. Under Schultz's leadership, Starbucks expanded beyond coffee, introducing lifestyle products and global initiatives. His emphasis on innovation led to the launch of Starbucks' mobile app, drive-through stores, and new product offerings, ensuring the company stayed ahead in a competitive market.

Legacy and Social Impact

Howard Schultz's journey didn't stop with business success. He used Starbucks as a platform to promote social change, supporting initiatives in education, veterans' employment, and racial equity. After retiring as CEO in 2018, Schultz considered a foray into politics, seeking to inspire others with the belief that business leaders can contribute to societal change. His life is a testament to the power of vision, empathy, and resilience in transforming an idea into a global brand that redefined not just coffee but the customer experience.

Howard Schultz's story shows that business success is not only about profit but also about purpose, proving that companies can thrive while making a meaningful impact on society.

Elon Musk's Success Story: From Dreamer to Disruptor

"Mastering ChatGPT isn't just about technology, it's about transforming how we think and interact in the digital age." — ELON MUSK, ENTREPRENEUR AND VISIONARY

"Getting through the incorporation process is like setting the cornerstone of a building. It's your first real commitment on paper, legally speaking, that you're in it to win it." — ELON MUSK, CEO OF TESLA AND SPACEX

"As technology continues to evolve, so too must our approach to copyright. It's about staying ahead of the curve to ensure our creations are protected in a digital age." — ELON MUSK, CEO OF SPACEX AND TESLA

"Juggling multiple contracts is like conducting an orchestra; each has its part to play, and it's your job to ensure they harmonize perfectly to create a symphony, not a cacophony." — ELON MUSK, CEO OF TESLA AND SPACEX

Elon Musk is the ultimate example of someone who thinks big—*really* big. From wanting to colonize Mars to revolutionizing the auto industry, his journey to becoming one of the most successful entrepreneurs of our time is nothing short of extraordinary. But how did this South African-born visionary go from a kid with big dreams to a billionaire at the helm of multiple game-changing companies?

Early Life and First Ventures
Born in 1971 in Pretoria, South Africa, Elon Musk was always a curious kid. By the age of 12, he had taught himself computer programming and created a video game called *Blastar*, which he sold for $500. That early knack for technology was a sign of things to come, but Musk's ambitions were far bigger than just video games.

After attending the University of Pretoria for a short time, Musk moved to Canada, where he attended Queen's University. He later transferred to the University of Pennsylvania, where he earned degrees in both physics and economics. But academia wasn't enough for Musk—he wanted to be part of the action.

Zip2: The First Big Break
In 1995, Musk headed to Silicon Valley during the internet boom, and his first company was born. Along with his brother, Kimbal, he co-founded Zip2, a software company that provided business directories and maps for newspapers. The company grew rapidly and caught the attention of big players. In 1999,

Compaq acquired Zip2 for a whopping $307 million, giving Musk his first major payday—a cool $22 million from the sale.

X.com and the Birth of PayPal

With cash in hand, Musk wasn't about to sit still. In 1999, he founded X.com, an online payment company. X.com quickly evolved into what we now know as PayPal, thanks to its focus on simplifying online money transfers. Musk's vision of digital payments was ahead of its time, and it didn't take long for PayPal to become the go-to service for e-commerce.

In 2002, eBay saw the potential and acquired PayPal for $1.5 billion in stock. Musk made $165 million from the deal, but PayPal was just the beginning. He had much bigger plans.

SpaceX: The Quest to Reach Mars

After the PayPal sale, most people would have retired on a private island—but not Elon Musk. He had his eyes on the stars, quite literally. In 2002, he founded SpaceX (Space Exploration Technologies Corp.), with the goal of making space travel affordable and eventually colonizing Mars.

At first, SpaceX was an underdog in the space race. It struggled with early rocket failures, and many thought Musk's dream of interplanetary travel was impossible. But Musk poured his heart, soul, and much of his fortune into SpaceX, refusing to give up.

In 2008, after three failed launches, SpaceX successfully sent the Falcon 1 into orbit. This was a game-changing moment. NASA took notice and awarded SpaceX a $1.6 billion contract to supply the International Space Station. Fast forward to today, and SpaceX has redefined the space industry, becoming the first private company to send humans into orbit with the Crew Dragon in 2020.

Tesla: Electric Cars for the Masses

Around the same time SpaceX was taking off, Musk set his sights on revolutionizing the auto industry. In 2004, he became involved with Tesla, an electric vehicle startup, investing millions of his own money and eventually becoming its CEO.

Tesla's goal? To make electric cars mainstream. It wasn't an easy road—production delays, financial struggles, and skeptics all tried to bring Tesla down.

But Musk persisted, believing that the future of transportation had to be sustainable.

Tesla's Model S became a breakthrough product, proving that electric cars could be fast, stylish, and desirable. Under Musk's leadership, Tesla continued innovating with the Model 3, the world's best-selling electric vehicle, and introduced technologies like Autopilot, pushing the boundaries of what cars can do. Tesla is now the most valuable automaker in the world, and Musk's vision of a cleaner, electric future is becoming a reality.

SolarCity, The Boring Company, and More

But wait, there's more! Elon Musk didn't stop at rockets and electric cars. He also co-founded SolarCity, a solar energy services company (later acquired by Tesla), to promote clean energy solutions. And then there's The Boring Company, which aims to build tunnels to reduce traffic congestion, and Neuralink, a company focused on brain-machine interfaces to connect humans and computers.

The Unstoppable Entrepreneur

So, what's the secret to Elon Musk's success? It's not just his ability to think big, but his relentless determination, risk-taking, and ability to push through failures that have made him a titan in multiple industries. Musk has faced countless obstacles, from financial ruin to technical failures, but he never backs down. He's driven by a desire to change the world and to do so on an epic scale.

From revolutionizing online payments to launching rockets and electric cars, Elon Musk is proof that if you can dream it, you can build it—as long as you're willing to work relentlessly, embrace risk, and see failure as just another stepping stone to success.

And with his eyes now set on Mars, Musk's journey is far from over.

Charles Duhigg's Success Story: Unlocking the Science of Habits and Productivity

"Understanding your own habits and particularly your weaknesses can help transform the abstract concept of time management into practical, everyday victories." — CHARLES DUHIGG, JOURNALIST AND AUTHOR

Charles Duhigg is a master storyteller and investigative journalist whose work has profoundly reshaped how we understand habits and productivity. From his early days at *The New York Times* to becoming a best-selling author, Duhigg has shown a remarkable ability to blend science with practical advice, making complex psychological concepts accessible to the public. With his books *The Power of Habit* and *Smarter Faster Better*, Duhigg empowers individuals and organizations to harness the power of small changes, improve decision-making, and unlock their potential. His insights have become essential reading for anyone seeking personal and professional transformation.

The Early Spark

Charles Duhigg's journey to becoming a renowned author and journalist began with a curious mind and a relentless pursuit of understanding human behavior. After studying history at Yale University and earning an MBA from Harvard Business School, Duhigg initially ventured into journalism. His fascination with uncovering the "why" behind everyday actions and societal patterns led him to work at *The New York Times*, where he reported on complex subjects such as business dynamics, economics, and personal productivity.

The Birth of a Best-Seller

Duhigg's breakthrough came when he stumbled upon intriguing research about habits while working on an investigative piece. Recognizing the profound implications this research had on both personal success and organizational growth, he began to explore how habits shape our lives. This journey culminated in his first book, *The Power of Habit: Why We Do What We Do in Life and Business*. Released in 2012, the book became an instant sensation, offering readers a deep dive into the mechanics of habit formation and transformation, with actionable insights for self-improvement.

Shifting Focus to Productivity and Performance

Riding the success of *The Power of Habit*, Duhigg continued to investigate the intersection of psychology and performance. His second book, *Smarter Faster Better: The Secrets of Being Productive in Life and Business*, delved into how individuals and organizations can harness motivation, creativity, and decision-making to achieve extraordinary results. His ability to blend scientific research with captivating storytelling resonated widely, solidifying his reputation as a thought leader in the field of productivity.

Legacy of Insight and Influence

Duhigg's influence extends beyond books. His insights into habits and productivity have inspired corporate leaders, entrepreneurs, and individuals striving for personal growth. He has become a sought-after speaker, delivering talks at conferences, universities, and organizations worldwide. Through his writing and speaking, Duhigg has transformed complex psychological concepts into practical strategies, empowering people to rewire their habits and achieve meaningful success.

A Lasting Impact on Self-Improvement

Charles Duhigg's career exemplifies the power of curiosity, storytelling, and rigorous research. By decoding the hidden forces behind habits and performance, he has given readers the tools to take control of their lives and achieve lasting change. His work serves as a guiding light for those eager to unlock their full potential, leaving a profound impact on the self-improvement landscape.

Pierre Omidyar's Success Story: From Online Auction to Global E-Commerce Giant

"Access to opportunity is key—not just for a few, but for everyone. That's how we create real, lasting change." — PIERRE OMIDYAR, VISIONARY ARCHITECT OF ONLINE MARKETPLACES

eBay, one of the world's largest and most successful e-commerce platforms, began as a simple idea in the mid-1990s but quickly evolved into a global marketplace that transformed how people buy and sell goods online. Here's how eBay got its start and became the massive success it is today.

The Humble Beginnings: AuctionWeb

eBay's story starts with Pierre Omidyar, a French-born Iranian-American computer programmer. In 1995, while working at General Magic in California, Omidyar had the idea to create an online auction site where individuals could buy and sell items. He initially launched the site, called AuctionWeb, as a side project. The first item ever sold on the platform was a broken laser pointer for $14.83, a moment that surprised Omidyar and highlighted the potential of a marketplace where people could find value in what might otherwise be overlooked.

The idea behind AuctionWeb was simple but innovative: a peer-to-peer marketplace where people could list items for auction, and others could bid on them. This concept of online auctions resonated with the early internet users who were excited about the opportunity to buy and sell directly to other individuals, often finding rare or niche items.

Early Growth and Name Change

As the platform gained traction, Omidyar realized it was more than just a side project. The traffic and transactions on AuctionWeb rapidly increased, and in 1996, Omidyar hired his first employee and began charging users to list items on the site. By 1997, AuctionWeb was hosting 2 million auctions every month.

Realizing the platform's potential, Omidyar renamed AuctionWeb to eBay, which was short for "Echo Bay," a name he originally wanted for his consulting firm. The domain EchoBay.com was already taken, so he shortened it to eBay.com, and the name stuck.

The late 1990s marked eBay's explosive growth. The platform expanded internationally and began to attract collectors, hobbyists, and bargain hunters looking for everything from antiques to electronics. eBay also expanded its categories to include cars, real estate, and consumer goods, making it a one-stop shop for a wide variety of products.

Building a Trusted Marketplace

One of the key factors behind eBay's early success was its focus on trust and community. Omidyar recognized the importance of creating a safe and reliable marketplace where buyers and sellers could feel confident. To achieve this, eBay implemented a feedback system, which allowed users to rate their experiences with buyers and sellers. This was a revolutionary idea at the time and helped to build trust between users.

eBay also emphasized self-policing within the community, encouraging users to report fraudulent activities. These measures made eBay one of the most trusted platforms for online transactions, and its reputation for reliability helped attract more users.

The PayPal Acquisition and Further Expansion

In 2002, eBay made one of its most important acquisitions: PayPal. PayPal, which started as a secure payment system, was widely used by eBay buyers and sellers because of its simplicity and safety. By acquiring PayPal, eBay made transactions even smoother, removing many of the previous hurdles in online payments.

The PayPal acquisition allowed eBay to focus on its core strength—facilitating transactions—without worrying about the complexities of managing payments directly. PayPal quickly became the platform's dominant payment method, contributing significantly to eBay's continued growth.

Over the years, eBay acquired other companies as well, including StubHub and Skype, although it later sold off some of these businesses. eBay's global reach expanded as it launched localized versions of the platform in countries around the world.

Adapting to a Changing Market

In the 2000s, the internet landscape began to change with the rise of competitors like Amazon, which offered a more retail-style shopping experience. eBay had to adapt from being known primarily as an auction site to a broader e-commerce platform where fixed-price listings became more common. The company shifted its focus from the "garage sale" image to a marketplace where small businesses and individual sellers could thrive.

While eBay faced competition from other online marketplaces, it continued to stand out due to its unique blend of consumer-to-consumer and business-to-consumer transactions. The company also embraced mobile commerce, launching its own apps and making it easy for users to buy and sell on the go.

eBay Today

Today, eBay is a multibillion-dollar company with over 185 million active buyers worldwide. It remains one of the largest e-commerce platforms, providing a space for people to buy and sell everything from electronics to collectibles. Though the auction format still exists, the majority of listings on eBay are now fixed-price, and the platform has increasingly focused on businesses and individual entrepreneurs.

The success of eBay is a testament to Omidyar's vision of a global marketplace where anyone can become a seller, and where items of all kinds can find a buyer. Even though the online landscape has changed, eBay continues to thrive by adapting to new technologies and market trends while staying true to its core mission of connecting buyers and sellers around the world.

Conclusion

eBay's story is one of vision, community, and innovation. What started as a small side project to help people sell a few items has turned into a global marketplace that has transformed online shopping. With its focus on trust, convenience, and adaptability, eBay remains a central player in the e-commerce world, continuing to influence how we buy and sell online.

Sam Walton's Success Story: Building an Empire from Small-Town Roots

"Capital isn't scarce; vision is. Effective capital management aligns financial resources with visionary goals to turn ambitions into reality." — SAM WALTON, FOUNDER OF WALMART AND SAM'S CLUB

Sam Walton, the visionary founder of Walmart, transformed the retail industry through his relentless focus on customer service, operational efficiency, and low-cost products. Born into modest beginnings, Walton's journey from managing a single store in rural Arkansas to building a global retail empire is a story of resilience, innovation, and entrepreneurial spirit. With a keen understanding of market needs and a willingness to take risks, Walton redefined how retail business operates, turning Walmart into a household name. His ability to leverage technology, streamline supply chains, and empower employees laid the foundation for one of the largest and most influential companies in the world. Walton's legacy endures, inspiring business leaders to prioritize customers, embrace innovation, and remain adaptable in the face of change.

Early Life: A Foundation in Hard Work

Sam Walton, born on March 29, 1918, in Kingfisher, Oklahoma, was raised during the Great Depression. Growing up in a rural farming community, he learned the value of hard work and frugality at a young age. His family struggled financially, so Walton took on various odd jobs to support them, including delivering newspapers and milking cows. These early experiences instilled in him an understanding of customer service and the importance of meeting people's needs.

Walton attended the University of Missouri, earning a degree in economics in 1940. Following graduation, he joined J.C. Penney as a management trainee, where he gained firsthand experience in retail operations. Though he enjoyed his work, Walton left after 18 months to join the U.S. Army during World War II. His time in the military further developed his leadership skills, preparing him for future entrepreneurial challenges.

The First Venture: A Humble Beginning in Retail

After the war, Walton married Helen Robson, whose father helped him secure a loan to purchase his first store—a Ben Franklin variety store in Newport, Arkansas, in 1945. Walton worked tirelessly to make the store a success, using innovative ideas to increase sales. However, due to a lease dispute, he lost the store. Undeterred, Walton and his wife moved to Bentonville, Arkansas, where they opened another Ben Franklin store.

During these early years, Walton developed the skills that would define his career—keeping costs low, stocking shelves with affordable merchandise, and putting the customer first. He also studied his competitors closely, learning what worked and what didn't, setting the stage for the revolutionary retail model he would soon create.

Founding Walmart: A New Model for Retail

In 1962, Walton opened the first Walmart store in Rogers, Arkansas, with a simple mission: provide customers with quality products at the lowest possible prices. He realized that small-town customers needed access to affordable goods just as much as those in big cities, and he was determined to build a retail model that could serve them effectively.

Walmart's strategy was revolutionary at the time. Walton focused on cutting costs through efficient logistics, a focus on volume buying, and minimizing overhead. Unlike his competitors, Walton chose to open stores in rural areas rather than metropolitan cities, believing that small towns were an untapped market. This decision proved to be a masterstroke, allowing Walmart to grow without facing immediate competition from established urban retailers.

Scaling Success: Innovations in Supply Chain Management

Walton was an early adopter of technology to optimize Walmart's operations. He pioneered the use of just-in-time inventory management and invested in computer systems to track sales and streamline the supply chain. This allowed Walmart to restock shelves quickly and efficiently, keeping products affordable and readily available.

Walton's focus on cost efficiency extended to everything—from distribution centers to store layouts. He also implemented a unique profit-sharing program for employees, believing that happy workers would create a better shopping experience for customers. This employee-first philosophy fostered a strong corporate culture that became a hallmark of Walmart's success.

Becoming a Retail Giant

Throughout the 1970s and 80s, Walmart expanded rapidly, opening stores across the southern United States. By 1980, Walmart had become a billion-dollar business, thanks to Walton's relentless focus on efficiency and customer service. In 1991, Walmart surpassed Sears as the largest retailer in the U.S., cementing its position as a dominant force in the retail industry.

Walton continued to push for growth, venturing into new markets by launching Sam's Club, a membership-based warehouse model, and expanding into grocery retail with Walmart Supercenters. His ability to adapt and innovate ensured Walmart stayed ahead of competitors.

Legacy and Influence

Sam Walton passed away in 1992, but his legacy lives on. Under his leadership, Walmart became a global retail giant, known for its commitment to low prices and operational efficiency. Walton's focus on serving customers, empowering employees, and embracing innovation set a standard for retailers worldwide.

Walmart remains one of the largest companies in the world today, with thousands of stores in multiple countries. Walton's vision of affordable shopping continues to shape the retail landscape, influencing countless entrepreneurs and businesses. His story serves as a testament to the power of persistence, innovation, and putting the customer first.

Lessons from Sam Walton's Success

- **Frugality and Cost Control:** Walton's focus on keeping costs low was a driving force behind Walmart's competitive pricing.

- **Customer-Centric Approach:** He believed that serving customers well would always lead to long-term success.

- **Innovation in Logistics:** Walton's early adoption of technology and supply chain management became key differentiators.

- **Persistence and Adaptability:** Despite early setbacks, Walton's resilience and willingness to adapt allowed him to build one of the most successful retail empires in history.

Sam Walton's life is a testament to the power of entrepreneurship, vision, and determination. From a small-town store owner to the founder of one of the world's largest retail chains, Walton's story continues to inspire generations of entrepreneurs to think big and serve customers better.

Conclusion

Your Turn to Build an Empire

A s we close this collection of extraordinary business success stories, let's take a moment to reflect on the immense wisdom and inspiration these narratives offer. The journeys chronicled within these pages are not just about financial milestones or market dominance—they are about resilience, creativity, innovation, leadership, and, above all, the human spirit's ability to overcome challenges and create something truly meaningful. Each entrepreneur, visionary, and leader featured in this book has charted a unique course, shaped by their values, decisions, and circumstances. Their stories serve as roadmaps for those of us looking to build our own path toward success.

A recurring message throughout these stories is that success is personal and nonlinear. No two journeys are alike. Some achieved greatness after years of trial and error; others stumbled into success almost by accident. Yet, in each case, we see a willingness to adapt, learn, and pivot when necessary. This is one of the most valuable lessons in business: there is no one-size-fits-all formula for success. What worked for one entrepreneur might not work for another, but the principles of persistence, thoughtful action, and strategic planning are universal. These stories remind us that failure is not the opposite of success—it's often a key ingredient in the process.

Moreover, success is deeply tied to mindset. Many of the leaders featured in these pages emphasize the importance of clarity, focus, and purpose. Visionary figures like Simon Sinek, Richard Branson, and Indra Nooyi show us that knowing *why* you do something is just as important as knowing *how* to do it. Their stories demonstrate that business is not merely about generating profits—it's about creating impact, solving problems, and delivering value to others. It is about building legacies that extend far beyond the bottom line. In today's competitive environment, the ability to connect your personal vision to your business goals is what will set you apart.

The diversity of industries and insights covered in this book also reveals another crucial truth: opportunities exist everywhere. Whether it's writing, technology, branding, or product development, there is room for innovation in every field. We've seen authors who turned their words into movements, tech pioneers who disrupted entire industries, and marketers who transformed brands into cultural phenomena. Each chapter has been a reminder that the only real limitations are the ones we impose on ourselves. The world of business is dynamic and constantly evolving, and those who embrace change as an opportunity rather than a threat will find themselves ahead of the curve.

It is also worth noting that none of the success stories featured here were achieved alone. Behind every triumph lies a network of collaborators, mentors, partners, and supporters. Business success is inherently relational—it thrives on connections, trust, and shared vision. As you build your own empire, remember that no one succeeds in isolation. The relationships you nurture along the way—whether with your team, customers, or fellow entrepreneurs—are as valuable as any financial investment. Collaboration amplifies success, and partnerships can often unlock doors that may otherwise remain closed.

This book has also explored the essential role of storytelling in business. Each entrepreneur we've profiled has, in their own way, mastered the art of narrative. They've used stories to communicate their vision, connect with audiences, and build brands that resonate deeply with customers. Their journeys remind us that your success story is not just a personal triumph—it can inspire and empower

Conclusion

others. As you move forward, think about the story you want to tell. How will your journey inspire others? What legacy do you want to leave behind?

Now, the question remains: *What will you do with the lessons you've learned?* The power of these stories lies not just in the inspiration they offer but in the actions they compel you to take. Business success doesn't come from passive reflection; it comes from bold, decisive action. It's easy to read about others' achievements and assume that greatness is out of reach, but the truth is, the same potential for success lies within you. It begins with an idea, followed by careful planning, relentless execution, and the courage to keep moving forward, no matter what challenges arise.

Building an empire, whether in business or in life, requires both strategy and heart. The path forward won't always be easy. There will be setbacks, unexpected twists, and moments of doubt. But as these stories have shown, success is not about avoiding challenges—it's about facing them head-on and growing through them. The leaders featured in this book have all encountered failure at some point, but they refused to let it define them. They adapted, learned, and emerged stronger. You can do the same.

What's more, success isn't a final destination—it's a journey. It's a series of small wins, steady progress, and constant learning. Some of the most influential figures in business view success not as a place to arrive but as a process to be embraced. The goal isn't just to build a business—it's to build a life that aligns with your values, passions, and purpose. Success is about crafting a legacy that reflects who you are and the impact you want to have on the world.

Now that you've explored the journeys of these remarkable entrepreneurs, innovators, and thought leaders, it's time to start writing your own success story. What will your empire look like? How will you use what you've learned to create something meaningful? You don't need to have all the answers right now—every journey begins with a single step. The key is to start.

The business world is waiting for your unique ideas, talents, and contributions. Whether you're launching a startup, growing an existing business, or exploring new opportunities, remember that the insights from this book are not just meant to inspire—they are meant to guide you. Use them as tools to build the foundation of your success. Revisit these stories whenever you need motivation, and let them remind you that if others have done it, so can you.

Your empire begins with action. Take that first step today, and keep moving forward, one decision at a time. The road ahead may be long, but the rewards are worth the journey. It's time to make your mark, create your legacy, and build a story worth telling. Your success story is waiting to be written—go out there and write it.

The next chapter in your business journey is yours to create. And the world is ready for what only *you* can offer.

Resources

The Empire Builders and Blueprint Series

Welcome to the Resource section of the Empire Builders Series: Masterclasses in Business and Law. Here, we provide a carefully curated collection of practical tools and materials designed to complement the strategies and insights discussed throughout the series. This section is your gateway to deeper understanding and application, offering everything from sample agreements and checklists to detailed case studies and guidelines. Whether you're forging a new business, protecting intellectual property, or planning for expansion, these resources are intended to empower you with the necessary tools to effectively implement and navigate the complex landscape of business and law. Embrace these resources as your companion in building and sustaining a robust empire.

Empire Builders Series:
Masterclasses in Business and Law

In the dynamic world of business, where innovation intersects with opportunity, success often hinges not only on creativity but also on a deep understanding of the legal and operational landscapes. The Empire Builders Series is meticulously designed to arm aspiring entrepreneurs, seasoned business owners, creative professionals, and legal experts with the comprehensive knowledge and strategies needed to navigate these complexities and build lasting empires.

Each book in the series serves as a foundational pillar, offering expert guidance and actionable insights in specific areas of business and law; tailored to foster growth, innovation, and success in today's competitive marketplace:

1. **Brick by Brick**: This guide acts as your blueprint for building a business from the ground up. It offers essential strategies, legal insights, and operational tactics crucial for establishing a solid foundation for any business venture.

2. **Mark Your Territory**: Dive deep into the world of trademarks with this essential guide, designed to help you protect and effectively leverage your brand in today's competitive market.

3. **From Idea to Empire**: Transform your entrepreneurial dreams into reality with this exhaustive guide to business planning. Learn how to craft a compelling business plan that not only attracts investors but also sets the stage for a successful enterprise.

4. **Beyond the Pen**: Safeguard your creative works and master the intricacies of copyright law with this expert guide, tailored specifically for writers, artists, musicians, and digital content creators.

5. **Legal Ink**: Demystify the complex legal landscape of publishing with practical advice on negotiating contracts and protecting intellectual property, essential for authors and publishers.

The Empire Builders Series stands as a testament to the power of knowledge and the importance of mastering the strategic and legal aspects of business management. Each book is designed not merely to inform but to inspire action and lead to success. Embark on this journey to build your empire, one masterclass at a time.

Brick by Brick:
The Entrepreneur's Guide to Constructing a Company

The first book in the Empire Builders Series: Masterclass in Business and Law is "Brick by Brick: The Entrepreneur's Guide to Constructing a Company."

Summary: "Brick by Brick" is an indispensable resource for entrepreneurs who are poised to transform their innovative business ideas into successful enterprises. This comprehensive guide meticulously outlines the complexities of business formation, providing detailed, step-by-step instructions and vital insights into the legal, operational, and strategic aspects of starting and running a thriving company.

Part 1: Laying the Foundation – Focuses on selecting the appropriate business entity, delving into the legal implications of each option and the economic considerations vital for establishing a solid foundation for your business.

Part 2: Operational Mechanics – Discusses the operational aspects of setting up partnerships and LLCs, navigating corporate governance, maintaining corporate records, and managing capital and shareholder relationships effectively.

Part 3: Advanced Strategic Planning – Offers insights into managing structural changes, handling stock and ownership issues, expanding operations across state lines, and deploying tax strategies to ensure compliance and optimize financial performance.

Part 4: Implementation Tools and Resources – Provides practical tools such as sample agreements, startup task checklists, and comprehensive guidelines for drafting business plans and the incorporation process, enabling entrepreneurs to effectively implement their business strategies.

"Brick by Brick" not only serves as a guide but acts as a complete blueprint for building a robust business capable of thriving in today's competitive market. It arms aspiring entrepreneurs with the necessary knowledge and tools to navigate the complexities of business formation. From drafting your first business plan to preparing for incorporation, this book delivers invaluable insights and practical advice to establish a strong foundation and sustain growth.

Mark Your Territory:
Navigating Trademarks in the Modern Marketplace

The second book in the Empire Builders Series: Masterclass in Business and Law is "Mark Your Territory: Navigating Trademarks in the Modern Marketplace."

Summary: "Mark Your Territory" provides an indispensable resource for anyone involved in the branding and legal aspects of their business, offering a comprehensive guide to understanding, acquiring, and effectively managing trademarks. This book is crucial for ensuring that trademarks, which are vital assets to any business, are properly protected and leveraged.

Part 1: Fundamentals of Trademarks – Introduces the basics of trademarks, including their legal framework, the process of trademark selection and registration, and their importance in identifying business sources and ensuring product quality.

Part 2: Strategic Trademark Management – Focuses on the ongoing management of trademarks, detailing strategies for maintaining rights, monitoring for infringements, addressing challenges in digital marketing, and managing global trademark portfolios.

Part 3: Advanced Topics in Trademarks – Delves into more complex issues such as preventing trademark dilution, managing renewals, understanding the specific needs of service marks in advertising, and navigating the intricacies of trademark licensing and emerging legal trends.

Part 4: Practical Tools and Resources – Provides practical aids like sample trademark filings, management checklists, and insightful case studies, equipping readers with tangible tools and real-world examples to apply the concepts discussed effectively.

Designed for entrepreneurs, business owners, and legal professionals, "Mark Your Territory" equips readers with actionable strategies and essential tools for effective trademark management. It ensures that readers can maintain their brand's uniqueness and legal protections, thus securing a competitive edge in the marketplace.

From Idea to Empire:
Mastering the Art of Business Planning

The third book in the Empire Builders Series: Masterclass in Business and Law is "From Idea to Empire: Mastering the Art of Business Planning."

Summary: "From Idea to Empire" offers an indispensable roadmap for entrepreneurs eager to transform their innovative ideas into successful businesses. This comprehensive guide equips readers with a strategic blueprint for drafting robust business plans that attract investors and serve as a roadmap for navigating the transition from startup to thriving enterprise.

Part 1: Conceptualizing Your Business – This section lays the groundwork by assisting readers in defining their business vision, understanding market needs, analyzing competitors, and setting clear business objectives. It also guides readers in selecting an effective business model that aligns with their long-term goals.

Part 2: Strategic Planning – Delve into creating detailed marketing strategies, operational plans, and financial projections. This part covers risk management and technological integration, ensuring the business plan is both innovative and executable.

Part 3: Articulating Your Plan – Focuses on the actual drafting of the business plan, including how to write an engaging executive summary, develop compelling proposals, and master communication and negotiation tactics with potential investors and partners.

Part 4: Execution and Review – Outlines the necessary steps to launch the business successfully, monitor its performance, and make adjustments based on real-world feedback and market dynamics. This section also explores strategies for sustainable growth and long-term viability.

"From Idea to Empire" is more than a mere planning manual; it's a strategic guide that provides budding entrepreneurs with the necessary knowledge, tools, and confidence to build a business capable of facing today's market complexities. With practical advice, real-world examples, and essential resources, this book is a vital tool for anyone ready to evolve their business concept from idea to a profitable empire.

From Idea to Empire: Abridged Edition

The third book in the Empire Builders Series: Masterclass in Business and Law is "From Idea to Empire: Abridged Edition."

Summary: "From Idea to Empire: Abridged Edition" delivers the essential roadmap for turning business ideas into successful enterprises—streamlined for readers seeking concise and actionable insights. While the original edition provides an expansive resource with success stories and detailed case studies, this abridged version focuses solely on the strategic elements of business planning, offering the tools needed to conceptualize, design, and execute a winning business strategy.

By eliminating supplementary stories and focusing on the practical frameworks, this edition is perfect for readers eager to dive straight into the mechanics of business planning without distraction. It provides the knowledge required to develop robust business models, articulate compelling proposals, and successfully launch and grow a business in today's dynamic marketplace.

Part 1: Conceptualizing Your Business – Laying the Foundation – In this section, readers learn how to define their business idea, identify market needs, analyze competitors, and set clear objectives. It introduces essential business models and helps entrepreneurs align their vision with long-term goals.

Part 2: Strategic Planning – Mapping the Path to Success – Here, readers will discover how to design effective marketing strategies, operational plans, and financial projections. Topics like risk management and technological integration are covered to ensure every business plan is both realistic and innovative.

Part 3: Articulating Your Plan – Communicating with Precision and Impact – This section emphasizes the importance of clarity in communication. Readers will learn how to craft compelling executive summaries, develop strong proposals, and master negotiation strategies for working with investors and partners.

Part 4: Execution and Review – Launching and Scaling with Purpose – The final section covers essential steps for launching a business successfully, monitoring performance, and making real-time adjustments. It also addresses strategies for sustainable growth, long-term resilience, and market adaptation.

About This Edition:
The Abridged Edition is crafted for readers who prefer a focused, no-frills approach to business planning. By presenting the core methodologies from the original book in a concise format, this version allows entrepreneurs to absorb key concepts quickly and efficiently. Whether you're a first-time entrepreneur or a seasoned business owner, this streamlined guide provides the essential tools needed to transform an idea into a thriving business.

Why This Edition Matters:
"From Idea to Empire: Abridged Edition" underscores that great business planning doesn't require lengthy explanations—it requires clear strategies and actionable frameworks. This edition emphasizes the importance of focus, discipline, and adaptability in building a successful business.

Designed to complement busy entrepreneurs, it delivers the same powerful strategies as the original book but in a more accessible format. Readers can quickly refer to specific sections, apply the knowledge, and move forward with confidence in their business endeavors.

"From Idea to Empire: Abridged Edition" is the perfect companion for entrepreneurs who need to move swiftly from concept to execution. With straightforward advice and practical insights, this edition equips readers to create robust business plans and take decisive action toward building their own empire.

Beyond the Pen:
Copyright Strategies for Modern Creators
The fourth book in the Empire Builders Series: Masterclass in Business and Law is "Beyond the Pen: Copyright Strategies for Modern Creators."

Summary: "Beyond the Pen" serves as a crucial guide for artists, writers, musicians, and digital creators who seek to effectively navigate the complexities of copyright law and protect their creative assets. This comprehensive resource provides a deep dive into the mechanisms, legal frameworks, and strategic practices necessary to safeguard intellectual property in today's rapidly evolving digital landscape.

Part 1: Understanding Copyright Law – This section lays the groundwork by covering the essentials of copyright, including how to register works, the extent of legal protection available, and the nuances of international copyright laws. It equips creators with the crucial knowledge needed to assert and defend their rights.

Part 2: Navigating Use and Fair Use – Focuses on the vital concept of fair use, offering real-world scenarios and detailed guidance on how to handle copyright infringements and resolve disputes effectively without compromising creative freedom.

Part 3: Licensing and Monetization – Explores strategic approaches to structuring and managing licensing agreements, understanding diverse revenue models, and handling collaborations, ensuring creators can monetize their works effectively while maintaining control over their usage.

Part 4: Copyright in the Digital Age – Addresses the challenges and opportunities presented by new technologies, digital rights management, and online content sharing platforms. This part also examines the impact of social media on copyright and anticipates future trends that could influence creators' rights.

"Beyond the Pen" is more than just a legal manual; it is a strategic resource that empowers creators to protect, manage, and prosper with their intellectual property in today's interconnected market. Packed with practical examples, expert advice, and actionable strategies, this book is an indispensable tool for anyone looking to navigate the legal challenges and seize the opportunities in the modern creative landscape.

Legal Ink:
Navigating the Legalese of Publishing

The fifth book in the Empire Builders Series: Masterclass in Business and Law is "Legal Ink: Navigating the Legalese of Publishing."

Summary: "Legal Ink" offers an indispensable guide for authors seeking to navigate the complex world of publishing contracts. This comprehensive book demystifies legal jargon and provides a clear roadmap to understanding and managing the intricacies of publishing agreements effectively.

Part 1: The Grant of Rights – This section explains the various types of publishing rights, offering guidance on how to negotiate and manage these rights effectively to safeguard the author's interests.

Part 2: Your Obligations – Details the commitments authors must uphold under publishing contracts. It emphasizes the implications of these obligations for an author's literary career and advises on managing multiple contractual commitments.

Part 3: Getting Your Book to Market – Covers the practical aspects of the publishing process from the final manuscript preparation to marketing and distribution. This part ensures authors understand the steps involved and their roles in bringing their book to market.

Part 4: Follow the Money – Breaks down the financial components of publishing contracts, including advances, royalties, and accounting clauses. It offers crucial advice on how to negotiate for fair compensation.

Part 5: Parting Ways – Discusses strategies for effectively managing the conclusion of a publishing agreement, including rights reversion and contract termination, providing tactics for authors to regain control of their work.

"Legal Ink" acts as more than just a guide—it's a strategic tool for any author looking to deeply understand and master the legal framework of publishing contracts. With this book, writers are equipped to make informed decisions, negotiate better terms, and ensure their rights are protected throughout their publishing journey. It is an essential resource for anyone looking to confidently handle the legalities of publishing and secure the success of their work in the competitive marketplace.

The Empire Blueprint Series:
Case Studies for Business Success

Welcome to the Case Studies section of The Empire Blueprint Series: Case Studies for Business Success. This collection serves as an essential companion to the theoretical knowledge presented in the earlier volumes. Here, we delve into real-world applications and successful business practices through detailed case studies, showcasing how various entrepreneurs and businesses have navigated challenges, seized opportunities, and achieved success in their respective fields.

In this series, you will encounter a variety of scenarios that illustrate the practical implementation of business strategies and legal frameworks. Each case study not only highlights successes but also discusses the obstacles faced and lessons learned along the way. Whether you're a budding entrepreneur, a seasoned executive, or a legal professional, these insights will provide you with invaluable perspectives and tools to enhance your own business endeavors.

Each book in the series includes:

1. **70 Case Studies in Vision, Strategy, and Personal Branding**: This volume explores the journeys of entrepreneurs who have effectively crafted their visions and built strong personal brands. It highlights strategies for aligning personal values with business goals and creating a lasting impact in the marketplace.

2. **70 Case Studies in Leadership, Innovation, and Resilience**: This volume examines leaders who have driven innovation and fostered resilience within their organizations. The case studies showcase their approaches to overcoming challenges and inspire others to cultivate a culture of adaptability and forward-thinking.

3. **74 Case Studies in Growth, Digital Presence, and Legacy Building**: This volume delves into the strategies employed by businesses that have successfully navigated digital transformation and growth. It emphasizes the

importance of establishing a strong online presence and building a legacy that resonates with future generations.

Each case study in The Empire Blueprint Series: Case Studies for Business Success is crafted to offer actionable insights and inspiration for readers. By examining these real-world examples, you will gain a deeper understanding of the strategies that drive business success and how to apply these lessons to your own ventures.

70 Case Studies in Vision, Strategy, and Personal Branding: The Foundations of Success, Volume 1

The first book in The Empire Blueprint Series: Case Studies for Business Success is "70 Case Studies in Vision, Strategy, and Personal Branding: The Foundations of Success," Volume 1

Dive deeper into the essential elements of business success with Volume 1: 70 Case Studies in Vision, Strategy, and Personal Branding. This volume not only presents a wealth of real-world examples but also serves as a practical toolkit for aspiring entrepreneurs and seasoned professionals alike. Here, you will find a curated collection of resources designed to complement the case studies and enhance your understanding of effective business practices.

From strategic planning templates and personal branding frameworks to time management guides and storytelling techniques, these resources empower you to implement the insights gleaned from the case studies. Explore practical tools for optimizing your online presence, launching impactful marketing campaigns, and engaging audiences across various platforms.

With a focus on innovation and adaptability, this resource section is your go-to companion for navigating the complexities of today's business landscape. Whether you're looking to craft an inspiring vision, develop effective strategies, or build a standout personal brand, the materials provided will equip you with the actionable insights needed to achieve meaningful success. Embrace the tools and inspiration within these pages, and take your entrepreneurial journey to new heights.

70 Case Studies in Leadership, Innovation, and Resilience: Building a Thriving Enterprise, Volume 2

The second book in The Empire Blueprint Series: Case Studies for Business Success is "70 Case Studies in Leadership, Innovation, and Resilience: Building a Thriving Enterprise," Volume 2

Enhance your understanding of effective leadership with Volume 2: 70 Case Studies in Leadership, Innovation, and Resilience: Building a Thriving Enterprise. This resource section is designed to complement the rich insights presented throughout the volume, providing you with practical tools and frameworks to elevate your leadership journey.

Within this section, you'll find a variety of resources that address the core themes of this book—leadership, innovation, and resilience. From templates for developing effective communication strategies to guides on fostering a collaborative corporate culture, these materials are crafted to support your growth as a leader. Explore negotiation techniques, emotional intelligence assessments, and frameworks for ethical leadership that will help you build trust and loyalty within your teams.

The resources also include practical tips for embracing digital transformation and integrating innovative technologies into your business practices. Learn how to leverage these tools to drive growth, enhance customer engagement, and maintain a competitive edge in today's dynamic market.

With a focus on creating lasting value and building a legacy, this section equips you with actionable insights and strategies to navigate challenges with confidence. Whether you are an entrepreneur launching a new venture or an executive steering an established enterprise, these resources will empower you to lead with purpose and resilience.

Dive into these valuable tools and insights, and discover how to turn challenges into opportunities, fostering an environment where innovation and sustainable growth thrive.

74 Case Studies in Growth, Digital Presence, and Legacy Building: Strategies for Long-Term Success, Volume 3

The third book in The Empire Blueprint Series: Case Studies for Business Success is "74 Case Studies in Growth, Digital Presence, and Legacy Building: Strategies for Long-Term Success," Volume 3

Unlock the secrets to sustainable success with Volume 3: 74 Case Studies in Growth, Digital Presence, and Legacy Building: Strategies for Long-Term Success. This resource section is designed to enhance your understanding and application of the powerful insights shared throughout the volume, providing you with practical tools and strategies for thriving in today's competitive landscape.

In this section, you'll find a wealth of resources that align with the key themes of this book—growth, digital engagement, and legacy building. From templates for strategic goal-setting and growth frameworks to guides on optimizing digital marketing efforts, these materials will help you implement the actionable insights gained from the case studies.

Explore best practices for storytelling and community engagement in the digital realm, along with practical tips for leveraging social media to amplify your brand's presence. Discover frameworks for navigating the complexities of innovation and operational efficiency, ensuring your business not only grows but flourishes sustainably.

The resource section also emphasizes the importance of legacy building, offering tools for effective succession planning and community involvement. Learn how to align your everyday decisions with your long-term vision, ensuring that your enterprise leaves a lasting impact for future generations.

Whether you are an entrepreneur embarking on a new venture, an executive scaling operations, or a professional seeking to elevate your digital presence, these resources will empower you to lead with purpose and confidence. Dive into the practical tools and insights provided here, and equip yourself to navigate challenges, innovate boldly, and create a meaningful legacy.

In conclusion, the Resource section of the Empire Builders Series and Empire Blueprint Series serves as valuable extensions of the learning journey you've embarked upon. By utilizing these carefully chosen tools and materials, you are better equipped to apply the principles and strategies discussed in the series to real-world scenarios. Each resource has been tailored to enhance your understanding and effectiveness in the realms of business and law, ensuring you have the practical support necessary to navigate challenges and seize opportunities. We hope these resources prove instrumental in helping you build and sustain your business empire, transforming knowledge into actionable success.

L. A. Moeszinger also known as simply "L" is the face behind the AuthorsDoor Leadership Program: AuthorsDoor Series: *Publisher & Her World*, AuthorsDoor Advanced Series: *Publisher & Her World*, and AuthorsDoor Masterclass Series: *Publisher & Her World*. The program comprises, books, courses, and workbooks. The courses expand upon the books. The workbooks go into further detail, outlining step-by-step instructions. Courses are *free*; books and workbooks are available for purchase on Amazon and other retailer sites. She has been launching the careers of self-publishers since 2009, and she also writes the AuthorsRedDoor.com blog on writing, publishing, and marketing. L is also the co-founder of The Ridge Publishing Group and its imprints.

She is an American author, publisher, and creator who resides in Coeur d'Alene, Idaho, with her husband and two dogs. She writes under the pseudonyms: Ann Patterson and Ann Carrington for her business law pieces; L. A. Moeszinger for her writing, publishing, and marketing pieces; Lori Ann Moeszinger for her biblical books and personal pieces; and a handful of others for her Manhattan Diaries series. She believes strongly in faith, blessings, and working her butt off . . . and she thinks one of the best things about being an author-publisher—unlike the lawyer she used to be—is that she can let her passion out.

Original Package Design
© 2024 AuthorsDoor Leadership Program
Cover Design: Eric Moeszinger
Author Photo © 2023 Edwin Wolfe

Parent Website: https://www.RidgePublishingGroup.com and

blog site https://www.PublisherAndHerWorld.com

Publisher Website: https://www.GuardiansofBiblicalTruth.com and

blog site https://www.Jesus-Says.com

Author website: https://www.LAMoeszinger.com and New Youniversity sites:

https://www.NewYouniversity.com, https://www.ManhattanChronicles.com

Bridge Website: https://www.AuthorsDoor.com and

blog site https://www.AuthorsRedDoor.com

Entertainment website: https://www.EthanFoxBooks.com and

blog site https://www.KidsStagram.com

Want More?

The ideas in this book are expanded upon throughout the AuthorsDoor Leadership Program of books, courses, and workbooks. Follow our Facebook page. Join our Facebook private group. Watch our YouTube channels: AuthorsDoor Group, Authors Red Door #Shorts, and Publisher and Her World at Ridge Publishing Group. Listen to our Podcast channel: Publisher's Circle; or email me: *Hello@AuthorsDoor.com*

AuthorsDoor Hubs

Get insights from the articles we write on our *website* (AuthorsDoor.com). You'll find more publications to help authors sell better, pitch better, recruit better, build better, create better, and connect better. You are also invited to visit our *blog* and find out what we're talking about now. Sign up for our *AuthorsDoor Leadership Program Newsletter* and join the conversations going on there with our private community (Publisher's Circle); visit: *www.AuthorsRedDoor.com*

Publisher & Her World Blogs

Enter a world where the sometimes shocking and often hilarious climb to the top as an author-publisher is exposed by a true insider. Faced with on-going trials and tribulations of the world of self-publishing, L. A. Moeszinger is witty and sometimes brutally candid in her postings. If you enjoy getting the inside scoop on the makings and thoughts behind self-publishing, this is the blog for you! *www.PublisherAndHerWorld.com*

This
book was art
directed by John Jared.
The art for both the cover and the
interior was created using pastels on toned
print making paper. The text was set in 10 point Times
New Roman, a typeface based on the sixteenth-century type designs
of Claude Garamond, redrawn by Robert Slimback in 1989.
The book was printed at Amazon and IngramSpark.
The Managing Editor was Jack Clark. The
Production was supervised by
Jason Reed and Ed
Warren.

www.ingramcontent.com/pod-product-compliance
Lightning Source LLC
Chambersburg PA
CBHW031842200326
41597CB00012B/241